6

# THE BOOK OF CRICKET

# THE
# BOOK OF CRICKET

### BY
## SIR PELHAM WARNER

" No human institution is perfect; it will always tend to excess or defect. But how nearly perfect in its own way is cricket. . . . It is a game which keeps boys out of mischief. It is a training of youth for a manly life. It lays up a store of strength and health against old age. It makes individual men lifelong friends. It unites whole schools and universities. . . . The truth is, that athletics are an integral part and a powerful support of all Education: they make it popular."

Professor Thomas Case in Prince Ranjitsinhji's *The Jubilee Book of Cricket.*

*Illustrated with Thirty-two Photographs*
*and Fifteen Diagrams*

## LONDON
# SPORTING HANDBOOKS LTD.

PRINTED IN GREAT BRITAIN BY
UNWIN BROTHERS LTD., THE GRESHAM PRESS, WOKING

# CONTENTS

# LIST OF ILLUSTRATIONS

# DIAGRAMS

# AUTHOR'S PREFACE TO THE FOURTH EDITION

THIS book covers a space of fifty years and more but it seems only yesterday that I was sitting as a small boy in the crowd at Lord's thrilled by the cricket and feeling the history and tradition of the famous ground round and about me.

P. F. W.

*April,* 1945

# PUBLISHERS' NOTE TO THE FOURTH EDITION

FOR more than thirty years this book has been one of the standard works on Cricket. The war has provided the opportunity for a complete and final revision, and the type has been reset.

Sir Pelham Warner, in his capacity as England cricketer and captain, Test Match selector, Editor of *The Cricketer*, and in his work at Lord's during the war, is exceptionally qualified to write on the game, and with this fourth revision the book has crystallized into a classic.

Every chapter has been brought up-to-date, many have been enlarged, particularly with reference to Empire cricket and cricketers. The chapter "An Honours School of Cricket", in which Sir Pelham and an anonymous circle of selectors have set out their ranking of past and present cricketers will create discussion the world over.

# CHAPTER I

## BATTING

It has been said that good batsmen are born and not made, but my experience is rather to the contrary. There are certain gifts of eye and hand which all really good batsmen must possess, but early practice and sound coaching have much to do with the acquiring of all-round skill. The late A. E. Stoddart, the famous Middlesex cricketer, was the only batsman, I believe, to reach the front rank who did not start to play the game early in life, and he is the exception that proves the rule. The first essential is a thoroughly good wicket on which to practise, and this is not difficult to obtain nowadays; the second is the absolute necessity of practising in earnest from the very beginning. Practice should be carried on as keenly and earnestly as if it were a match, and the rattle of the ball against the stumps should cause almost as keen a feeling of disappointment as if a similar fate had befallen one in a game. Pay attention to details, and, if you make a bad stroke, notice where your mistake lay and remember it. Practise, too, new strokes, and try experiments—though this applies rather to the finished than to the embryo batsman—and if you are a keen cricketer batting at a net may be made most enjoyable. It is, of course, necessary to have good bowlers to bowl, but it is not necessary that they should be of the class of Verity, or Clark, or Larwood, or Freeman. A good way to get the best out of a bowler at a net is to play an imaginary match, the position of the fieldsmen being ascertained beforehand. Then ' last man in and thirty runs to make to win ' is often productive of great fun.  Having obtained a good wicket and a keen and intelligent cricketer—not necessarily a great one, but one possessed of patience and tact—to coach you, see that a suitable bat is in your hand, one suited to your strength and style.  And here I may mention that it is a thousand times better to play with too light a bat than too heavy a one, for with too heavy a bat one cannot cut or time the ball correctly.  Besides, it is hardly possible to play straight with too heavy a bat, and a straight bat is the essence of sound batting.  A man must decide for himself what weight of bat suits him best, but a boy up to sixteen ought not to play with one weighing more than 2 lb. unless he is exceptionally strong.  A shorter handle than usual is often an advantage.  Giving our young cricketer a good driving and well-balanced bat, see that he puts on two pads, and at any rate one, if not two batting gloves.  Thus equipped he will be ready to take his place at the wicket, and the first thing our imaginary coach will have to teach him will be his *position at the wicket.*  No fixed rules can be laid down as to the position a batsman should take up at the wicket, but undoubtedly the best advice that can be given him is to take up the position most natural to him. The most popular way of standing is to place the right foot just inside the popping-crease, with the left just outside it, pointing towards the bowler or mid-off; the *right toe should be pointed slightly behind point in the direction of third man*; this will be found a great help in getting the left leg well across for the off-drive.  But no two players stand exactly alike.  The object of every coach should be to lay a sound foundation upon which young cricketers can build up a style not only correct in principle, but also in conformity with their own individual methods and powers.

Now for a famous batsman's comments on the left elbow and left shoulder forward, and for this we turn to C. B. Fry in *Great Batsmen.*  Here we read:

There is no doubt that the principle is sound, but it applies only to certain points in certain strokes; really, as an absolute rule, it applies only to the forward stroke, and especially to the forward stroke which is played with push. But insistence on the principle of left elbow and left shoulder forward has caused batsmen, or some of them, to think that it is a universal principle which must as far as possible be obeyed always. Consequently, some batsmen in taking up their first position at the wicket think more of left elbow and left shoulder than of anything else. What it comes to is this, that in standing at the wicket waiting for the ball they more or less rigidly congeal themselves into a set position, which is suitable, or will be suitable later, for a forward push stroke. Evidently such a set position is premature. The ball may not be suitable for that particular stroke; it may be a ball which ought to be cut or pulled. Thus it appears that this set position, as it were, compromises the batsman. But it has a further disadvantage. If the batsman is standing with his left shoulder and his left elbow artificially urged towards the bowler, he cannot look at the ball fair and square without twisting his head into rather an uncomfortable position, so that his chin is nearly touching his shoulder point. In point of fact, batsmen who stand in obedience to the left-elbow and left-shoulder principle as a rule slightly exaggerate their obedience, and finding it difficult to turn their eyes full to the ball, content themselves with a more or less skew-eyed view of it. Indeed, some batsmen, in waiting for the ball, really see it with one eye only, for the simple reason that the bridge of the nose obstructs the line of sight.

A full view of the ball from the bowler's hand right on to the bat is of the first and paramount importance, since everything depends upon an accurate judgment of the flight of the ball. Therefore the batsman should stand so that he can see the ball fair and square. This at all costs. But the principle of left elbow and left shoulder forward can still be obeyed—when alone it requires to be obeyed, that is, in the actual making of the stroke; for this position of shoulder and elbow is part of the action of certain strokes if correctly played, and does not necessarily belong to what may be described as the attitude of rest from which these strokes originate. There is no doubt whatever, however, that one of the great difficulties, if not the greatest, which a batsman has to overcome is to combine a full sight of the ball with what may be called correct bodily mechanism. It is worth suggesting that what is usually known as the blind spot is a spot created by the batsman himself when his head is in such a position with regard to the ball that his eyes have no chance. Indeed, it is scarcely an exaggeration to say that some batsmen keep their left shoulder so far forward, pointing across the wicket to the off-side, that if a ball pitches a good length on the leg-stump they can only see it out of the tail of the left eye, if at all; it is quite possible that the left elbow and the left shoulder entirely obstruct the ball from view directly the bat begins to swing forward.

So much for the opinions of one of the most accomplished batsmen that ever lived. 'Can you possibly cut or drive as well when you are facing the bowler as when you have the left shoulder up?' Many thought that the answer must be 'No.' But a photograph of R. E. Foster at the wicket shows him to be very much facing the bowler, with his left shoulder pointing almost to forward short-leg, and if ever there was a magnificent off-driver and late-cutter it was he. But then Foster was a genius, and for the less gifted player it may surely be said that if he exaggerates his position in facing the bowling he must lose in off and straight driving, if not necessarily in cutting. The happy mean is what each batsman must discover for himself.

The batsman who overdoes the left elbow and left shoulder forward will, as C. B. Fry says, often find that the bowler pitches the ball on the blind spot, and I remember H. K. Foster, who when he first went up to Oxford adopted this style very considerably, telling me that after bowling to him at the nets the late Alfred Shaw made him alter his position to one which brought both eyes on to the ball throughout its flight. 'A good-length ball on the middle- and leg-stump always puzzled me; I seemed to lose sight of it,' said Foster, and he added that from the time he adopted a position which gave a fuller view of the ball his batting improved. An even more famous bowler than Shaw, the great Spofforth himself, liked bowling at what he called a 'one-eyed batsman'—that is to say, the exaggerated left shoulder forward—as he generally succeeded in getting him caught at mid-on off a good-length ball on the leg-stump.

The late Lord Harris thought that a batsman strengthens his defence at the beginning of his innings by getting in front and facing the bowler, when the bowler is such a one as Hirst, who swerved from the off at a fast pace. My own experience is, however, that the fast-swerving ball as bowled by the famous Yorkshireman did not necessitate one's facing the bowler so much as does the ball from a right-handed bowler who is breaking back on a sticky or crumbling wicket. If anything, I stood rather squarer to Hirst than to Haigh, but, *under the conditions mentioned,* I did not often play forward to either, believing that if one played forward one was very likely to miss the ball and be clean-bowled or bowled off one's pads.

Bowlers who break or swerve from leg, like Barnes of Staffordshire, demand of a batsman that he should have both eyes well on him so as to have a clear view all the way of the leg-stump good-length ball, otherwise a blind spot may very soon arise. But what Lord Harris railed at was the jumping in front and dangling the bat in front of the legs in playing back, and the predisposition to get in front for this stroke before the batsman can possibly tell what the length of the ball is going to be. Here, of course, a batsman's freedom of action is necessarily curbed, and when the ball is turning quickly and occasionally getting up, those who use it are at a disadvantage, as they have not their wrists in reserve for sudden emergencies.

No one would dream of condemning the really first-class batsman for adopting what may be considered unorthodox practices, but it cannot be too strongly insisted that in coaching the young player, the 'face the bowler' theory should be discouraged. It is an evolution of the game resulting, possibly, from the prevalence of leg-break bowling a few years ago—and the only exception ought to be defensive play against such bowling; but for the young player to adopt that position against the ordinary straight or off-side bowling (left or right) must bring disaster. It is impossible to see how he can possess any certainty in his off-side strokes or straight drives. No one advocates the left shoulder and hip forward in an exaggerated manner, so that the left eye seems to be squinting over the shoulder, but it is possible to have both shoulder and hip forward to such an extent that *both eyes* can get a good sight of the ball by a turn of the head. There used to be a difference of opinion as to whether a batsman should stand with his weight equally balanced on both legs or on the right leg only; but nowadays the accepted theory is that the weight should be chiefly on the right leg. Personally, I was a great believer in standing according to the bowling one has to face. If the bowling was fast, I threw the weight of my body on the right leg; if the bowling was slow, I stood almost, one might say, on my toes—ready to jump in to drive, especially if the wicket were difficult. A slight easing of the knees is of advantage, as it enables one to get a quick start at the ball—and quickness of foot is one of the essentials of batting. It is advisable to stand as near as possible to the bat, without being in front of the wicket, for the reason that the nearer one is to the bat the more chance is there of playing absolutely straight and getting well over the ball. I am quite aware that there are one or two first-class batsmen who do not play with a straight bat, but they are men of wonderful eyesight, and their success has not altered my conviction that a boy should be taught to play with a straight bat; as straight, indeed, as Euclid's famous definition. As for taking guard, you can take middle, middle and leg, or leg-stump. It is a mere question of inclination. The bat should be held in the manner most natural to the batsman, but the most common method is with the left hand nearly at the top of the handle and the right hand somewhere about the middle.[1]

The first principle to instil into our young batsman is that he *must never move his right leg in the direction of short-leg*. He may move it to jump out to drive, or to cut, or to play back, *but never should he move it away from the wicket*, except to hit a rank long hop on the off-side. This is the first point to be mastered by the beginner, for if the right leg is withdrawn away from the wicket it is impossible to play with a straight bat. The second is that a *straight bat is essential to success in batting*, though I do not mean to say that the bat should be held straight for every stroke, for the cut and the pull, for instance, are not made with a straight bat; but what I mean is that for defensive strokes, and in some scoring strokes, the bat must be held straight. A batsman who plays with an absolutely straight bat is nearly always a strong defensive player. The third principle is: *watch the ball*. Watch the bowler's hand as he runs up to bowl, and then the ball as it leaves his hand. Watch it closely right on to your bat, and do not start with a preconceived idea of where the ball is going to pitch, and do not make up your mind to make a particular kind of stroke before the ball is delivered.

A minimum amount of movement is essential. If the body moves too soon the head must also move, and the eyes will lose the focus of the ball. The head should therefore be kept steady as long as possible: this is the fourth principle. The bat should be held firmly when the stroke is made, but the muscles in the arms and shoulders should be loose to enable the stroke to be completed without losing balance or finish. If the muscles in the arms and shoulders are rigid,

---

[1] It is of supreme importance that the bat should be raised straight and *not in the direction* of extra-slip. In playing an off-drive the bat should swing from the leg-stump or even from outside it. A free, easy flowing swing is also essential. There should be no ' stabbing ' at the ball—no curtailed back lift. A short back lift militates against the wrists acting freely.

the bat will be dragged by the body and will not finish the stroke properly; balance also will be lost. The forward shoulder should move loosely under the chin, especially in off-play. The forward elbow should bend and point at the bowler when the upward part of the stroke is being made. Here we have principle number five.

All strokes may be conveniently divided into two kinds, back and forward, and back and forward play may be further divided into back and forward play for defensive purposes, and back and forward play with the object of making runs. Let us take *Forward Play,* and imagine that a good-length ball has been delivered on a hard, true wicket. Some batsmen are so strong in their back play that they can play back to almost any good-length ball, but for the moment we are dealing with the young batsman, and to play this ball correctly the batsman should get his left leg well out in the line of the ball, and then bring his bat as close as possible to his leg. This is the secret of all forward play, and the young cricketer cannot be too often urged to ' get the left leg well out to the bat ' when playing forward. Care should be taken not to over-balance oneself; but if body, wrist, and legs work correctly, the ball may be forced past the fielders, and it is really quite extraordinary the power that may be put into the stroke. Some coaches urge that the right foot should not be moved from its original position before the stroke, but this is a theoretical rather than a practical point. Some of the best off-drivers do not move the right toe; but others, and by far the greater number, allow the right foot to follow through with the stroke after the ball has been hit, so that at the finish of the stroke the right foot is either dragged a few inches over the line or moved right up to the other foot. If the right foot is kept flat on the ground *with the heel down*, it is impossible for the right shoulder to come through with the bat. The best advice is to ' allow the right heel full play

W. R. HAMMOND

'Past cover for 4'

DON BRADMAN

The beginning of an off-drive

*G. W. Beldam*

VICTOR TRUMPER JUMPING OUT TO DRIVE

*G. W. Beldam*

HON. F. S. JACKSON
About to 'push' the ball between mid-off and cover-point

without displacing the right toe.' The ball must, of course, be kept down, and in order to do this the left shoulder must be kept well forward, pointing in the direction in which the stroke is made, and the bat must be at such an angle that the top of the handle is nearer to the bowler than the bottom of the handle. The whole weight of the body should be brought to bear on the stroke, and the batsman must make the most of his reach, and the whole thing should be one action and in one motion. The right shoulder should follow round with and after the right arm, otherwise there is no freedom about the stroke, and an off-drive should be played with a free swing. At the moment of actual contact with the ball, the bat should be just behind the left leg. The off-drive may range anywhere from the left of the bowler to just in front of point, and the ball to be thus driven is one that is fairly well pitched up on the off-side of the wicket, but not necessarily a half-volley. The great thing is to get well to the pitch of the ball, watch it, and not slash wildly at it. Care must be taken not to have a ' go ' at too wide a ball, for this is a favourite trick of slow bowlers, especially left-handers, and often results in an easy catch on the off-side. Some critics hold the opinion that no ball within reach should be left alone, but even old Nyren recommends the batsman to have ' nothing to do with ' too wide a ball, and thought that Beldham's habit of cutting at it was ' dangerous play.' There is one stroke which is neither a genuine cut nor a genuine off-drive, and which may be called the ' slash.' The left leg is brought across in the line of a shortish-pitched ball, the right foot being kept still, and the ball being hit with a horizontal bat. This is a stroke which requires a perfect wicket and very accurate timing, but when well timed often goes to the ring with the speed of thought. It is of course dangerous, for should the ball hang or bump unexpectedly, an uppish hit will in all probability follow.

I remember H. K. Foster making two such strokes off successive balls from E. Jones's fast bowling in the match between Oxford and the Australians on the Christ Church ground in 1896. In each case the ball went flying first bounce into the ring. After the second stroke Jones turned round to me—I was in at the other end—and said, ' Does this cove often make strokes like this? ' Jones never forgot those two strokes of Foster's. Many years afterwards, in Australia in 1911, he recalled them in a conversation with me.

A good-length ball on the off-stump should be played in the direction of mid-off, a ball just wide of the off-stump in the direction of extra-cover, and a ball about a foot wide of the off-stump should be played towards cover-point. The farther the ball is pitched outside the off-stump the farther ought the left leg to be thrown across the wicket, and the farther ought the left shoulder to be thrown forward. The wider the ball is the more difficult it is to play; and a mistake common amongst beginners is that, without considering the direction of the ball, they advance the left leg straight down the wicket, just as if, in fact, the ball had pitched on the off-stump, and not, for instance, a foot outside it. *The left leg should be thrown across the wicket almost in a line with the flight of the ball.* If the batsman plays forward at a ball a foot outside the off-stump with his left leg straight down the wicket, he will find that the weight of his body will play no part in the stroke, and that should the ball break back he will be bowled. But in forward strokes, as indeed in all other strokes, the great thing is to watch the ball carefully, for should you be playing forward with ' your head in the air,' that is to say, not looking at the ball, which at the last moment does something unexpected, either bumping or hanging on the pitch, you will find yourself in trouble; and therefore until you are thoroughly well set and have got the exact pace of the wicket, there should be a margin for emergencies, so that it should be possible to alter one's stroke at the last moment. The best way of playing a ball which one has gone forward to, and which one finds one cannot reach far enough to smother at the pitch, is to adopt the 'half-cock' stroke. It is a most excellent defensive stroke, and the proper way to play a ball whose length one has slightly misjudged. It is made by holding the bat quite straight just over or slightly in front of the popping-crease and letting the ball hit it. Dr. Grace and Sir F. S. Jackson used this stroke frequently, and nearly all the best 'moderns' have it in their armoury.

In making a forcing forward stroke the arms should swing freely, and the stroke be carried right through. Some batsmen play this forcing forward stroke so hard that it is difficult to distinguish from a genuine drive. In offensive forward play great care should be taken not to bend the right knee, for with the bending of the right knee comes the sinking of the right shoulder, and if the shoulder sinks the batsman is very likely to get under the ball. It requires no great physique to be a powerful off-driver, for a man of very slight build, for example, Bradman, if he is timing the ball well, can make it travel as fast as a strongly built man. There are few better moments at cricket than when one has forced a good-length ball through the fielders on the off-side, standing well balanced where one is, and the ball speeding to the ring. Amongst the finest off-drivers to-day are Hammond, Bradman, D. Compton, L. Hutton, and E. R. T. Holmes.

## BACK PLAY

This is the age of progress, and that cricket has progressed, and is better and certainly more scientifically played than it was, is generally admitted. The game has advanced so much in popularity, and so much more energy and thought are given to it, that at a time when men were never less willing to take for granted the maxims of their predecessors, but rather desire to know the why and the wherefore of everything, it would have been strange if alterations of style and methods had not crept in.

In batting there has been little short of a revolution. While both the old and the modern school are agreed that in forward play it is essential to get the left leg out to the ball, fifty or sixty years ago there was disagreement between the two schools as to the best method of playing back. The old school contended that the right leg should never be moved in playing back, while the modern generation maintained that a quick movement of the feet was the very essence of sound back play. The contention of the old school may be all very well as an elementary principle for a boy who is just starting cricket, but experience has proved that it is altogether wrong when applied to one who has got over the initial difficulties of the game, though, for myself, were I coaching a boy, however young, I should tell him to move his right leg in playing back, though of course I would not allow him to move it away from the wicket in the direction of the square-leg umpire, unless to hit an atrocious long hop on the off-side. With a moment's thought it will be seen that a batsman who moves his right leg towards the wicket must have a better chance of playing the ball correctly than one who stands with his right leg glued to the ground. In the first place, by moving back towards the wicket he makes the ball he is playing at shorter by the distance which he steps back, and he has more time to watch it from the pitch. By a forward movement the batsman can alter the length of a ball, why then should he not be allowed to alter the length of a ball by a backward movement? The late Arthur Shrewsbury used to move so far back that on occasions one wondered why he did not tread on his wicket.

Secondly, just as in forward play the golden rule is to get the left leg well forward in the direction the ball is taking, with the bat well up to the leg, so in playing back the right leg should be placed in the direction the ball is taking, with the bat as near as possible to the leg. The nearer the batsman's body is to the ball the more likely is he to make a correct stroke, for the reason that his eye is nearer to the object he is striking at.

Supposing the ball pitches on or just outside the off-stump, the batsman will assuredly play that particular ball more correctly if he moves his right leg across the wicket in a line with the off-stump than if he keeps it firmly planted just off the leg-stump; for it stands to reason that if he moves his right leg across the wicket in a line with the ball, he will be nearer the direction the ball may take after pitching than if he adheres to his original position. Again, should the particular kind of ball we are discussing break an inch or two from leg, the odds on his being caught at slip or the wicket are very great should he not move his right leg across the wicket; whereas should he bring his right leg across to the off-stump and watch the ball closely after it has pitched, he will stand a far better chance of playing that ball in the middle of the bat than if he had remained with his right leg rooted to the earth. Then should the ball break back the batsman is equally well prepared for it, for he is well over the ball and better able to contend with the break because more easily able to get into position to play the stroke than if he were standing firmly fixed on his right leg.

Let any cricketer compare the two methods of playing back. If he follows the advice of the old school he will find that he feels uncomfortable and unnatural, in direct contrast to the easy natural movement of the feet which the present generation hold is the essence of successful batsmanship. It is curious that those who deny the necessity of moving the

right leg in playing back are very strong on the ' left leg
out to the ball ' maxim in the case of forward play. The
old cricketer thinks that an action for trespass should lie
against those batsmen who place their legs in ' the bowler's
territory '—meaning thereby the space between wicket and
wicket—but he forgets that in forward play the left leg is
moved across the wicket right down the line of the middle-
and off-stump.  If the principle of moving the body as near
as possible to the line of the ball applies to forward play,
there would seem to be good ground for applying the same
principle to back play. Though they all have this in
common, that they move their right leg both back and
across the wicket in playing back, different batsmen play
back in different ways.  Some walk right in front of the
wicket, face the bowler, and push the bat out in front of
them somewhat stiffly with the hands wide apart.  This is
a good though somewhat ungainly method of defence on
good fast wickets, and on those which are slow and easy,
but when the ball is turning quickly and occasionally getting
up, those who use it are rather at a disadvantage, as they
have not their wrists in reserve for sudden emergencies.
Others, again, frequently play back with the weight on the
right foot entirely and the left shoulder pointing straight
down the wicket, and this I believe to be the best method
to insist on in coaching boys. *I would, I repeat, have no
facing the bowler.* That may be all very well for the finished
batsman; to a beginner it would probably spell ruin. A
third class have the power of playing their stroke at the last
possible moment, which enables them to deal with each ball
on its merits.  The old school complained that batsmen like
Hirst and Hayward, having once determined on a defensive
stroke, allowed the bowler to see very little of the wicket;
but genius must have full scope, and every man must decide
for himself which method is likely to bring him most success.

On a difficult wicket back play is everything; in fact, it

may safely be said that a good rule to bear in mind on a sticky wicket is *to play back or hit*. It used to be thought that ' get out or hit ' was a sound maxim to adopt when the turf was false, but this idea has long been knocked on the head, and the good back player with, of course, some hitting power may confidently expect to do well under these conditions.

The men who can play on the on-side are certain to be the most successful on sticky wickets, for, except when facing left-handed bowlers, the ball is always breaking in to the batsman—though the old theory that a leg-break bowler is not formidable on wet wickets has been scattered to the winds. Against right-handed bowlers who rely on an off-break the ball comes back so much that the cut and the off-drive are to a large extent eliminated, though a really skilful wet-wicket batsman will occasionally be able to make use of the openings on the off-side, bowlers being only human after all and occasionally bowling a bad-length ball. By making use of their legs and bringing all their knowledge of back and on-side play into use against them, batsmen do not fear right-handed bowlers as they used to do in the days when defence was concentrated almost entirely on forward play, and backing up with one's legs was an art not greatly in vogue. A left-handed bowler, however, presents as difficult a problem as ever, and the best method of meeting him is to be ever ready to jump out to drive anything the least over-pitched, and to beware of playing at the good-length ball which pitches just outside the off-stump. For the ball which pitches on the middle- and left-stumps the batsman must work out his own salvation!

Many years ago it was almost heresy to move the right foot when playing back, and the 1904 edition of the Badminton Library[1] lays down the commandment ' never to move the right foot,' and adds: ' Some modern players

---

[1] *Vide* 1920 edition.

move their right leg in front of the wicket in playing back, and under the present rule of l.b.w. this often protects the wicket; but we do not think this sound play, and if the l.b.w. rule were altered it would probably never be seen.' Then Dr. Grace,[1] in one of his books says: ' On no account must you move the right leg.  But you must keep as firm as if it were riveted to the ground, or you will very likely be driven on to your wicket.'

' W. G.,' indeed, is often cited by those who still pin their faith to this rigidity-of-leg theory as a batsman who played back without moving his right foot towards the wicket; but according to the admirable series of photographs taken by G. W. Beldam, the Middlesex cricketer, for *Great Batsmen: their Methods at a Glance*, those who maintain that back strokes should be played without moving the right leg cannot claim W. G. as a supporter.  On pages 15, 16, 19, and 20 of that really wonderfully artistic work W. G. is seen moving his right leg very decidedly in the action of playing back; and we know that the camera, certainly Beldam's camera with its exposure of 1-1000th of a second, does not lie! Look through that book, and it will be found that W. G., K. S. Ranjitsinhji, V. Trumper, C. B. Fry, A. C. MacLaren, F. S. Jackson, M. A. Noble—in fact, the then greatest players in the world—moved the right foot towards the wicket in playing back unless the ball was very short, and then they hit where they pleased from any position they pleased.

I played on several occasions with and against W. G., and he certainly moved his right leg in playing back.

In moving the foot back towards the wicket the great batsmen vary in how much they turn towards the bowler.

In all these various methods the left shoulder is not turned away from the ball in such a way as to pull the left hand with it, for if the shoulder pulls the hands there is difficulty in keeping the bat straight.

[1] W. G. did not always write his own books!

But while the improvement in back play is the reason why many more runs are made nowadays on sticky wickets than used to be the case, there is some danger of this line of defence being overdone on hard true wickets; and I have seen batsmen, and good batsmen too, clean bowled on a perfect wicket through playing back at balls which they should obviously have gone forward to. Forward play is still a very important weapon both of defence and offence on easy wickets, but quite apart from this, it would be the greatest pity if so attractive a stroke as the forward stroke were to die out.

I do not think boys ought to be taught to try to *hook* short balls round to leg, though it is an invaluable stroke on slow wickets; but a rank ' long hopper ' may be hit to any point of the compass with a horizontal bat, though, however short and bad a ball, it should be carefully watched all the way, in case of an unexpected hang or rise. Tom Emmett's advice was the best: ' I won't teach you the hook stroke, but if you *can* do it, well, it will bring you runs. You must judge for yourself.' In making the hook stroke the batsman should move back towards the wicket, turn almost square to the ball, and hit with a horizontal bat, with elbows well away from the body. Hooking a fast bowler is fraught with no little danger, for often the ball comes shoulder high to the batsman. The finest exponents of the hook are Sutcliffe, Bradman, Hendren, R. E. S. Wyatt, S. J. McCabe, and D. Compton. A. C. MacLaren, too, was particularly good at this stroke, as was George Hirst.

## LEG STROKES

A ball rather short of a good length pitching just outside the leg-stump should be played away on the leg-side with a backward movement, the right leg being drawn back some-

c

what towards the wicket with the left foot close beside it, the ball being forced away by a turning movement of the wrists or arms at the last moment as the ball rises from the pitch. The ball must be watched right on to the bat.

To a ball fairly well pitched up that invites forward play the left leg should be thrown down the wicket in a line with the ball, and the moment the ball touches the bat, the bat should be pushed forward by a quick turn of the wrist, the whole weight of the body being put into the stroke, and the body being thrown well forward. ' Lean on her, Sir,' as Tom Emmett used to tell us at Rugby.

For myself I believe in following up the turn of the bat with shoulders and hips, allowing the right leg to come forward over the crease, sometimes bringing it well past the left leg, and thus making a nearly complete half-turn. This stroke may be described as forcing, and pays tremendously against fast and medium right-handed bowlers, and is a particularly effective stroke at Lord's when batting at the end opposite the pavilion, for the slope in the ground tends to accentuate the off-break of any bowler who is on at the pavilion end. These two forcing strokes have practically taken the place of the leg hit, though occasionally one is offered an opportunity of putting it into practice against leg-break or googly bowlers. Hendren was probably the best genuine leg hitter of his day, and I shall not easily forget one magnificent stroke of this kind at Canterbury off D. W. Carr's bowling. Against the ordinary style of bowling I am inclined to think that the forcing stroke is preferable to the square-leg hit, for it is quite as good for scoring purposes, and the ball can be watched right on to the bat, and placed and kept down with far greater certainty.

The *pull* differs from the hook in that it is more in the nature of a drive; indeed, as Fry says, ' it is nothing more or less than the hitting of a ball pitching on the wicket or just outside the off-stump round to square-leg, or to the on-side, just as though the ball had pitched on the leg-side of the wicket.' It is a dangerous stroke, for the ball which can thus be treated requires very careful choosing and timing, and is not to be recommended to boys; it is only for the experienced batsman. The left foot should be thrown out to the pitch of the ball, and just as the ball rises from the ground it should be hit round on the on-side with a horizontal stroke. It is often a very useful stroke on a sticky wicket to a right-handed bowler who is breaking back, though there is a risk of being caught at deep square rather in front of the wicket. On a sticky wicket a right-handed bowler who is making the ball break back will often have six men on the on-side. Indeed I have seen slip done away with under certain conditions, and seven men stationed on the on-side.

A straight half-volley is a ball which every player ought to be able to drive, and it should always be hit in the most natural direction. It is a mistake to try to pull a straight half-volley. The chief point to remember in hitting a half-volley is to get as much swing as possible into the stroke. One or two batsmen swing the bat so far back that they occasionally hit their heads with the back of the bat. The shoulders should come greatly into play in the drive, for they give added power to the swing of the arms, and throw the weight of the body with great force on to the left leg at the moment of hitting the ball. There are various ways of playing the straight drive. Sometimes it is played with a preliminary jump, then a stride, and then a follow-up with the back foot. Again, the feet may be kept rather close together in a series of short jumps to the ball, so that the follow-up with the back foot is almost part of the last jump. Batsmen who are quick on their feet often jump out to the pitch of a ball, and thereby make it a half-volley. Trumper was the great exponent of this stroke, as are Hammond and Bradman, and the rapidity with which they get to the ball is astonishing.

In on-driving the same canons of style hold good as in the straight drive. This stroke is played to balls pitching on or just outside the leg-stump, and, if properly timed, causes a batsman intense satisfaction. Jackson, Fry, Hendren, and Larwood were perfect masters of this stroke, as are Ames and D. Compton.

There are two classes of cuts: the 'square' cut and the 'late' cut. The forward cut is not really a cut at all; it is often described as such, but it is really a 'slashing' stroke, as has been said, and not technically a cut. The *square cut* sends the ball just behind point, and is made by moving the right leg across the wicket in a line with the off-stump, and just as the ball is passing the batsman's body, the bat is brought down by a quick movement of the arms, while more power is added to the stroke by a sharp flick of the wrist. The bat should be slanting downwards towards the ground, in order to get well over the ball. J. T. Tyldesley played this square cut better than anybody else. He brought his bat down from a great height, with an action which may be described as 'throwing the bat at the ball without letting go of the handle.' In the *late cut* the right foot is moved across to the same position as in the case of the square cut, but the ball is hit *after* it has passed the batsman's body. Care must be taken to avoid cutting at a ball too near the wicket. In cutting, the 'hammer principle,' as G. A. Faulkner called it, should be stressed; i.e. the bat should be up and behind before the stroke, and almost touching the ground at the finish. No ball must be cut with the bat *parallel* to the ground. There are few players who cut really well, for the stroke requires the greatest nicety in timing and a strong, flexible pair of wrists. K. S. Ranjitsinhji, Trumper, C. G. Macartney, Tyldesley, Tarrant, Sir F. S. Jackson, R. E. Foster, Duleepsinhji, Bradman, Hobbs, Hutton, Headley, and D. Compton are perhaps the finest cutters ever seen.

So much for the different strokes; but when all is said and done the real difference between an ordinarily good batsman and a great batsman is that the latter knows just a shade sooner exactly what the ball is and is not. Ranjitsinhji was pre-eminent for this quickness of judgment. He knew the fraction of a second sooner than other people the exact length of the ball, and therefore had more time to get into position to play his stroke. A batsman must use his brains as well as his bat, and by constant practice and attention so perfect himself that batting becomes a kind of instinct. Different wickets require different styles. That is what is meant by adaptability in batting. A Lord's wicket in dry weather is different to a Taunton or a Worcestershire wicket. At Lord's the ball will often kick up and occasionally keep very low; at Taunton and Worcester it will come along half-stump high. Then a sticky wicket requires a different game to a perfect wicket. On the former kind you will be playing back at practically every ball which you do not attempt to drive or pull, while on a perfect wicket you will be playing forward, off-driving, and cutting. There has in recent years been a great improvement in on-side play, and this improvement has made the placing of the field more difficult. In days when it was not only bad cricket, but absolutely immoral, to pull or hook a ball, the placing of the field was an easy matter; but nowadays, when nearly all the great batsmen play strongly on the on-side in addition to possessing what may be called the more orthodox strokes like the cut and the off-drive, a captain often finds eleven men far too small a number for his purposes. Formerly a stereotyped affair, the placing of the field is to-day a scientific matter which always demands the utmost care and, therefore, circumspection from a captain. All bowlers whose length is very accurate do their utmost to confine the batsmen to one stroke or to a special set of strokes; and the Test Match at Lord's in 1905 between

*Plan showing position of fieldsmen for right-hand bowler who is making the ball break back on a sticky wicket:*

Long-field

Long-on

Mid-off

Bowler

Mid-on

|||

Cover-point

Deep
Square-leg

Short-leg

Point

|||

Wicket-keeper

Short-leg

*Placing of the Australian field, as viewed from the pavilion, to the bowling of Noble or Laver, June 1905.*

England and Australia will not easily be forgotten, if only for the fact that the Australians bowled without a third man on an easy-paced wicket for the greater part of the first day, and the England eleven contained such superb cutters as Sir F. S. Jackson and Tyldesley. But so accurate was the Australian attack, which, in the hands of medium-paced, right-handed bowlers with an off-break like M. A. Noble and F. Laver, was concentrated almost entirely on the middle- and leg-stumps with six fieldsmen on the on-side, that only one ball was cut past the spot where the third man would have been. And yet late cutting is far from becoming a lost art, as some critics are heard to maintain, only people exercise a wiser discretion and cut at the right ball. Many famous batsmen do not make the late cut a strong point of their game, but every cricketer has his favourite strokes, and any one who thinks that cutting is not the fashion should see Bradman, Hutton, or D. Compton well set on a good wicket.

There is a much-neglected factor of batting, and that is running between the wickets. Remember to run wide of the wicket, and never attempt a run if you feel any doubt as to its safety; for it is far better to lose a possible single than to run out either one's partner or oneself. At the same time I do not think that English cricketers as a rule run well between the wickets. The Australians can give us points in this part of the game; they are extraordinarily quick. It has been laid down that if it is the striker's call, and he calls you, you must go at any cost. I think this dictum fundamentally wrong, for the reason that if there is a prompt and decisive ' No ' to the call to run, ninety-nine times out of a hundred the latter can get back with ease. No batsman that I have ever met objected to being sent back if *the refusal to run was made known immediately*. Many runs are lost by not running the first run fast, but many more are lost in the shape of singles just in front of the batsman, as when the wicket-keeper is standing back, or short of mid-off or mid-on, and to the right or left of point. Again, there is nearly always a run if the ball is going a little to either the right or left side of third man, and I venture to think that an eleven who were masters of the art of running between the wickets would make ten to fifteen per cent more runs in a season than an eleven who adopted the somewhat casual and lifeless manner of running which is prevalent to-day. Hobbs, Sutcliffe and Rhodes were the best of English runners, as are Washbrook and Paynter of to-day.

Many batsmen, when nearing their 50 or 100, attempt the most absurd runs. The fault is more common amongst professional cricketers than amongst amateurs, probably due to the old talent money, or £1 for every 50 runs, now happily done away with, a better and fairer substitute being provided in the shape of marks. By this system each professional is ' marked ' for his work in a particular game. Each mark represents five shillings, and 25 runs on a bad wicket or even 10 not out in a one-wicket victory would be rewarded. A fine bowling feat or a fine catch is similarly rewarded. There is one thing that no coaching will teach a young cricketer, and that is confidence. Time and experience alone can give him that. I do not believe the cricketer who says he is never nervous, but nervousness will gradually disappear as a batsman gains confidence in himself. Too much confidence is a mistake, but too much is better than no confidence. Nervousness is largely a matter of health, at any rate with the seasoned cricketer, who, even if only occasionally, if he is honest, will admit to feeling nervous. If one is fit and well, and there are no worries to disturb one's peace of mind one goes in to bat with little nervousness. Even then every cricketer worth his salt is *keen* to do well, which, however, is a very different thing from being nervous.

Then there are the extra-superstitious men who think they

cannot make runs unless they go in to bat in a particular place. These men should be humoured, because if they really believe what they say a captain will get the better out of them, and *thereby the side will benefit*. Many cricketers are extremely particular in regard to what cap, shirt, or trousers they wear. I know several men who have lucky trousers, and as for myself, I never dreamt of going in to bat wearing any other cap than a Harlequin. The first time I wore it at Oxford it brought me good luck, and, taking one year with another, it did not belie that reputation. Also I used to believe in having my pads cleaned before every match—'rubbing some runs into them,' as Philip Need, the dressing-room attendant at Lord's, used to say; and finally, I used to like George Bean to bowl to me at the nets before a match. Not once or twice but several times I made a big score after he had given me some practice.

Public school cricket seems at the moment to be in a satisfactory condition, but I cannot help thinking that an even higher standard of excellence would be obtained if the pitches throughout the various schools were better. To my mind the first and most important essential in teaching boys cricket is a good, indeed a perfect, pitch, and for this reason every practice wicket in every game in every school should be prepared with marl, if the turf is not naturally, as it seldom is, capable of producing a really good pitch. There will be some, I am aware, who will disagree with me on this point; but I maintain that rough and dangerous wickets murder the chances of a good batsman; and, moreover, on such wickets boys will neglect the art of slow and 'heady' bowling, and will bowl as fast as they can, irrespective of spin, break, length, or flight, for they will discover that on such wickets the fast 'plugger' will be the most successful. I am, therefore, advocating the perfect wicket in the interests of the bowler as well as of the batsman.

Why are the Australians, with a population of only seven

millions, able to hold their own with us? The reason is that Australian boys are taught the game on absolutely perfect pitches, with the result that they acquire an easy, natural style, that they learn all the strokes, that they gain confidence, and that the game is a delight to them. Far too often in our great schools the pitches are very far from good, with the result that the small boy, fresh from the good wickets of his preparatory school, is often hit, he loses his strokes, and his confidence, and his delight in and enthusiasm for the game goes. I would earnestly urge on those responsible for the cricket at our Public Schools the *absolute necessity* of a good pitch. The pitch on which an actual game is played need not be quite so good—it must not, however, be bumpy or in any way dangerous—and if pitches were as good as I would have them, we should, with our natural aptitude for the game, produce and continue to produce a splendid array of amateur cricketers, and many a natural cricketer who now turns in disgust and disappointment from the game would be found and not lost.

It is a fallacy to say that bad pitches encourage bowlers. They encourage the wrong type of bowler, the brute force type, not the artist; and on this point I would like to quote from an article which was written by the Hon. Ivo Bligh, later Lord Darnley, in James Lillywhite's *Cricketers' Annual* for 1884, after his famous pilgrimage to Australia to recover the ashes:

The standard of Australian cricket must always be a high one, for one all-powerful reason—the Australian cricketer will always pass through the earlier stages of his cricket career with good wickets to play on, and the advantages arising from that condition are immense. The young batsman will always have every inducement to practise a free and upright style, and the young bowler will have to make use of every wile in his power of twist and change of pace, to break through the defence of batsmen on the easy wickets. Boys cannot acquire the necessary confidence and style on wickets where a rough and ready slogger, who would hit up his 25 regardless of catches, could afford to laugh at the player who, adopting a more scientific style, would soon have to retire, caught off the inevitable bumpy one.

As regards coaching, much harm is often done by a coach worrying a boy. Boys need encouraging, and men too, for that matter, and they should be taught in a happy spirit and not ' sträfed.' My own experience is that the best coaches talk the least. They say little at the time, but after the practice is over a few quiet words will be of value. A coach should be on the look-out for individuality, and beware of cramping a natural style. You cannot turn out batsmen on one pattern; and often the fact is lost sight of that no two boys, or men, bat exactly alike. Build, strength, arm, and wrist have all to be taken into consideration. A coach who tried to make a Jessop bat like a Jardine or a Hobbs would be depriving us of a genius. If a batsman become ' stale '—all cricketers experience this—he should have a complete rest from cricket for three or four days, and then be taken to a net and half-volleys on his legs and outside his off-stump bowled to him.

A coach must, of course, be enthusiastic and possess a sound knowledge of the game and all its varying phases and ideas; and if to these he adds encouragement and a pleasant method of instruction he will soon find himself the proud maker of a good side.

## SOME SUGGESTIONS TO COACHES

1. Do not try to make every boy bat alike. Encourage individuality. If his coaches had insisted on Jessop batting in the orthodox style, a great player would have been lost to the world. Be on the look-out for genius.

2. *Orthodoxy*, with the above exception, should be the great object. Just as the recruit is taught to turn to the

right and left, and to march properly, before he engages in field exercises, so the young cricketer should be taught to walk before he can run.

3. Remember that batting on a hard, true wicket and on a sticky one are two entirely different things. Roughly speaking, the rule should be forward play on good wickets, *back* play or hit on bad wickets.

4. Boys should be taught to play back as well as forward. Back play is probably more useful, taking one day with another, than forward. In many instances back play is not taught to boys at all.

5. Get out of your head the old idea about *not* moving the right leg. It is extinct. A boy should be encouraged to move his feet about, *so long as he does not move them away from the wicket in the direction of short-leg*. Encourage quickness of foot. It is the keynote of batting, and remember to *get sideways*.

6. If a boy exhibits hitting powers but lacks defence, encourage him in his hitting. Defence can be taught afterwards, and is largely a matter of experience.

7. Do not, on any account, allow a boy ' to face the bowler ' in playing back.

8. Don't talk too much at the time the boy is batting. Point out his mistakes quietly, and after he has left the net much may be taught him.

9. If a boy is playing back with a crooked bat, make him play with one hand for five minutes at a time every day. This is the method the splendid coaches which Harrow enjoy adopted when MacLaren was found to be playing back with a crooked bat.

10. When jumping out to drive go the whole way. You may just as well be stumped by two feet as by two inches should you miss the ball. ' If you come to her, come ' (Tom Emmett). And *chassé* to the ball—that is with the right foot moving behind the left heel. This will get you quicker

to the pitch of the ball and moreover will help to bring your left shoulder well over the line of the ball.

11. Physical co-ordination will make a slightly built man a strong player, for it means timing the ball.

12. Neatness, precision and accuracy all help, and balance is vital. J. T. Tyldesley used to say: ' Get into the ball-room in the winter.' Dancing will improve your balance and quickness of foot.

13. A word of encouragement at the right time is worth a great deal.

14. Never allow a boy to bat on a bumpy wicket. On a sticky one—yes; but *never* on a dangerous one.

15. All strokes should be played, at the moment of impact of bat and ball, *under the nose*. ' Smell her, sir, smell her,' as Tom Emmett used to say.

16. At the first practice of the year it is rather a good plan to cast aside orthodoxy for the time being, and to allow the boys to have a good ' slog ' in order to loosen arms and shoulders.

17. Do not, as is occasionally done, allow a white line across the pitch to mark the dividing line between balls to be played forward and balls to be played back. This encourages a mechanical and stereotyped style of play, is too theoretical, and takes no heed of the fact that the pace of the bowler and the pace of the wicket make a difference as to whether a ball should be played back or forward.

18. If possible, arrange for the boys to see an occasional day's first-class cricket. Much may be learnt by watching a great batsman or bowler.

19. Boys do not smoke at school, at least they are supposed not to. Men may note the fact that Grace, Trumper, Ranjitsinhji, and Bradman, four of the greatest batsmen that have ever lived, have been non-smokers.

20. Finally, try to make boys understand what a beautiful game cricket is, and how much good there is in it.

F. T. Badcock, the New Zealand cricketer and an admirable coach, has been good enough to give me his ideas on the art of training young cricketers:

The essentials are that a good coach should possess good temper, unlimited patience and the ability to ' get inside ' his pupil, so that he can readily work out the puzzles that the latter is bound to create in his own mind. Some boys are very hesitant in asking questions and it is to them that the above applies more particularly.

In addition it is obvious of course that he should have a very intimate knowledge of *all* departments of the game, including captaincy. Whenever you tell a boy anything, the reason for it must be explained. For instance, it is of little use to tell him to keep his right foot still when playing forward on the leg-side, unless you tell him why he has to do so and what happens if he doesn't. Something after this style. Imagine the crease to be the base of a protractor with your right foot on the 90 degree mark. In playing forward on the off-side, your left foot is put forward into the various lines of degrees radiating from the base, but the right foot remains in its place. Similarly on the leg-side the same thing should occur. If, however, the right foot is drawn back in the direction of square-leg, the ball becomes a *straight one* as far as the batsman is concerned and must be played as such, thus depriving you of your scoring stroke on the leg-side and there are plenty of runs to be had in that direction.

No two boys are exactly alike in their play or in their ability to absorb instruction, and a coach should be a man of many methods. Some boys are very quick in the uptake. To them a quiet word or a gesture is sufficient, but to others it may be necessary almost to hammer it in. This can be done with a smile, but you have to make the boy realize you mean to get him right, and a word of praise now and again works wonders. It is a mistake, however, to remain too long on the same stroke. Far better to leave it, go on to something else, and then come back to it. Very often the pupil gets it right without knowing he has done so. Once that happens you should have little difficulty in keeping him right. When the stroke has been mastered, it should be explained to the pupil the various times it can be played, having regard to the state of the wicket and the type of bowling. Try and conjure up a picture in his mind that he may recognize when he meets it. Experience will teach him the rest.

Your disappointments will be many, but you have to realize that you can only go so far with your pupil and then it is up to him to use his brains to reproduce your instructions and the successful result is your reward.

Most coaches will pay attention to the position of the feet, and this is admirably described in the chapter on Batting, but no mention has been made of the position of the hands. It is amazing what positions a pupil will adopt. Remember always that the most natural is the best position. A simple way of ensuring this is as follows:

Take your guard and then, standing upright with the feet in the position already described, let the handle of your bat rest against your left thigh. The hands are at your side, palms inward and if you like ' thumb in line with the seam of the trousers! ' Without changing the position of your hands, lift your arms in front of you, and then stooping slightly, bring your hands down on to the handle of the bat. Grip with your fingers, lift up the bat and you will find you have free movement of your wrists whatever you play. It will ensure, too, a natural ' pick up.' Try it and see for yourself. You will see that the top hand lies in a position midway between being too far round in front of the handle, and too far behind the handle with a locked wrist and forearm. In nearly all strokes, especially when driving, the hands should be kept close together, but in back and forward defensive play (see plate of Warren Bardsley) the bottom hand should be slipped down to the bottom of the handle, with only the thumb and forefinger holding it. The batsman has full control as by straightening his top wrist and holding back with the bottom hand he can ' kill ' the ball practically dead when required.

In back play this position of the bottom hand ensures that the left elbow is not cramped into the body but has freedom of movement clear of it.

*Feet.* The whole essence of batting lies in correct footwork. If you watch a good batsman you will probably be struck by the ease with which he makes his strokes. He always seems to have plenty of time. This is because he has already decided on his stroke and has completed the movement of his feet to the correct position, whereas a mediocre batsman would be still moving into position.

With the young batsman two main faults in the positioning of his feet emerge. Though his stance at the crease is fundamentally correct as already described, it is an extraordinary thing that, when it comes to moving his feet, he should try and change their relative position by pointing the toe of the forward foot straight towards the bowler when playing forward. Unless he is a contortionist, the continuation of the stroke must swing the right shoulder forward and the left shoulder and elbow away. Result—the bat is brought clean across the line of the ball, with the inevitable result.

When playing back, the same thing occurs if, when the back foot is moved across the wicket, the toe is turned to point up the wicket. The next movement is to bring the forward foot back and the whole body is turned with the shoulders square to the bowler.

Another fault is, I think, the direct result of golf. In making his forward stroke the batsman allows his rear knee to bend and point towards the ground, the heel being raised and pointing upwards. The result is to force the rear hip forward, turning both shoulders square to the bowler. A genuine finish to a golf stroke but not conducive to a correct stroke at cricket.

There are a number of pictures of famous batsmen jumping out to drive. In every case it will be seen that the weight of the body is *backward*. This is perfectly in order where these men are concerned, but not as far as a young pupil is concerned. The tendency of this movement is to throw the head back, balance is lost with both feet off the ground, and invariably the amount of ground ' made ' toward the ball can be measured in *inches only instead of feet*. I believe it is very much better to make the pupil use his feet to get to the ball, not by jumping, but by walking out sideways, crab fashion, the weight of the body always on the forward foot. If necessary the rear foot can be brought past and behind the front foot on the second step, assuring that a considerable amount of ground is covered. The movement is smooth, there is no jerk to disturb the focus of the eyes, and the batsman arrives in a perfectly balanced position for the completion of his stroke.

When two moving objects are travelling in the same straight line but in opposite directions they must meet. In this case it is bat and ball. On this assumption, and to keep the bat straight, coaches insist on their pupils keeping their forward elbow ' up.' Too much insistence on this however is apt to prove *too* correct in so far as loss of power of stroke, especially in driving. It should be impressed on the pupil that keeping the elbow up does not necessarily mean keeping it bent. The arm can be straight with the point of the elbow on top of the arm. The use of the wrists in driving is essential, but if the follow-through is continued in the same direction as the ball, the elbow is on top as already described. There is a tendency,

C. G. MACARTNEY
Back play, feet right back

*G. W. Beldam*

R. H. Spooner
Beautiful finish of an off-drive

however, of bringing the hands up short towards the forward shoulder which allows the under wrist to ride over the upper and the elbow is then definitely underneath. This is the wrong finish for the beginner who cannot do better than to copy the stroke of R. H. Spooner in this book.

D

# CHAPTER II

## BOWLING

BOWLING is as important a feature of the game of cricket as batting. There is, and always has been, as much fame in store for the successful bowler as for the successful batsman; but in spite of this the number of really good bowlers in the history of the game is far smaller than the number of really good batsmen. This would seem to show either that the art of bowling is more difficult of attainment than its sister accomplishment, or that sufficient attention is not devoted to it. That the cultivation of bowling was somewhat neglected in past years I believe to be true, but the discovery of the off-breaking leg-break ' googly ' bowling has given a stimulus to a department of the game which sadly needed it; and nowadays it is probably safe to say that great pains are taken to teach the young generation that bowling is quite as interesting and quite as fascinating as batting. The success of Bosanquet, D. W. Carr, Schwarz, Faulkner, Vogler, and G. C. White opened the eyes of the cricketing world to the fact that there is no such thing as finality in bowling, and the spread of new theories and ideas must benefit the game all round considerably.

I do not propose to deal with the theory and practice of bowling, as it has been dealt with before in previous cricket books. My idea is that boys and young men will learn more about the art of bowling if they study carefully the styles and methods of our greatest bowlers. For this purpose I have selected Bosanquet and Carr as representatives of the ' googly ' and leg-break school; Barnes, of Staffordshire, and

J. T. Hearne as the two medium-paced right-hand bowlers; W. C. Smith, of Surrey, as the slow right-hander; Rhodes and Blythe as the slow left-handers; Larwood and G. O. Allen as the fast right-handers; Hirst and F. R. Foster as the fast ' swerving ' left-handers; and Simpson-Hayward as the ' lob ' bowler. These men, I think, represent every style of bowling known to English cricket.

Years ago the Australians taught us that steadiness of length was not the only thing to be aimed at in bowling; that it was even worth while giving away a few runs if there was a definite object in view; and that, in fact, mere mechanical accuracy was but one of the means, and not the sole means, towards the discomfiture of the opposing batsmen. Bosanquet has been called the ' Googly King '—it is certain that he invented the googly—and it is not too much to say that when he started to bowl his off-breaking leg-break he opened a new era in our national game. Few indeed were those who could tell for certainty, when batting against Bosanquet, which way the ball was going to break. After the third Test Match at Adelaide in 1904, when the Australians defeated the M.C.C. team by 216 runs, Clement Hill remarked that 'Bosanquet would not get another wicket in Australia, as they had all discovered his secret'; and yet in the next Test Match he not only had Hill stumped but took four other wickets, and Hill candidly confessed that he was still in the dark as to which direction the ball would take after pitching. And then in a Gentlemen *v.* Players at the Oval, Lilley, who was some 20 runs not out, remarked at luncheon-time to Bosanquet: ' Well, anyway, you won't get me out. I know you too well.' Immediately after lunch, however, he clean bowled him with a ball which the Warwickshire wicket-keeper thought was breaking from the off and which broke from leg!

Luckily for batsmen, Bosanquet had his off days, when full penalty was exacted from him.

Playing ' Tisty Tosty ' over a table with a tennis-ball was
the origin of the now famous googlies, and the moment he
discovered that it was possible with a leg-break action to
put on the opposite spin he set to work to perfect the new
discovery. In the nets, between the fall of wickets in a
game, at stump cricket, on board ship—wherever, indeed,
he had the chance—he practised.

When he first attempted to put his new-found theory into
practice in county matches he was laughed at by scores of
sound judges, and I remember a very well-known cricketer
remarking that it was not only absurd but positively immoral that such ' stuff ' should be allowed in first-class
cricket.

A remark which Hill made to me at Adelaide a day or
two before we left Australia may be worth while repeating,
as throwing light on the success of the 1903-4 M.C.C.
team.

'If you had not had Bosanquet on your side,' he said,
'we should have won the rubber. Our first few batsmen
generally made a good start, but there were five or six on
the side who were practically certain to be got out by
Bosanquet. They were all good bats, and in reality we had no
tail, for those men who failed against Bosanquet would have
made their thirties and forties against Rhodes, Hirst, Arnold,
and Braund. It was the peculiarity of Bosanquet's bowling
which won you the rubber.'

Bosanquet told me that he first worked out the principle
with a tennis-ball over a table. ' I used to bowl it at
stump cricket with a rubber ball, afterwards practised it in
nets and between the fall of the wickets off and on for four
or five years before I bowled it in a match. It took a lot
more practice after that to get it any good, and I always
required constant practice if I wished to keep any control
over the ball. The whole secret of it lies in turning the
ball over in the hand by *dropping the wrist* at the moment

of delivery, so that the axis of spin is changed from left to right to right to left, thus converting the spin from being an ordinary leg-break into an ordinary off-break. That is the whole secret, and the *only way* the ball can be bowled. It is simply an off-break delivered in a new way, and obtained by a different method. The spin is the same for both breaks (leg and off), and is obtained by the same movement of the fingers, *but* its direction is altered. *Voilà tout!*'

Every googly bowler will admit that it is easier to bowl in a warm climate like Australia and South Africa, and that a matting wicket is a great help, for the ball not only gets a good grip on the matting, thus enabling it to break to a surprising extent, but it also takes the break and does its work very quickly, and at the same time gets up to a good height. I only once saw Bosanquet bowl on a matting. This was at San Francisco, and his analysis worked out at eleven wickets for 37 runs. The batsmen opposed to him were very weak, but he made the ball dance!

*D. W. Carr* was originally a medium-paced right-handed bowler, but after seeing Bosanquet bowl, ' just for a rag ' he practised googlies in the winter. It took Carr a long time to find out the idea, but as all the world knows, he finally obtained a complete mastery over the ball, and his case goes to show what energy and perseverance, coupled with intelligence, can do. When bowling a googly Carr put the spin on with the third finger as if he were about to send down a *leg-break*, turned the hand well over, at the same time dropping the wrist, and let the spin come off the same finger. *The actual grip of the ball was the same for both spins —off and leg.* The leg-break was put on by the third finger, which began to act on the ball *before the arm reached the top of its swing*, while the googly break came off the third finger,

*Field for Bosanquet's bowling:*

*Showing position of various fieldsmen*

Long-on                                    Long-off

      Mid-on

                    Mid-off

            Bowler

            III

                            Cover-
                            point

Deep
Square-leg

     Short-leg

         III

                   Point, deep

       Wicket-keeper

               Slip

*Occasionally short-leg would drop back to deep square-leg, and cover-point would move back deep to save the 'four.'*

which did not impart any spin to the ball until the *arm had nearly reached* the top of its swing.

The actual googly which I bowled [writes Mr. Carr], was more an *arm action* break than a true finger spin, the spin being put on more by cutting under the ball with the third finger, the ball coming out from behind the hand with the back of the hand facing downwards. My tactics were to place the field for the leg-break, and to use the googly as an incentive to make the striker get himself out off the leg-break; quite seventy-five per cent of my wickets were obtained by the leg-break, and I do not think that the googly in itself will be of very much use in the future without a good leg-break to help it.

Carr believed in a low delivery *for a leg-break*, as in his opinion it gives the bowler much more scope for variety both in pace and elevation, while the ball comes off the wickets faster in comparison to its pace through the air than the same break delivered with a higher action, the reason being that it is possible to impart more top spin with a low delivery than with a high one. This is not a generally accepted theory, and does not apply to any other type of ball; but Carr gives sound reason for his opinion, and batsmen generally found it very difficult to 'get to' his leg-breaking ball. On the other hand, 'it is,' says Mr. Carr, 'very difficult to get any googly spin on the ball with a low delivery.' The idea is common that the googly comes off the pitch much the faster of the two breaks, but I fancy that this has been somewhat exaggerated. When a batsman playing for a leg-break receives a googly, and is bowled by it, he is apt to think that it has come very fast off the pitch, just as when he is bowled by an unusually fast ball he is apt to think that ball has kept low.

It is not so difficult, in Carr's opinion, to keep a moderate length as people think. 'If the wicket is a trifle worn, both breaks take their spin quite easily and without any extra effort. This is certainly not the case when the wickets are absolutely plumb like those I have met more than once at the Oval—and never elsewhere. On this class of wicket my googly did not turn at all, and the leg-break very little. It is just that extra effort to impart more spin than usual to the ball that is absolutely fatal to a steady length.

' The actual finish of the bowler's delivery is so entirely different that viewed from the pavilion it is comparatively easy to distinguish between which is the leg-break and which the googly. The pavilion, however, is a long way from the wickets, and at the moment the bowler is " giving the googly away " by his finish, the batsman has to have his eye fixed on the ball. *The pavilion critic need not look at the ball at all; he simply watches the bowler's action.*'

In writing of googly bowling something must, of course, be said of the South African cricketers, who brought this style of attack almost to perfection.

Until the visit of the South Africans to England in the summer of 1907 the Australians were generally regarded as the only possible challengers of our skill in the cricket field, but the results of that tour showed conclusively that yet another rival from His Majesty's Dominions across the seas had arisen to dispute our supremacy. For thirty years we had been accustomed to think that the only country outside England where cricket attained to anything like our own standard was Australia, when lo and behold the South Africans appear, and their googly bowlers at once proceed to puzzle our famous batsmen, and to establish for themselves reputations equal to those of Spofforth, Palmer, Turner, and Trumble, the great Australian bowlers.

Those cricketers who had been to South Africa in the winter of 1905–6 were prepared for something of this sort, but to the majority of people the success of the South Africans came as a positive shock. Could Spofforth, they asked, have been more difficult to play on a sticky wicket than was Faulkner in the Test Match at Leeds, when according to an old hand, ' it was like playing Briggs through the air and Tom Richardson off the pitch,' and was Palmer, or even Spofforth, a better bowler than Vogler?

All the trouble Vogler, Faulkner, and Co. caused English batsmen may be traced to Bosanquet. Bosanquet taught Schwarz, Schwarz found imitators in South Africa, and the pupils proved better than their tutors. Schwarz was not really a googly bowler, for he broke only from the off, though always with a leg-break action; but Vogler, Faulkner, and White were genuine googly bowlers.

On sticky wickets, of which there were a great many in the season of 1907, the South African bowlers were seen to tremendous advantage, and it was the general opinion that on such wickets they were the finest *combination* of bowlers that ever lived, though I fancy that Spofforth and Barnes in their best days were just as good, if not better, under similar conditions.

I have heard it suggested that the South Africans were handicapped by the wet summer, and that their bowlers would have done even better in a dry season, but with this view I do not agree, for the following reason. They played four matches in genuine summer weather—the first Test Match at Lord's, the Surrey match, the Notts match, and the match at Scarborough—and in the first of these England scored 428, Surrey 239 and 225 (Surrey winning by 85 runs), Notts 296 and 164 for five wickets (Notts winning by five wickets), and at Scarborough C. I. Thornton's XI scored 397 and 232 for two wickets. These facts and the high scoring of the Australian batsmen against the googly seem to prove that the South African bowlers were not invincible on true wickets, and should be borne in mind in comparing them with the best Australian bowlers.

In his article in *Wisden's Almanack* for 1908 R. E. Foster gave an admirable description of these South African bowlers, who in their methods were so essentially up to date. Foster thought Vogler 'the greatest bowler in the world' at that

*Field placed for Carr's bowling (or R. V. W. Robins, Free-man, or Mitchell):*

*Showing position of various fieldsmen*

Long-on

Mid-off

Bowler

Mid-on

|||

Cover-point

Square-leg

Point, deep

|||

Wicket-keeper

Third Man

Slip    Extra-slip

*Occasionally extra-slip is moved across to short-leg, in front of the umpire, and when the googly is on its way, by prearranged signal slip often dashes across on the leg-side to a sort of fine short-leg. Occasionally, too, Carr would have another long-field instead of the extra-slip.*

time, while he had a high opinion of White and Faulkner. Schwarz he thought the easiest of the four, 'as he only broke one way.'

All these South African bowlers sent down a ball which with an apparent leg-break action broke from the off. Schwarz, who possessed the most pronounced leg-break action of the four, always, as I have already said, broke from the off, and the secret of his success lay in the extra-ordinary pace and height at which the ball came off the ground. On matting wickets and on a crumbling grass wicket Schwarz's deliveries were like 'a thing possessed,' so great was the spin on them, while the ball on pitching often described what might be called a parabola, and certainly came at quite a different height to the ordinary bowler's off-break. Schwarz could make the ball break anything from six inches to two and a half feet; perhaps he often broke too much and did not use the plain straight ball enough.

At the beginning of his run up to the wicket, Vogler seemed almost certain to get out of his stride, but the last few steps were easy and natural. He had a difficult flight through the air, and usually bowled a leg-break of a very accurate length. Every now and again he would bowl with the same action as for a leg-break, an off-break, which came off the pitch at a wonderful pace. This off-break rarely turned more than three or four inches, and sometimes came perfectly straight through.

Faulkner and White bowled practically alike. They both bowled the googly, but Faulkner was quicker through the air and came off the pitch rather faster, while his off-break did a good deal more than White's, which more often than not went straight on.

Undoubtedly these unorthodox South Africans afforded a most interesting study. Possibly they had too much googly bowling. The ideal side on a perfect wicket would, in my opinion, contain two googly bowlers, one medium right-hander, one left-hander, and one fast right-hander—say Vogler, Faulkner, Barnes, Lockwood, and F. R. Foster.

The best way to play the googly is to play each ball on its merits, and not to try to spot which is the leg-break and which the googly. Of course, if you do find out which is which, so much the better, but it is a mistake to 'worry.' Hobbs told me that he *never knew for certain which way Vogler and Faulkner were going to break the ball*, and his batting in South Africa for the M.C.C. team was described as equal in skill and brilliancy to that of Trumper's in the English season of 1902.

S. H. Emery, who was here with the Australian XI of 1912, was, potentially, the most difficult googly bowler I have ever seen. He bowled medium pace varied by an occasional really fast yorker, and being immensely strong in the forearm and wrists, and possessing long and powerful fingers, used to impart tremendous spin to the ball. When he struck a length he was a great match winner, but he was uncertain. M. A. Noble held a high opinion of his possibilities.

A. A. Mailey, the Australian who had such startling success against us shortly after the Great War, was for a time without an equal in this type of bowling, the best English exponents of which are, or were, Freeman and Wright, of Kent, R. W. V. Robins, I. A. R. Peebles, and Mitchell, of Derbyshire. Of these Freeman was the best, his length being very accurate.

It is not easy to assign the palm to any one of these googly bowlers. Perhaps Faulkner, or Vogler, in his day was the actual best, but the Australians, H. V. Hordern and A. A. Mailey, would be strong rivals to either of the two South Africans. Hordern never came here with an Australian XI, but when quite a young man he was a member of the Haverford College, U.S.A., eleven, which played a series of matches *v.* our Public Schools, and in 1908 he was here with the Philadelphian team. On returning to Australia, the country of his birth, he met with great success. For New South Wales and for Australia against the South Africans who toured Australia in 1910–11, and against the M.C.C. Australian team in 1911–12, Hordern kept a perfect length and made the ball appear to be farther up to the batsman than it really was. He bowled at a pace rather similar to that of R. W. V. Robins, delivering the ball right over his head. To the regret of all he retired after the Australian season of 1911–12.

If our budding left-handed slow bowler lived in the north, he could not have done better than watch *Verity* bowl; or he might have been fortunate enough to have seen *Rhodes* in action. Coming out for Yorkshire in 1898—his first match being against the M.C.C. at Lord's in May of that year—Rhodes was one of the great figures of English cricket from that time up to 1931. No bowler, with the possible exception of A. G. Steel, has performed so brilliantly in his first year of county cricket. Rhodes in his prime was superb; for he was accurate in his length, had a deceptive flight, and on a sticky wicket could make the ball 'talk.'

His action was fascinatingly easy; it seemed literally part of himself. He took three steps up to the wicket, placing the weight of his body chiefly on the heels, and delivered the ball on the fourth step. He was easier to see than Blythe, who began his swing with his arm right round his back, and had a quick finish to his swing. Verity was Rhodes' successor, and a very good one, too, with a style modelled on Rhodes.

The late *Colin Blythe*, of Kent, was the very model of what a slow left-hand bowler should be. No finer bowler

*Field placed for Rhodes, Blythe, Verity, James Langridge,*
*or Parker, slow left-hand:*

*Showing position of various fieldsmen*

Long-off

Mid-off

Bowler

Mid-on
Deep
Extra-cover

|||

Extra-cover

Extra-cover

Short-leg
Cover-point

|||

Point
Wicket-keeper

Slip

*On a sticky wicket these bowlers would have two slips, short-leg*
*coming across to extra-slip.*

of his kind has ever appeared. Peel, Briggs, Peate, Rhodes, and J. J. Ferris, the Australian, were, in their day, great bowlers, but he would be a rash man who would aver that even Peel, for instance, was a *greater* bowler than Blythe. On a sticky wicket Blythe did exactly what he liked with the ball, and on wickets which favoured the batsmen I have seen him keep runs down and get men out as well. Over and above everything else he was a 'flighty' bowler— a master of varieties of pace. Every slow left-hander should cultivate 'flight.' 'Bowling,' to use Blythe's own words, 'an occasional ball from a yard or two behind the crease is a very good plan to adopt, and by bowling to a quick-footed batsman a slow left-hander will learn that he will have to bowl slightly faster to some batsmen than to others.'

Here are seven rules for our embryo Blythe to remember:

1. Obtain a thorough command of length, as it is no good varying the pace and flight of the ball without a good length to follow.

2. Try not to be put off if you are hit.

3. Perseverance and patience are essential.

4. Never be annoyed if catches are missed, as it is certain to upset your bowling. In the long run things generally level themselves up, and you will find that many brilliant catches are caught.

5. Don't worry too much about breaking the ball, as a left-hander has a natural break.

Bowl the ball that comes with the arm every now and again—Blythe bowled a very distinct swerver with a new ball—but be careful not to overdo it; twice in every three or four overs is ample. With a new ball you may attempt it more frequently.

6. Keep your arm as high as possible.

7. No two batsmen play exactly alike, therefore watch

carefully the style of each man as he comes in, altering your field to suit his style.

Blythe began to bowl when he was about eleven years old, and the first time he saw Kent play was the means of his adopting the game as a profession. Kent were playing Somerset at Blackheath. 'I don't think,' says Blythe, 'there were many more spectators than players. Walter Wright came out to practise and asked me to " bowl him a few." Captain McCanlis happened to be present, and took my name and address.' The result was an invitation to the Tonbridge Nursery, and up to the end of 1914, the summer before the war, Blythe, who first appeared for Kent in 1900, was the mainstay of his county's attack. He was killed in France in 1917.

*W. C. Smith*, of Surrey, was for many years regarded as a slow-wicket bowler pure and simple, but one season, 1910, he excelled on every kind of wicket. On a sticky wicket I think he was just about the most difficult bowler I have ever played, with the exception of Barnes. He differed in method entirely from the great majority of slow right-handers, for he relied chiefly on the ball that broke from leg to get men out on sticky wickets, and not on the break-back like most of his class. Smith had a difficult flight, spun the ball so much that the batsman could hear the snap of his fingers, and was altogether such a brainy and interesting bowler that I shall go into some detail in describing his methods.

When bowling an off-break Smith placed the top joint of the first finger alongside the seam, while the third finger was underneath the ball, the top joint in this case being

---

NOTE. The left shoulder of a right-handed bowler should be pointed almost towards short-leg in delivering the ball. This gives body-swing and consequent fizz off the pitch. A left-handed bowler should point the right shoulder towards extra-slip.

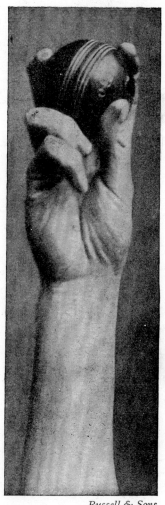

*Russell & Sons*

W. C. Smith

Leg-break

*Russell & Sons*

W. C. Smith

Off-break

C. BLYTHE IN THE ACT OF DELIVERING THE BALL
Note how far the left arm is swung behind the back

bent across the seam, the top of the thumb and the whole of the second finger being used to keep the ball in position. As he ran up to the wicket Smith worked the ball with his left hand up into the tips of his fingers, and then with a turn of his wrist from left to right flicked the ball from his fingers much after the style of a man spinning a billiard ball, his fingers at the moment the ball was delivered making the snapping sound mentioned above. The more noise he made the more spin did he get on the ball. Smith was gifted with very long fingers, which assisted him enormously in spinning the ball in this peculiar way, and the spin seemed part of the action. 'I could not have bowled a slow ball,' writes Smith, 'without spinning it, to save my life.'

Then as to the ball which 'runs away from the bat,' which Smith declared tired his shoulder! When about to bowl this, Smith held the ball with the ball of the thumb on the seam exactly underneath, and the first and second fingers close together on top *across* the seam. This ball, which was faster than the leg-break, was bowled without intended spin of any sort, and yet on a sticky wicket it took such a decided turn from leg that it was nothing short of a fast leg-break. Smith once asked Dr. W. G. Grace what caused this particular ball to turn without his spinning it, and the reply of the champion was characteristic: ' Never mind, youngster, what causes it; if you try to discover how you do it, you will very likely lose it '—and ' the youngster ' took his advice. Smith thinks that his shoulder came greatly into play in bowling this ball, for on a fast wicket, when he bowled about one an over, he could bowl all day without fatigue, but on a sticky wicket, when he bowled four or five an over, two hours' bowling would make his shoulder so tired that he could 'hardly move it.' It is a very curious fact that although Smith knew nothing of how he actually made the ball break so quickly from leg, he knew as soon as he had finished his delivery whether he had bowled the

E

*Field placed for W. C. Smith, of Surrey, slow right-hand:*

*Showing position of various fieldsmen*

Long-on           Long-off

Mid-off

Bowler

Mid-on

|||

Deep                                       Cover-
Square-leg                               point

Short-leg   |||

Point

Wicket-keeper

Slip

*On a sticky wicket Smith would do away with long-off, have two slips and point quite close up.*

ball that will go straight or turn from leg by the fact that if it was the latter ball 'I found a sort of over-reaching pain in my shoulder, but if the straight one I didn't have this feeling at all.' This leg-break nearly always kicked up, whereas the straight ball never did. It will be seen that, normally, Smith's leg-break was faster through the air than his off-break, and in order to prevent the batsman telling which was which for certain, he often bowled the off-break at a faster pace than was his usual habit.

If one may quote from one's own experience, I fancy Smith halted for a moment on the crease when he was about to bowl the off-break, and came on with his run and action when about to bowl the leg-break.

The name of *J. T. Hearne* is honoured at Lord's, as well it may be, for through many long years he rendered great service to Middlesex and to the Marylebone Club. Who that has been to Lord's does not at once picture to himself, when he hears the name of Jack Hearne, that easy, graceful run up to the wicket, that swinging, rhythmical action, and the superb length, and quick break-back? In the course of his career Hearne obtained no fewer than 3,473 wickets at a cost of 16·44 runs each.

Hearne took just sufficient length of run up to the crease to bring his whole body into action, and it is probable that no bowler ever had more absolute control of the ball as to direction, length, and variation of pace than he. Hearne was a great believer in the slight variation of pace—and here he resembled Trumble, the great Australian, who got many a wicket with balls just a little faster or a little slower than the preceding one. Too pronounced a change of pace may defeat its object. 'It is the little difference that often does so much.' 'Change of pace,' writes Hearne, 'is obtained at the moment of releasing the ball, a slower ball leaving the hand sooner than a faster ball, but much more depends

*Field placed for J. T. Hearne, Goddard, or V. W. C. Jupp,
medium right-hand:*

*Showing position of various fieldsmen*

Long-field

Mid-off

Mid-on                 Bowler

‖‖

Extra-cover

Cover-point

‖‖

Point

Wicket-keeper

Third man

Slip    Extra-slip

*Very often on a good wicket extra-slip would be dispensed
with and put in the long-field; it all depends on who the
batsman is.*

*On a sticky wicket Hearne, Goddard, or Jupp would have their field like this:*

*Showing position of various fieldsmen*

                    Long-on


                                        Mid-off
                    Bowler
                     |||
           Mid-on

    Deep
    Square-leg                              Cover-point



            Short-leg
                     |||
                                    Point
            Short-leg    Wicket-keeper

                        Slip


*Sometimes slip and point are dispensed with and placed in the long-field and at short-leg.*

upon the degree of spin imparted at the time of delivery; just as spin again has an important influence on the flight of a ball.' Jack Hearne was a master of spin, as of length, and when added to his naturally quick off-break he could also bowl the dead straight ball or the ball that goes just a little with his arm, his success was not to be wondered at. He may be taken as the beau-ideal of a medium-paced right-hand bowler.

*Barnes* had every attribute of a great bowler. He brought the ball from a great height, broke both ways, kept a perfect length, and had a deceptive flight. He possessed a remarkable power of hand and finger, and his leg-break especially went very quickly off the pitch. On first going in to bat one was apt to think, judging by the flight of the ball, that his leg-break would pitch off the leg-stump, while as a matter of fact, eight times out of ten it pitched on the wicket. This was probably due to his bowling from the extreme end of the crease. Barnes may be called a fast-medium bowler, and as a rule bowled on or just outside the off-stump, and made the ball go first one way and then the other without betraying any difference in his delivery. Cross-examine any of the great batsmen of the day and they will tell you that the ball of all others they detest and abhor is the one which goes with the bowler's arm. Well, Barnes bowled this ball to such perfection that he made you play at it. Hence the many catches at the wicket and slip off his bowling. The leading Australian critics consider him the best bowler on a typical Australian wicket we have sent them. There can be little doubt that Barnes profited by playing comparatively little cricket, which enabled him to keep fresh and to come to each match full of life and energy; but for all that it was a pity he was not more often seen in first-class cricket. In my humble opinion he was, on all wickets, the finest bowler England has ever possessed.

*Field for Barnes or Maurice Tate:*

*Showing position of various fieldsmen*

Mid-off

Bowler

Mid-on

|||

Extra-cover

Cover-point

Short-leg

|||

Point

Wicket-keeper

Slip    Extra-slip    Third Man

*Tate would usually have a long-leg instead of an extra-cover.*

At Melbourne in 1912, at the beginning of Australia's first innings, he bowled 11 overs, 7 maidens, for 6 runs and 5 wickets, on a pitch that was in perfect condition. In more recent days the counterpart to Barnes has been *Tate*. Between 1922 and 1929 he was a really great bowler.

In the early days of cricket all bowling was under-hand. A. W. Ridley, Humphreys, of Sussex, and D. L. A. Jephson were all extremely good lob bowlers, especially the last two, but the general opinion seems to be that not one of these was the equal of *G. H. Simpson-Hayward*.

I got the idea of bowling lobs [Simpson-Hayward writes] from spinning a billiard ball. In my young days I was very fond of playing with small tops which you spin with your fingers on a tray, and this made my fingers very strong, which is a great help in bowling lobs. It struck me that if I could spin an ivory ball why not a cricket ball, so I set to work just about the time I was coming down from Cambridge to cultivate pitch, etc. At first I found I could not pitch the ball at all, so I tried from about twelve yards and as I improved I retired back until I got to the regulation twenty-two yards. This was done during the summer evenings at a net at home bowling to the members of the village club, and took me, off and on, about three years. I learn more every day I bowl, and I have to thank Humphreys for some excellent advice. The first time I bowled lobs in a match was at Johannesburg in 1897 when on tour with the Corinthians. I got eight wicket for 45 runs, I think.

Simpson-Hayward's lobs came off the pitch at a great pace—they seemed to 'fizz' off it, and this was especially the case on the fast matting wickets at Johannesburg. Here Simpson-Hayward, following up his initial success for the Corinthians, was a great success during the tour of the M.C.C. in South Africa in the winter of 1909–10, some of his performances being extraordinary  In the first Test Match, for instance, he took six wickets for 42 runs, and

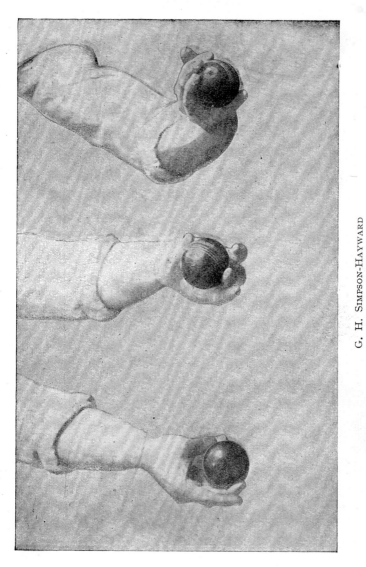

G. H. SIMPSON-HAYWARD

1. Leg-break
(Act of delivery, does not turn so much as No. 2)

2. Leg-break

3. Leg-break
(Act of leaving hand)

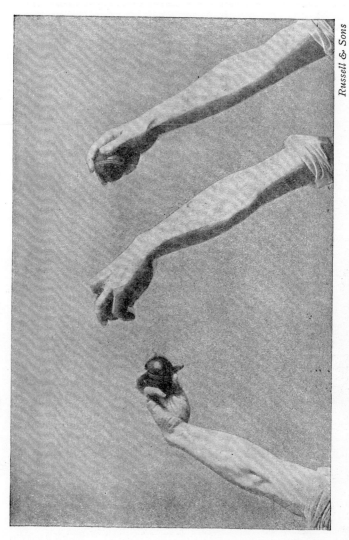

*Russell & Sons*

'Googly' taken from behind     'Googly' taken from front     Leg-break taken from front

D. W. CARR

*G. W. Beldam*

F. R. Spofforth
'The Demon Bowler

H. LARWOOD

Note the left foot, which he is about to 'pound' into
the ground

the crowd had roared with laughter when he first went on! Many batsmen seem to imagine that disgrace attaches to being defeated by a lob—why, I cannot imagine, unless it be that lobs look so easy from the ring. Certainly there was no disgrace in falling to Simpson-Hayward, for a cleverer bowler, of his kind, there never was. It was the off-break which spins off the wicket at such a pace which got Simpson-Hayward most of his wickets; but he was far from relying on one kind of ball alone. He bowled several different off-breaks, one turning a foot, another six inches, and a third an inch or two. These off-breaks were bowled off the thumb and second finger, as was the ball which went straight on, only in this case the fingers were held a little lower. On very fast wickets like Lord's or Johannesburg, Simpson-Hayward often bowled a slight leg-break by using the thumb and second-finger spin mentioned above, but holding the fingers lower and slightly turned over to the left.

Simpson-Hayward's ordinary leg-break was bowled off the thumb, first, and second fingers, while he had another leg-break up his sleeve (or in his hand, one should say) which, bowled off the third and fourth fingers, came out from underneath the hand and hung somewhat. Finally, there was the ordinary straight ball, and the one on the top of the stumps which soared a good height in the air.

Such was Simpson-Hayward's method of attack. No one will deny that he imparted plenty of variety to his bowling, and when to this variety was added a low trajectory and a tremendous spin, there is good reason for supposing him to be the best lob bowler that ever lived. Each batsman had to decide for himself which was the best way to play Simpson-Hayward. Some never played forward to him, but either hit him or played him back; others again, notably MacLaren, played him, and successfully too, like an ordinary slow bowler. In any case, Simpson-Hayward clean bowled all the best batsmen in England.

*G. H. Simpson-Hayward's field:*

*Showing position of various fieldsmen*

Fine Draw

Wicket-keeper

Cover, square

⦀

Square-leg

Deep
Square-leg

Deep cover

⦀

Mid-off

Bowler

Mid-on

Out-field,
on-side

Out-field,
off-side

Simpson-Hayward's advice to would-be imitators is best described in his own words:

To be a good lob bowler you must have *finger spin*, command of *pitch*, and control of *pace and break*. Risk something to obtain a wicket, and try to deliver different kinds of balls with the same action. Spin is the first thing to be worked at; and cultivate strong hands, which will help you in spinning the ball. Do not bowl a new ball in a match until you have got fairly proficient with it at practice. Keep your head, keep your temper, try to defeat your man.

*Larwood* may well claim comparison with any fast bowler of any age, his run up to the crease, action, delivery, and follow-through being models of rhythm and swing. Though much below the height usually associated with fast bowlers, Larwood has very long arms, and is powerfully built about the back and shoulders. I cannot recall a more accurate fast bowler. He had such complete control of the ball that G. O. Allen stood nearer in at forward short-leg to him than any short-leg had ever before ventured to stand, and escaped injury. When bowling 'leg theory,' 'in full blast,' he had only two men on the off-side—a deep third man and a silly-point, though the off-side was strengthened on occasions, e.g. for Bradman when a backward point was used and silly-point dropped back to cover-point—almost square. To a left-handed batsman, four or five men were placed in the slips; the field assuming what may be called a more 'ortho-dox' appearance. His bowling in 1933 was undoubtedly the chief factor in the recovery of the Ashes, and his figures —splendid as they are—would have been even better but for several catches being missed off him in the first innings of the last Test Match at Sydney, when for once the fielding fell away from a previously high level of excellence. He owed much of his success as a bowler to his captain, who managed him most ably, seldom bowling him for more than four or five overs at a time, and thereby keeping him

*Larwood's (Australian) field:*

*Showing position of various fieldsmen*

Long-leg

Deep Third Man

Fine-leg

Wicket-keeper

Short-leg

Short-leg

▥

Short-leg

Cover-point, near in

Deep square-leg

Short mid-on

▥

Bowler

*The wicket-keeper, Ames, stood slightly on leg-side.*

*Larwood's field with a new ball:*

*Showing position of various fieldsmen*

Deep Third Man

Long-leg

2nd Slip  Slip

3rd Slip

Backward point    Wicket-keeper

‖‖

Cover, near in    Short-leg

Mid-off

‖‖

Bowler

*Mid-off would sometimes be transferred to mid-on.*

fresh through a long innings.  He is also a very fine fielder, and a competent batsman.

*G. O. Allen* is another fine fast bowler.  Like Larwood he is on the short side, but he is strongly built and, at times, is only slightly less fast than Larwood.  He has a beautiful action, and puts every ounce of energy into his work.  He never uses an excessive leg-side field; and 'body-line' bowling was never attributed to him, his field being set with only three men, occasionally four, on the leg-side.  He was a great factor in the success of the 1932-3 M.C.C. team in Australia, for his fielding within two or three yards of the bat at short-leg was magnificent, and he made many useful scores in a free attractive style, the drive, both on and off, being his best strokes.

Allen also did very well in Australia in 1936-7, not only as a player but as a captain.  His leadership indeed was praised on all sides, such good judges as C. G. Macartney, 'Third Man,' and Neville Cardus paying him many compliments.  He has a sound knowledge of the game and is never stereotyped in his tactics.  He bowls with tremendous zest and energy, but though strongly built he is very apt to suffer from strained and pulled muscles, and this has handicapped him not a little at various times and has caused selection committees a good deal of anxiety.  There is no doubt that thoroughly fit he is a fine all-rounder and his performances in Test matches and in Gentlemen *v.* Players bear this out.

I have often been asked: 'Who is the fastest bowler you ever played?'  Opinions differ as to which was the fastest of Kortright, the Australians E. Jones and Cotter, and the South African Kotze.  Personally I think Kortright at his best was just a shade faster than anyone else.[1]  Tall, loosely

[1] Larwood was probably as fast as any one in the history of the game, and Constantine, in his prime, was also extremely fast.

built, and very strong in the back, Kortright, with his long, springy run up to the wicket, was at times almost terrifying. One had to shut one's teeth very tight, and to remember that for honour's sake one could not run away, to face him on a rough wicket. Some of the professionals, in particular, feared him with a mortal fear! Kortright's muzzle velocity was, to use a musketry term, about 2,000 feet per second, that of Jones, Kotze, and Cotter about 1,950 feet per second, so that in reality there was little difference between the four. The first ball Jones bowled in the Test Match at Lord's in 1896 pitched short and went through ' W. G.'s ' beard against the screen for four byes, whereupon the champion 'said something'; and the Middlesex eleven had a nasty experience against Kotze on a fiery Lord's wicket in June 1904. The wicket subsequently toned down, as it often does at Lord's, but in the first hour the batsmen were being constantly hit, Tarrant receiving one on the shoulder and two in the ribs in the course of ten minutes!

Cotter had rather a low trajectory, but his arm had a nice free swing, and there was nothing low about the ricochet of the ball after leaving the ground. He was one of the few fast bowlers who could stand up on a wet wicket. In England, after heavy rain, we do not as a rule utilize our fast bowlers, the idea being that they cannot get a proper foothold; but in Australia, whether it is that the wet does not penetrate so far into the earth, and that consequently it is easier to get a foothold, or whether Cotter possessed unique powers, the fact remained that on wickets affected by rain he was very successful, the ball bumping about 'all over the place.'

*Tom Richardson*, of Surrey, was in the matter of consistency, the finest fast bowler England has ever had. In four seasons, 1894, 1895, 1896, 1897, he took over a thousand wickets in first-class cricket, and it goes without saying that he was a man of immense physique; C. B. Fry, indeed, has written that he had 'Damascus steel fittings' to his shoulders. He was a natural fast bowler with a lovely swing and an extraordinarily quick break-back. From the pavilion end at Lord's he was a terror. He was the idol of the Surrey crowd, and well deserved his immense popularity, for he was a fine fellow who always apologized when his superb break-back hit one on the thigh. He seldom bowled short, aiming at clean bowling the batsman with a good-length off-break. A splendidly-built man, with a swarthy countenance and a delightful smile, he never knew when he was beaten.

Richardson was great, but *Lockwood*, also of Surrey, was, in his day, even his superior. In the Gentlemen *v.* Players match at Lord's in 1901 the Gentlemen had at lunch-time on the second day scored 206 for one wicket, with Ranjitsinhji and Fry well set; and yet an hour after play was resumed the Gentlemen were all out for 272—Lockwood having taken five of the wickets. It was a great piece of bowling, that wonderful slow ball of his, deceiving batsman after batsman—no fast bowler in the world ever had a better.

Cricketers as a rule do not carry in their minds the memory of any one particular ball which they have seen bowled, but there is one ball which I shall never forget.

England were playing Australia at Lord's in July 1893, and Lockwood was bowling from the pavilion end.

Lyons went in first, but after making 7 runs Lockwood clean bowled him. It was a good ball, a very good ball, but nothing like the one which George Giffen, the next batsman, was asked to play.

This was an exceptionally fast one, which pitched about four inches outside the off-stump, kept very low, and hit the leg-stump. Of course Giffen had no chance—that ball would have bowled any man in the world.

The slope in the ground and the little bit of fire and life

*G. W. Beldam*

J. T. HEARNE JUST AFTER THE BALL HAS LEFT HIS HAND

*G. W. Beldam*

Tom Richardson
Full steam ahead!

there always is in a Lord's wicket unmistakably help a bowler of Lockwood's type, but probably one of the finest things he ever did was his seven wickets for 70 runs in the Test Match at the Oval in August 1899. The wicket was of the most perfect Oval type, and the Australian eleven of that year very powerful in batting.

Richardson scarcely ever varied his pace. Lockwood bowled a most deceptive slow ball, and also that particularly nasty fast ball which, pitching just on the off-stump, gets up and comes in to the batsman—the sort of ball which often produces a catch to the wicket-keeper. His off-break, too, was very abrupt, and was obtained, as was Richardson's, by body as well as by finger-break. Lockwood had not Richardson's serene temperament, but when the spirit moved him he has never had an equal.

In the chapter on 'Cricket Captaincy' in the *Badminton Library*[1] one comes across the following sentence:

Let any one look at an old bowler who has to begin the bowling; his first action is to rub the ball on the ground in the hope of taking off even a little of its slippery newness; it is not, however, till after its surface has been considerably worn that it begins to take much notice of any twist—at any rate on a hard ground.

The words were written nearly sixty years ago, when the possibility of imparting a swerve to a cricket-ball was undreamt of by the vast majority of bowlers, though before this the American baseball 'pitchers' had made the ball take such extraordinary flights through the air that even the best and most experienced batsmen were deceived. Nowadays every cricket eleven has its 'swerver,' actual or reputed, and almost excessive care is taken to keep the newness and shine on the ball as long as possible in order that he may have every chance; for it is a well-known fact that a new ball will invariably curl more than one which has had thirty or forty runs scored off it.

[1] 1888 edition. *Vide* 1920 edition.

F

Science has told us that when a ball is advancing rapidly through the air there is formed in front of it a small aggregation or cushion of compressed air which causes it to curl. The heavier the air the greater the cushion, and in the thick smoke-laden atmosphere of Sheffield or Bradford *Hirst* would swerve infinitely more than in the clearer and brighter climate of Sydney or Adelaide. The Yorkshireman was the greatest modern exponent of this style of bowling, and on certain days his fast left-handers would curl so much that he would place five and, on occasions, six fieldsmen on the on-side. There would be a mid-on, a wide mid-on, a short-leg in front of the umpire, another behind the umpire, a long-leg, and, finally, what amounted to a short-slip on the leg-side, though many captains did not like to see him bowling without an orthodox short-slip. The wicket-keeper would stand back, and I have seen Lilley and David Hunter effect many a fine catch off a genuine leg-glance.

The best baseball 'pitchers' are not only able to curl the ball from leg and from the off, but can also impart a decided downward swerve to it, and Albert Trott, who was well known in Australia as a baseballer before he came to England, used in his first two or three seasons here to bowl a ball which, swerving from leg, dropped in the air just as the batsman was about to play it. Leg-before-wickets were numerous, as an apparent full pitch to leg often landed on the striker's toe.

Before Trott and Hirst, Wright, a medium-paced to slow left-hander, who played for Kent in the eighties and nineties, Rawlin, the Middlesex professional, and W. E. W. Collins used to impart a curl to their bowling; and J. B. King, of Philadelphia, had a tremendous swerve from the off; but the first cricketer to practise this art was Noah Mann, of the famous old Hambledon Club. John Nyren says of him, ' He was left-handed, both as bowler and batter. In the

*Here is a diagram of the field when Hirst was in his best swerving mood, the wind blowing from the direction of extra-cover:*

### Showing position of various fieldsmen

Long-leg

Deep
Third Man

Wicket-
keeper.

Slip on
leg-side

Short-leg

Short-leg

Cover-point

Forward
Short-leg

Mid-off          Bowler

Mid-on

*Direction of wind*

former quality his merit consisted in giving a curve to the ball the whole way.' (Here he was different from Hirst, who curled the ball in the last two or three yards of its flight.) ' In itself it was not the first-rate style of bowling, but so very deceptive that the chief end was frequently attained.' Noah Mann was a wonderful horseman, and stooping from his horse would pick up a handkerchief while going at full speed. He was extraordinarily active in the field, and used to stand behind the long-stop that he might cover both long-stop and slip. In this position he and little George Lear, the long-stop, would play many a trick on the inexperienced batsman. He once hit a ball on Windmill Down for 10 runs, and as a batsman possessed great nerve and self-possession. Mann was short in stature and swarthy as a gipsy, and had, according to Nyren, 'large hips and spider legs.' His end was sad. 'After a free carouse' he could not be persuaded to go to bed, but persisted in sleeping all night in his chair in the chimney-corner. During the night he fell into the hearth, and burned himself so severely that he died within twenty-four hours. Such was the first swerver, though, be it remembered, in his day the bowling was under-hand. Many a long day was to elapse before even round-arm was to be legalized.

But Hirst was really two bowlers rolled into one; for when he had finished swerving with the new ball he would bowl in the orthodox style with seven men on the off-side; and when the day came for him to give up bowling fast, he was a rare medium left-hander. At any rate, I have seen him bowl very well in this style in the nets at Eton, where he was at one time coach.

Hirst varied the pace of his swervers from fast to almost slow. Personally I disliked the slow swerver more than the fast one, for in proportion to its pace through the air it came extraordinarily quickly off the ground.

When about to bowl the swerver the seam of the ball is

held vertically, two fingers on each side of it on the top, and the thumb directly underneath. For the left-hander's natural break-back Hirst had the tips of the first two fingers across the seam.

*F. R. Foster* was one of the most brilliant all-round cricketers of his age that England ever possessed. With a slim active figure he batted, bowled, and fielded quite naturally, and it is sad indeed to think that, owing to a broken leg sustained in a motor-bicycle accident, he will never play cricket again. It was his splendid all-round cricket, coupled with his enthusiasm and judgment as captain, that led Warwickshire to the top of the county championship in 1911, and never before had the Edgbaston grounds at Birmingham seen so many spectators. His bowling, and that of Barnes, was the principal reason of the success of the M.C.C. team in Australia in 1911–12, and on the hard true wickets at Sydney, Melbourne, and Adelaide these two formed the finest combination of bowlers England has yet sent to Australia. Ably backed up by J. W. H. T. Douglas, the bowling of the Englishmen on that tour attained a very high standard. Foster bowled left-handed with a beautifully easy action, and his pace was fast medium varied with an occasional very fast ball. His length was extremely accurate, he 'made haste off the pitch,' and he had a good head. As a batsman he was a natural hitter, his drives sailing away like a golf ball from a tee, and he was a capital field in the slips. Altogether a superb cricketer.

In any chapter on bowling it would be impossible to omit the name of *George Lohmann*, probably the greatest medium-paced bowler that ever lived. I actually played against him but twice, for his career was almost at an end when I was beginning first-class cricket; but as a little boy he was my cricketing hero, and many was the hour I spent at the

*F. R. Foster's field to C. Hill and W. Bardsley (left-handers):*

Bowler

Mid-off     ⫼     Mid-on

Cover-point

Short-leg

⫼

Wicket-keeper     Short-leg

Second-slip     Slip

Deep Third Man

Long-leg

*F. R. Foster's field to V. Trumper (right-hander):*

Bowler     Mid-off

Mid-on

||| (wicket)

Cover-point

Short-leg

||| (wicket)

Short-leg

Wicket-keeper

Short-leg    Short-leg

Deep Third Man

Long-leg

*N.B.—The wicket-keeper stood back to Foster. Occasionally the very fine short-leg would be moved to slip.*

Oval watching him bat, bowl, and field. His action had a suspicion of strain about it, but he made the most of every inch of his six feet, and he was the most 'flighty' bowler I have ever seen. The ball was constantly dropping feet shorter than one anticipated. Lohmann combined with this deceptive flight a quick off-break, and occasionally a faster ball that went just a little with his arm, and which he was very fond of bowling on sticky wickets. He loved cricket, and his bowling was a constant source of joy to him; he simply revelled in his art. In addition to his bowling he was the greatest extra-slip of his time, his activity being catlike and his hands supremely safe, while he was a free, dashing, and most attractive bat. The first time I saw him play was at Lord's in June 1887 for England v. M.C.C., when Stoddart and Arthur Shrewsbury played innings of over a hundred; and in the great match of those days, Surrey v. Notts at the Oval on the August Bank Holiday, I saw him make a wonderful catch at extra-slip off Bowley's bowling. I was a very little boy in Eton jacket and collar, and I remember being handed over the turnstile and taking up my position in the front row on the grass, where I was politely requested to remove my 'topper.' The crowd kept on increasing all the morning, and after lunch was twenty yards inside the ring. The police were powerless, and J. Shuter, the Surrey captain, had to come and ask us to go back. 'If you want Surrey to win, please go back.' We all cheered him, and somehow went back a bit. Those were the palmy days of the Oval. A year or two later I saw Lohmann and Maurice Read get 66 each on a bad wicket against Lancashire. Surrey had followed on, and five wickets fell before Barlow and Briggs for 25 runs, then Lohmann joined Maurice Read, and we had our money's worth. The wicket was still difficult, and Barlow, Briggs, and Mold were at their best. Mold made the ball jump every now and then, and both batsmen were hit; but the batting was perfect, and the Surrey crowd, always so keen and appreciative of any good thing, yelled with delight at every run-getting stroke. Lohmann has been much criticized for his action at the time of the 'strike' of the English professionals on the eve of the Test Match at the Oval in 1896. He was undoubtedly ill-advised in the position he took up on that occasion, and subsequently he fully admitted it. Lohmann went as manager to Lord Hawke's team in South Africa in the winter of 1898-9, and I got to know him very well and to like him very much. He used to talk cricket with an enthusiasm that was positively delightful. He was an intelligent man with nice manners, and every one who knew him felt keenly his early death from consumption in December 1901. He is buried at Matjesfontein, in Cape Colony, where he lived during the last few years of his life, and his death did not pass unnoticed even amid the clash of war. The Surrey Cricket Club have erected a handsome memorial over the grave of the greatest all-round cricketer that ever did battle for them.

I am indebted to F. T. Badcock for the following remarks on bowling:

It has often been said that a bowler is born and not made. Though this may sound a little drastic, it is, I think, more true in terms of bowling than of batting. Bowling is so much an individual effort both from a physical and far more from a mental point of view. You cannot *think* for a bowler on the field. Certain things can be shown him such as how to hold the ball to produce certain results, but even so it will not follow that he himself will achieve that result without some slight change. Above all it is quite impossible to teach anyone to bowl a length.

One can, of course, point to several famous bowlers in the history of the game who have by perseverance and sheer hard work pushed themselves into the front rank. These men had that 'infinite capacity for taking pains,' and it is only by such means that the really great bowler can produce his qualities. It takes all the wiles of genius to get rid of a good batsman on a plumb wicket.

Control of the ball in length, spin and flight is absolutely essential, and the first particularly can only be achieved by sheer hard work, that is apt to become monotonous if only for the very reason that there appears to be no definite result such as one can obtain when a ball is correctly timed and driven to the boundary.

In coaching the first thing one has to watch is the pupil's run up to the wicket and his action of delivery. The run up should be of such a length that he arrives at the crease in the best balanced position for his delivery. If you watch a racehorse or a sprinter, you will notice that it is not until they have travelled a certain distance that they can ' hit their gait,' when the balance of rhythm and movement is perfect. So it is with a bowler. It is almost as if one has been wound up to one's fullest tension and at the moment of delivery the spring is released. The run up should be practically mechanical; that is to say, you should never have to think about it.

In delivering the ball, one's arm should be as high as possible and tend to brush one's ear. This can be helped by placing the leading foot—so as not to confuse right and left—slightly across the line of flight of the ball. If you place it away, unless you are a contortionist it is impossible to get the arm up, and the higher the arm, the better the direction obtained. There should be no checking of the body after delivery. There should be a clean and fluent follow through. Be careful, however, to see that your follow through carries you clear of the wicket so as not to tear up the pitch.

The pupil should never be allowed to over-bowl as regards pace. Many boys have been spoilt in this way. The acquisition of length is paramount, so that he can pitch the ball on the proverbial sixpence, but that sixpence is moved up and down the wicket and across it so that it suits the type and state of the wicket, the pace of the bowler and the reach of the batsman. So many would-be bowlers start off with the theory that if you can spin the ball that is all that is required. All the spin in the world is of little or no avail without length. Once the length is there it only requires a very small amount of turn to beat the bat.

As regards flight this is something also that cannot be taught, in fact to go further, it is not easy to define. Really it is the bowler's ability to make the batsman think that the ball is going to land further up the pitch towards him than it actually does. Even the bowler who can achieve this, very often cannot say how he does it.

In these days when the word swing is closely allied to a form of dance music it might be better to speak of swerve rather than swing. Here again the effect is achieved before the ball pitches, but the bowler makes a definite use of the seam on the ball, and he should be able to control both the amount and direction. Atmosphere and wind play a large part in this department of the bowler's art.

It is well to remember in speaking of spin and swerve, that the ball that is going away from the bat is more dangerous and harder to play than the one that is coming into it. Neither, however, are much use unless the bowler has command of his length.

A bowler's attack is based on three things—temperament, reason, and intuition—none of which can be taught. No matter how badly things may be going for him, a bowler must at all times remember that it is he that is doing the attacking and the batsman the defending. He must never lose his attacking sense. He must cultivate a hostile atmosphere, and in this, of course, he can be very ably assisted by his field.

A bowler has two great assets—patience and control of the ball. Except on rare occasions when everything goes right, a bowler has to work very hard for success, but he has the knowledge that though he can make mistakes the batsman cannot afford to make one. At only one time is the former a definite loser: that is when matters come to a stalemate. Naturally the bowler tires first and has to be taken off.

*General considerations.* A bowler has by far the hardest work to do of any man in the side. He should therefore be as fit as possible and take every care of himself. Never hesitate if you feel inclined to bowl the first few overs with a sweater on, especially if it is a cold day. As long as it is fairly loose it will not hamper you at all. Cold means stiffness and a bowler can only do his best when he is warm.

Always put your sweater on after bowling.

Take care of your feet. Really thick-soled boots—especially for fast bowlers—and thick soft woollen socks give good protection. Always have a spare pair of socks to change into on leaving the field.

# CHAPTER III

## WICKET-KEEPING

I DO not think my best friend would call me a wicket-keeper. I have kept wicket, *in a first-class match, too*, M.C.C. *v.* Yorkshire at Lord's in May 1901, and in a total of 57 for four wickets let no byes and missed no catches—I did not have one!—and playing for the village of Leeds in Kent against the County Police a stalwart sergeant remarked: ' I should feel a deal happier, Mr. Warner, if you weren't behind those stumps '; but notwithstanding such feats as these I do not feel competent to write on the subject. The late A. A. Lilley, the England, Players, and Warwickshire wicket-keeper, however, very kindly gave me his views, and as he kept wicket for England from 1896 to 1909, taking part in no fewer than *thirty-five Test Matches*, there could be no greater authority. I have also been fortunate enough to obtain the views of J. C. Hubble, the excellent Kent wicket-keeper of the period between 1910–1924.

## WHY I BECAME A WICKET-KEEPER

### By A. A. Lilley

My earliest club cricket was in connection with the Bournville Cricket and Athletic Club. I was then employed at the works of Messrs. Cadbury Bros., and this club was formed by the foremen of the various departments in the works. Mr. George Cadbury engaged J. E. Shilton, the Warwickshire professional, to coach the young players, and the latter used to come up in the evenings for this purpose. On one occasion when we were practising under the guidance of Shilton, the regular wicket-keeper of the club happened to be absent, and so Shilton asked me to occupy this position for that evening. I had not previously acted in this capacity, having been played for bowling and batting, but after Shilton had given me a few hints as to the correct attitude to assume and the proper way of taking the ball, I soon became at home, and as he saw I had some natural aptitude for the position, I became from that evening the regular wicket-keeper for the club. It was therefore quite an accident that I first acquired my knowledge of or liking for wicket-keeping; and had the club's usual player been present upon that particular evening, it is quite possible that I might never have had the opportunity that subsequently meant so much to me.

## Methods of Standing—How to Take the Ball— and Hints to Young Players

In taking up position behind the wicket, the young player must always remember that whatever attitude he assumes he must always preserve free and easy movement. This is most important, and must be regarded as fundamentally necessary and to be zealously regarded. The necessity of free movement must indeed never be lost sight of, and I keep this particularly in mind in making the following suggestions. In taking up position the wicket-keeper should stand with the middle of the left foot in a line with the leg-stump. The right foot should then be extended only far enough to make the position a perfectly easy one. In extending the right foot it should be slightly drawn back so that the toe of this foot should come in a line with the ball of the left foot. This will give additional 'play' and greater freedom in movements of the right arm, and at the same time provide additional facilities in following the ball. When stooping, the utmost care should be taken that the feet are placed flat upon the turf, so as to provide as substantial a grip of the ground as possible. It affords a quicker and steadier start in making a rapid movement in order to take a ball on the leg-side or wide on the off-side; whereas, if he were on his toes he would be likely to overbalance in attempting to make either of these movements. He should not indeed move on to his toes for *any* action. It will naturally have the tendency to make a player overbalance himself, and so seriously handicap him in taking the ball properly. It has also a tendency to make him 'grab' at the ball, which should be carefully avoided, as not only does it make the catch more difficult to take, but is also very destructive to the hands. The hands, of course, should 'give' immediately on coming in contact with the ball, in order to break the pace of it, and that can only be done when the position allows the ball to be properly taken, which, of course, cannot be done when the body is in any way over-balanced, and causes the ball to be grabbed at. It will thus be seen how essential is free movement: in fact, free and easy movement of the feet is more essential to a wicket-keeper than a batsman, so it can easily be understood how impossible it is to impress this too strongly.

## WICKET-KEEPING

### By J. C. Hubble

The art of wicket-keeping is to make a difficult job look easy. It is delightful work when this can be done.

The necessities are a keen eye, steady nerve and a quick mentality.

Balance of body is the principal attribute and to attain this 'stance' is of the utmost importance.

The two feet should be firmly planted on the ground *flat* with perhaps the right toe 3 inches behind the left, and then move up and down with the feet flat.

As most of the work and chances are just outside the off-stump make the centre of the stance there, perhaps with an inswinging bowler it may be advisable at times to move a bit more to the leg-side.

The ball should be taken with the fingers pointed downwards.

There is no object in getting too low in the stance and most important of all do not get on your toes—this is fatal as it naturally leads to continually transferring the balance from toes to flat feet and is the cause of such things as snatching, bruised fingers, missed chances, and so on; in fact this stance will never lead to good wicket-keeping. I emphasize this point as I find unfortunately this stance is common, due no doubt to a misapprehension that unless one is perched like a frog behind the wicket one is not trying one's best.

As length is to bowling, and a straight bat to batting, so is stance to wicket-keeping.

---

By general consent J. McC. Blackham, the Australian, was the prince of wicket-keepers, and may, indeed, be said to have been the originator of the practice which has been prevalent for so many years of dispensing with a long-stop even to the fastest bowling. Like Lilley, Blackham had done no wicket-keeping until he was seventeen years old, which goes to prove the oft-repeated saying that a wicket-keeper is born, not made. His keeping to 'the demon' Spofforth with the 1878 Australian team was a revelation, and had an enormous influence on our cricket. With his ever-varying pace and flight Spofforth was a most difficult bowler to keep wicket to, and those who saw the combination of the two aver that the game has produced no greater spectacle.

G. MacGregor, Lilley, and Pilling, the Lancashire professional, must have run even Blackham close. Pilling was very good indeed, and the combination of S. M. J. Woods and MacGregor was almost as fine as that of Spofforth and Blackham. Who, too, that saw it could ever forget that marvellous right-handed catch low down on the off-side by MacGregor, who was standing up, off Kortright's terrific bowling in the Gentlemen and Players match at Lord's in 1893?

K. S. Ranjitsinhji says that MacGregor holds the record for tranquillity at the wicket. 'He is sphinx-like in his calm fixity.' The wicket-keeper has all sorts of returns to take—long hops, full pitches, half-volleys, wide returns, and straight returns. MacGregor had a wonderful knack of gathering them one and all and getting them into the wicket. The wicket-keeper sees much of the game, and MacGregor, by a quiet hint, obtained many a wicket for a bowler. 'You're bowling about two feet too short, Jack,' or 'Albert, a yard shorter,' often improved the analyses of J. T. Hearne and Albert Trott. The late Middlesex captain knew much about cricket. He had no fads, and pronounced judgment on merit. He was a great man for Middlesex; for apart from his superb wicket-keeping he was an admirable captain, and when runs were wanted at a crisis he was very apt to get them.

England has had many great wicket-keepers besides MacGregor and Pilling. For example, there was David Hunter, of Yorkshire, who retired with a record of 920 caught and 352 stumped. It is sad to think that we shall never hear in county cricket again his 'Well bowled, well bowled, Wilfrid.' A charming fellow was David, and very fond of his canaries. Huish, of Kent, though he never played for England in a Test Match, was one of the greatest wicket-keepers we have ever had, and in all matches for his county he caught 906 and stumped 356. Huish was equally good

W. A. OLDFIELD

LORD'S—THE MECCA OF CRICKET

standing back to fast bowlers, like W. M. Bradley or Fielder, and to slow bowlers, like D. W. Carr, Blythe, and Woolley, and I think the best catch I have ever fallen to by a wicket-keeper was made by Huish. The late Harry Butt, of Sussex, caught 927 and stumped 274 men during his career, but his hands in the end were terribly knocked about.

The late W. S. Bird, of Oxford and Middlesex, was a stumper of the MacGregor or Martyn class, and there was no one better in his day than Strudwick,[1] while G. E. C. Wood's form for some seasons was very good. Oates, of Nottinghamshire, was a wicket-keeper whose merits were not, generally speaking, recognized so highly as they deserved to be, and the same may be said of Murrell, of Middlesex, who, except for a very occasional off day, was both brilliant and safe and, being left-handed, very good at taking the ball on the leg-side.

In English cricket to-day, Ames is supreme, and there are several other very good wicket-keepers, Cornford, Price, W. H. V. Levett, W. T. Luckes, S. C. Griffith, H. Davies, G. Dawkes, S. Buller, and T. G. Evans. Indeed, almost every county can boast of a good wicket-keeper, and the standard is so high, that those old cricketers who remember the days of long-stops must rub their eyes at the sight of these daily exhibitions of skill in a position which is admitted to be the most difficult. Ames did wonderfully well in Australia in 1932–3, playing in every one of the five Test Matches. Standing back to Larwood, Voce, and Allen he was very safe, and his stumping on the leg-side of V. Richardson, off Hammond, in the fourth Test Match, at Brisbane, was a most brilliant piece of work. Fortunate indeed is the eleven which has so capable a batsman as a wicket-keeper.

P. W. Sherwell was born in England, but he made South Africa his home, and he has been a great asset in the rise of

---

[1] In first-class cricket Strudwick caught 1,235 and stumped 258, as compared to Hunter's figures of 920 and 352, and of Huish's 906 and 356.

G

his adopted country's cricket. Much practice made him the best 'taker' of googly bowling in the world, and he had a perfect style, with an entire absence of fuss.

Before Sherwell, E. A. Halliwell was the wicket-keeper in the various South African elevens. Here was a case of heredity, for Halliwell's father, R. Bisset Halliwell, kept wicket for the Gentlemen v. Players in 1870, 1872, and 1873, and more than one 'stumped Halliwell bowled Buchanan' appears in the score-books of those days. The son was an even better wicket-keeper than the father, for he used to stand up to Kotze, and he was both brilliant and safe. In taking a leg ball he did not jump across so as to be in front of the line of the ball, but strode, as it were, to the left and took the ball with a sideways reach, so that the hands were more easily swung across to the wicket than is the case when the wicket-keeper has jumped to the left and finds himself several feet wide of the stumps. Some of the finest exhibitions of wicket-keeping that I have ever seen have been given by E. A. Halliwell, and it is no exaggeration to say that in his prime he never had a superior. The late H. B. Cameron was another great South African wicket-keeper.

Lockyer, Pinder, and Pooley were long before my time; but in one of his books on cricket Mr. Ashley Cooper ranks Lockyer, I think, as the equal, if not the superior, of the great Blackham himself. This is a pretty tall order, and one to which few will subscribe. It must be remembered that in doing away with a long-stop even to the fastest bowling, and Spofforth was a very fast bowler in 1878, and different in this respect to 'the Demon' of later years, who bowled an occasional fast ball, Blackham created a revolution in our ideas of what a wicket-keeper could do, and in Lockyer's time a long-stop was an everyday occurrence, and as essential as a cover-point. No doubt in their day Lockyer, Pinder, and Pooley were all A1, for Lockyer 'kept' for the

Players on and off between 1854 and 1866, Pooley from 1866 to 1879, and Pinder from 1873 to 1877.

Of Australians, J. J. Kelly was very safe, and got through an immense amount of work. The catch with which he dismissed Tyldesley in a Test Match at Adelaide was one of the finest in the annals of the game. The Lancashire professional glanced a ball to leg, and Kelly, anticipating the stroke, dashed across and caught it quite four feet wide of the wicket. Kelly was pretty tough, but even his hands occasionally became sore after keeping to E. Jones for a few weeks. W. A. Oldfield, the Australian, was even better than Kelly. He is, perhaps, the greatest wicket-keeper of the day. He is neat, quiet and very efficient, and scrupulously fair in his appeals. Indeed, if he appeals a batsman may be sure he is out, or very nearly so. H. Carter, a Yorkshire-born Australian, was also a great wicket-keeper.

Mention has been made of MacGregor's marvellous catch when standing up to a bowler of Kortright's speed; but the common practice nowadays is for the wicket-keeper to stand back to very fast bowling. Experience has proved that there are three or four catches offered to every one of stumping, and that it is, comparatively speaking, fairly easy to hold catches standing back, as the ball generally comes into the hands on the long hop. Moreover, the wicket-keeper can cover more ground. He has not the opportunity given him of performing heroic feats, but he catches the other side out with greater certainty, and that, after all, is the point to be aimed at.

# CHAPTER IV

## FIELDING

CERTAIN natural qualifications are necessary to enable any cricketer to become a great fieldsman, but attention, practice, and experience are equally essential. 'Keep your mind on the game, and expect every ball to come to you,' is an excellent maxim, for once let your thoughts wander and it is extraordinary how often a catch will come your way with most unhappy results. Practice, too, is a means whereby one's fielding can be greatly improved, and is most interesting and amusing, especially off the iron-bound wooden catch-a-ball 'cradle' at Lord's, from which slip catches fly in all directions. Only two players are necessary, one throwing the ball into the cradle for the other to catch it, though three is a better number, as then it is possible to have two slips, a short-slip, and an extra-slip. Bouncing a ball off a roller, though injurious to the ball, gives fair slip-fielding practice, and catches may, of course, be hit from the bat, but no system or machine that I have ever seen is to be compared to the 'cradle'; Major E. G. Wynyard was an expert at throwing the ball into the ' cradle ' with an accuracy that produced ideal slip catches, and several of the M.C.C. professionals also possess the knack. A ship's deck is a splendid place for slip practice. The 1903-4 M.C.C. team enjoyed a great deal of it on the voyage to Australia. At least three players are required—one to throw the ball, one with the bat, and one to field, the thrower bouncing the ball in front of the batsman at a length which allows him to divert it to first, second, or third slip. R. E. Foster, Braund, and A. E. Relf used to give wonderful exhibitions, to the encouragement and applause of the rest of the passengers. Capital practice for long-field, cover, and mid-off catching may be had by getting someone to hit the ball to you at various distances, heights, and paces, but it is a mistake to hit long-field catches *too* high. Abnormally high catches are *not* wanted, one seldom or never gets them in matches, and they only tend to bruise the hands. A method of keeping the fieldsman on his toes is to hit the ball just a little short of him so that he has to come to the ball in order to make the catch, while in ground work the A B C of fielding is to advance to meet the ball, and not to allow the ball to come to you. Aim, too, at returning the ball to the striker on the first bounce and smartly. Do not practise fielding on very cold days; it is torture, and will only result in a bruise to the hands, missed catches, and consequent loss of confidence. Many catches are missed through sheer nervousness. Here practice does much good. As *The Jubilee Book of Cricket* says:

Nervousness often disappears as experience grows. After all, courage and nerve are largely matters of habit. A sailor would fear to tackle a herd of unruly cattle just as much as a stockman would fear to run up a high rigging. But both may be brave and steady enough in positions to which they are accustomed. So with cricket. A steeple-high catch in the country begins to lose its terrors when one has caught a dozen such the evening before at fielding practice.

The finest and most zealous fielders occasionally miss catches, sometimes because on our modern grounds it is often very difficult to follow the ball, sometimes because it is but human to err; but taking a season through, the great fieldsman will save literally hundreds of runs, and his energy and zeal will act as an inspiration to his comrades, and will inspire his side with a great enthusiasm. There is no better sight in cricket than that of an eleven fielding for all it is worth. One magnificent bit of catching or stopping evokes another, and the feeling of combination and supreme effort is delightful. Therefore let every cricketer strive to do his best—more than that he cannot—by practising diligently, and he will be surprised at the rapid improvement he will make. Some years ago fielding was little practised on first-class grounds. Nowadays it is a common sight to see men, early in the season, at any rate, practising fielding as keenly as if they were batting. People have come to realize that fielding is great fun, with the natural result that the general level of excellence in first-class cricket is high. And it would be higher if the ball could always be followed from the bat. Huge stands and pavilions crowded with spectators make up a poor background. Lord's is notoriously difficult to field on, and I have known men fielding in 'the country' at the end opposite the pavilion run the wrong way for a catch. They have imagined that the ball has been hit in a certain direction, and their surprise has been great, and their annoyance greater, when they have discovered, too late, the ball soaring yards away from them.

## THROWING

This is a gift of nature, and no rules can be laid down. It is possible, however, to improve one's throwing by practising; but never attempt to *throw far* when practising before the season begins, for the reason that the muscles of the arms and shoulders are very stiff after an English winter. Each day throw a few balls a little farther than the previous day; *festina lente* is the motto here. No wonder the Australians throw better than we do. They have none of the cold damp of a northern winter to contend with. One can throw fifteen to twenty yards farther in Australia than in England, so loose and supple are the muscles in that lovely climate.

## LONG-FIELD

Denton was one of the few cricketers about whom it could truthfully be said that he was worth a place in his team for fielding alone, and he has kindly given me his ideas on fielding in 'the country.'

'Never let your mind,' says Denton, 'go "wool-gathering" miles away from the cricket field, or a mistake is sure to be made. To be a real tip-top fielder you must practise. When you see the ball coming towards you, meet it, never stand still; get into your proper stride, pick the ball up clean, and throw in with the same action. No flourishes, please, and from the long-field throw straight to the bowler or wicket-keeper, as the case may be, *first bounce*. I have seen the Australians throw from the long-field straight into the bowler or wicket-keeper's hands, but in my opinion, from such a distance it is better to throw first bounce. In the case of cover, third man, etc., shy straight at the bowler or wicket-keeper without bouncing. As regards catching, some noted cricketers advocate holding your hands this way, others that way, but everything depends on the way the ball comes at you. My advice is, catch it the way it comes easiest to you, the way you have most confidence in.'

In reply to my question which was the best catch he had ever caught, Denton writes:

I hardly know which catch to single out as my best, but *one* I shall always remember (I have caught it scores of times since in my dreams!). Yorkshire were playing Somerset at Taunton. Haigh was bowling, and L. C. H. Palairet batting, when a ' skimmer ' came towards the pavilion straight for me. I rushed in, and going full tilt, caught it with my right hand on my boot. Another was when I caught C. E. de Trafford at Leeds. I was on the boundary edge near the pavilion, and it looked ten to one against me, but I jumped up, stuck out my hand, and there it was! One more, this time at Sheffield. W. McG. Hemingway, who played for Gloucestershire, hit one sky-high, and off I went. I must have gone twenty or thirty yards (I have the newspaper cutting by me now which says over thirty) and caught it when I was going full speed. I remember quite well being about two yards off George Hirst at mid-off when I had finished.

While waiting for a long-field catch Denton's hands were held well below the head, so that the hands did not interfere with the sight of the ball. As the ball entered his hands the catch was made just below the chin.

J. T. Tyldesley, some years ago, was the equal of Denton as a long-field and third man, and in his day K. L. Hutchings had no equal. He was a dead sure catch, and could throw with tremendous power, and as he also excelled in the slips, he may be ranked with A. O. Jones and Constantine as the best all-round fielder. Other very good long-fields are, or were, Hendren, whose energy, activity, and sureness of hand and eye have saved heaps of runs for Middlesex, Leyland and Holmes, of Yorkshire, Hardinge, of Kent, H. Ashton and A. P. F. Chapman, A. F. Bickmore, J. Douglas, K. G. Macleod, and Paynter, J. H. Hunt, H. G. Owen-Smith, Gregory, of Surrey, Barnett, H. Parks, of Sussex, and the Australians, Hill, Trumper, Ransford, Pellew, and Bradman. Hendren, like some few others, could field in any position, and I am not sure that his natural place was not at cover or extra-cover, while Hulme's work for Middlesex was always very notable. J. Douglas possessed as safe a pair of hands as any other long-field, but he had neither a very quick nor a very accurate return. One of the greatest catches I have ever seen was made by him on the Headingley ground, Leeds. Rhodes drove a ball into the long-field very hard and low, off C. M. Wells's bowling, and Douglas, racing along the boundary, caught it in his left hand just as it was clearing the ropes.

J. H. Hunt, with his big hands and huge reach, was an almost ideal fielder, and his left-handed catch in front of the pavilion which dismissed A. H. Hornby in the Middlesex *v.* Lancashire match in 1905 will be remembered at Lord's for many a long day. Ransford's long-fielding was a feature of the 1909 Australian tour in this country, the way in which he pursued, gathered, and returned the ball being a joy to behold, while Trumper and Hill were also very good. Forty years ago MacLaren was magnificent in the long-field and at third man, as those who witnessed the exhibition he gave in the Gentlemen *v.* Players match at Lord's in 1899 will testify.

Washbrook, Hutton, Hardstaff, Edrich, and D. Compton are also very good in the deep.

## THIRD MAN

Great long-fielders are very often great at third man, it being usual for long-field at one end to field third man at the other. Third man is a position which demands dash as well as watchfulness—dash to save the single, watchfulness to negotiate the curling, twisting ball. On a hard ground a ball cut clean will not twist until some of the pace has gone off it, but if the turf is slow the ball is almost certain to curl sharply from right to left on the second or third bound. Even when the ball is picked up smartly it is very difficult to prevent two really good runners from getting a run every time the ball goes in the direction of third man, and the least misfielding means a certain single. There is no more difficult ground to field third man on than Lord's at the pavilion end. The slope in the ground helps to impart a most worrying twist to the ball. C. J. Burnup, the distinguished Kent cricketer of some years ago, was as good a third man as ever lived. He was near the ground, very quick on his feet, and could throw in quickly and accurately. Trumper and Denton were very good here, as was Sandham. At short third man, ' the gully,' as it is called, a position invented and made for ever famous by the incomparable A. O. Jones, Jardine, Chapman, A. R. Tanner, Robins, J. W. A. Stephenson, and Peebles are the best modern exponents.

## SLIP AND EXTRA-SLIP

In the course of his career Tunnicliffe caught *over seven hundred catches* at short-slip, and it is probably safe to say that there never was a finer fieldsman in that position. Tunnicliffe has been good enough to lend me some notes he made on the subject of slip-fielding which, coming from such an expert, are naturally of great interest. ' The Pudsey Giant,' as the Sheffielders used to call him, thinks that a good slip is born in the same sense as a wicket-keeper, and that there is no place in the field where a man has to keep his mind and eyes more riveted on both batsman and bowler than at short-slip. He is against the bowler fielding slip because of the occasional sprints he may have to indulge in on the leg-side. 'It is a waste of good energy and cruel to a bowler, who requires all he has stored up in him for his own sphere.' Short-slip must think, for there are many problems connected with his work, and he must watch the bowler, who is for ever changing his method of attack, even more intently than the batsman.

It is bad policy, writes Tunnicliffe, to allow the regular short-slip of your side to field anywhere else, for if he does, 'he will lose that *very vital interest* which it is so important he should keep.' It is this intense interest in his work that enables a short-slip to gather up 'the unconsidered trifles' in the way of catches which win matches.

If our short-slip has had a decent training as a gymnast it will be all the better, because he will know how to fall with the least possible danger to himself. What a difference it makes to a man who knows that well! He can fling himself at a going-away ball with confidence, and gain a full yard in his reach, and though he may possibly rub the skin off his elbow or shoulder what does it matter if he has held a Trumper or a Ranji!

First slip should *not move* about after he has formed an opinion as to the pace of the wicket, for the ball which comes to him is the result of a false stroke on the part of the batsman, who does not intend to hit the ball in that direction. Extra-slip, however, may anticipate the flight of the ball by moving, because in this case there is more of an intended stroke on the batsman's part. Many a genuine late cut off the face of the bat has been held by extra-slips like Albert Trott, Seymour, Jones, or MacLaren.

Tunnicliffe's preliminary position at slip, with pads and gloves on, might pass for the position of a wicket-keeper, and there is no question that slip should stoop forward, for most balls keep low rather than rise into the air from a snick, and if they do rise slip can spring up more quickly and easily than he can bend down.

Some short-slips have a tendency to stand too wide. A captain should be always on the look-out for this, and at once see that slip gets to his proper place. It is always easier to cover to one's right than to one's left. The distance slip should stand away from the wicket depends entirely on the pace of the bowling and the pace of the wicket.

The best slips I have ever seen are Chapman, Tunnicliffe, Braund, R. E. Foster, Lohmann, Hammond, and Constantine. Hammond is the best slip-fieldsman in the world to-day.[1] A very fine slip to fast bowl-ing, he is, incomparably, the finest to slow bowling. A genius may do as he likes, and contrary to the precepts of Tunnicliffe, Hammond moves about to a slow bowler, but he invariably moves in the right direction. He has made some amazing catches off a slow left-handed bowler like

---

[1] Taking everything into consideration, Constantine ranks as the best all-round fieldsman in the world to-day—at all events Hammond and Hendren, who ought to know, are of that opinion.

Parker, of Gloucestershire, standing within a yard or two of the bat at second-slip, or at backward-point. Hammond, indeed, adorns any position in the field; and for Gloucestershire *v.* Surrey, at Cheltenham in 1928, he made ten catches —a record. R. E. Foster and Braund were a wonderful pair in Australia in 1903-4, and I have an instinctive feeling that the first Test Match was won in that second when Foster made his glorious left-handed catch which got rid of Trumper for a single. MacLaren and Albert Trott have brought off many superb catches, and so have those great fielders, A. O. Jones, Hutchings, and G. N. Foster, while J. R. Mason was as good as any one. Other admirable fielders in this position are, or were, Hubert Ashton, Seymour, of Kent, the two Relfs, John Langridge and 'Duleep,' of Sussex, J. Douglas and Hendren, of Middlesex, J. M. Gregory, the Australian, P. G. H. Fender, and Faulkner and Vogler, of South Africa. Next to the wicket-keeper slip is the most important place in the field, and it is the worst captaincy possible to allow anyone who is not accustomed to that position to go there even for one ball.

## POINT

Point is a position which requires a quick eye and a quick action. It is comparatively easy to be a respectable point, but there are great opportunities for fine fielding here. At one time, at any rate on good wickets, there seemed a likelihood that point would die out, but in the last two or three years it has come to be realized once again that a good point will make many catches. The cricketers of John Nyren's time set great store by point. Nyren himself was a great fielder there, and used to stand within three and a half yards of the bat; but wickets in those days were rough, and the ball must have been constantly getting up and giving point an easy catch. Nowadays, on a hard wicket and against fast bowling, point must stand at least eight or nine yards from the batsman. On a sticky wicket, to a slow left-handed bowler, he can come to within Nyren's distance, and off a leg-break bowler who can keep a fairly accurate length he will get many catches about five yards from the bat. Point should study closely the styles of different batsmen, and shift his position accordingly, and he should watch the ball all the way from the bowler's hand. Some points watch only the bat, but the balance of opinion seems to be in favour of watching the ball. Point must be quick on his feet and able to bend smartly, for he will get many catches within half a foot of the ground. It is often difficult to gauge the pace the ball is travelling off the bat, especially from a leg-break bowler; in this last instance it very often comes a little higher up than one expects. Point should stand much like slip, and, on the whole, should wait for things to take their course. A stroke to point is often a false stroke, as in the case of slip, and often comes off the edge of the bat. No man can anticipate the exact direction of a ball off the edge of the bat, and one has seen point dart away to the right and the ball fall gently and harmlessly in the place where a moment before he was standing. On the whole, then, it seems best that point should not jump about, but should wait until the ball has hit the bat, and then move accordingly. If he is nimble on his feet and ever on his toes he will 'get there' in plenty of time. Tradition says that E. M. Grace and R. T. King were very great at point, and in more modern days M. A. Noble, L. G. Wright, F. Laver, and Mitchell of Yorkshire, have been magnificent.

## SILLY POINT

On sticky wickets and with a left-handed bowler like Rhodes, Verity, or Parker, it is often advisable to have a 'silly' or forward point. It is a post of some danger, and the holder of it is not to be envied if the bowler is in the habit of bowling half-volleys. Let us hope he would not be asked to go there by his captain unless the bowler's length was to be relied on. Verity frequently had a silly point on the right kind of pitch, and Strudwick, the Surrey wicket-keeper, acting as a substitute, caught two men there off Rhodes in a Test Match at Melbourne. In Australia, where the ball ' pops ' up so much more quickly on a sticky wicket than it does in England, silly point is almost a *sine qua non* to a left-handed bowler.[1]

In recent years, point has to a large extent gone out of fashion. One is seldom seen nowadays, but silly point is very much in evidence and, I think, has been overdone on fast wickets. On sticky wickets to a left-hander, yes—but I am not a believer in a silly point on a true wicket. In the first four Test Matches v. Australia in 1926 in which a ' silly point ' was very frequently used, not a single catch was given in this position, and in the Test v. South Africa, at Lord's, in 1935, no chance went that way. It seems to me to give the bowler only ten fieldsmen, there being an obvious gap in the field of which batsmen can take advantage. I have seen a slow leg-break bowler bowling without a deep square-leg or without an extra-cover. Silly point gives great scope to a brilliant fieldsman to stop hard hits, but I am convinced that against good batsmen on a good wicket many runs are given away, while the chance of a catch is most unlikely.

## COVER AND EXTRA-COVER-POINT

There is no better place in the field than cover or extra-cover-point if you are anxious for work. There is plenty to do, saving singles, stopping drives, running after the ball to

[1] A. P. F. Chapman is a very fine silly point; the ' best ever ' probably, with Mitchell of Yorkshire *proxime accessit*, and A. B. Sellers, J. W. W. Davies and Andrews, the Australian, not far behind them.

save the four, making catches, and backing up. Cover's
position depends on the pace of the bowling and ground,
the style of the batsman, and whether there is an extra-
cover or not. Many catches to cover are much more difficult
than they seem, and a 'skier' nearly always has tremendous
spin on it; one can hear it buzz. Even a hard, honest hit
generally has a bit of spin on, and ground hits usually curl
from right to left. There is a world of difference between a
safe and a brilliant cover or extra-cover; the former will just
miss many balls, the latter will get to them and stop them.

The classic extra-cover is G. L. Jessop. He was so quick
in moving to the ball and so accurate in his pick up and
return that he could stand yards deeper than, in theory, he
should, and yet few dared run to him. He was remarkable,
as was S. H. Saville. Saville was recommended to me by
the Rev. H. von E. Scott who in writing said: ' I have seen
all the great cover-points from Royle to Jessop, and Saville
is inferior to none of them.' On the form Saville showed
when he played county cricket it is certain that Scott did
not exaggerate. The Rev. Vernon Royle enjoyed a reputation in the seventies and early eighties that lives to this day.
Even that consummate stealer of short runs, the late Tom
Emmett, never dared to run to him. ' It's gone to t' plaace
—Noa.' What a character Tom was! I shall never forget
the face of the then Head Master of Rugby, the Rev. John
Percival, when Tom remarked that New Bigside would be a
good ground 'if you would let me cut down those elms!'
He taught me all my cricket. ' See here, Mr. Warner,' he
would say, taking the stump out at the bowler's end and
proceeding to illustrate the stroke. He could still bowl in
his coaching days at Rugby, now and then sending down a
ball which pitched on the leg-stump and hit the top of the
off. 'Never mind,' he used to say, 'I bowled "W. G."
first ball with that one in Gentlemen *v.* Players at the
Oval.' Every Rugby boy who knew him loved him.

Of English cover-points Hobbs was *facile princeps* in his day; but younger men such as H. G. Owen Smith and R. W. V. Robins now stand out. Rhodes was another great off-side fieldsman, and so were Quaife, John Gunn, R. H. Spooner, S. E. Gregory, and A. P. F. Chapman, while Andrews, Macartney, and Pellew of the Australians were very fine; and others who may be mentioned are, Bradman, Fingleton, and Bromley, of Australia, Paynter, of Lancashire, W. J. A. Davies, J. W. A. Stephenson, and V. Richardson.

## MID-OFF

Mid-off must be active, brave, and possessed of large and strong hands. The ball rarely has much spin on a catch to mid-off, but it is often hit with terrific force. On a hard wicket and against a slow left-handed bowler mid-off will be kept busy. His exact position will depend on the state of the wicket, the pace of the bowler, and the style of the batsman, but roughly he will not be less than twenty yards and not more than thirty yards from the striker. The modern tendency is to have mid-off as deep as possible and yet near enough to save the single, at any rate on a hard wicket. When a left-hander is bowling round the wicket, mid-off should stand wider. Very great mid-offs have been the Australians, E. Jones and R. A. Duff, S. M. J. Woods, and Hirst. It is difficult to say who, actually, was the best. Jones, for such a big man, was extraordinarily quick on his feet, and seemed capable of stopping anything; Woods has caught the most wonderful catches off Tyler's slow half-volleys—how often has one seen him wringing his hands after stopping a more than usually fierce blow—and Hirst was brilliant. His glorious left-handed catch at Lord's from a very hard skimming hit off Albert Trott's three-pound bat is as fresh in my memory as if it had taken place yesterday;

L. N. CONSTANTINE AT WORK

Note the intenseness with which he is treating even this simple catch

Picking up          G. L. Jessop          Finish of throw-in

*G. W. Beldam*

and it is over forty years ago. No one, however, has ever surpassed Duff's work in the Test Match at Sydney in December 1903. R. E. Foster bombarded him hour after hour, but nothing within reach got by him, and at the end of a terribly tiring day his picking up and stopping were as wonderful as ever. Among other mid-offs may be mentioned Jayes, of Leicestershire, Mignon, of Middlesex, and Llewellyn, of South Africa. F. T. Mann, too, was very good, and Brown, of Hampshire, was probably the best of the lot, though A. E. R. Gilligan was a serious rival. Bradman and Victor Richardson, of Australia, are both great mid-offs.

## MID-ON

Mid-on is often assigned to a weak fielder, but in these days when there is so much on-side play the position is not always a sinecure, and may involve a good deal of running about, especially if there is no short-leg or deep square-leg. When he is the only fielder on the on-side, mid-on will have to back up both bowler and wicket-keeper, so that he will have to exercise judgment and be quick on his feet. Mid-on's exact position varies according to the state of the wicket, and the style of the batsman or bowler. For instance, on a sticky wicket, to a right-hand break-back bowler mid-on will stand wider, because the break tends to carry the ball after it is played in that direction. The position offers great scope for a clever fielder, and a good mid-on may make all the difference in the world in the matter of saving runs. The late H. F. Boyle, the Australian, made a speciality of the position, and on sticky wickets, to the bowling of Spofforth or Palmer, often stood within five or six yards from the bat. Such a place is only possible when bowlers of the highest class are on, men who can be relied on to keep a length and whose bowling is too fast to

H

allow a batsman to jump out to drive; otherwise, as the Hon. R. H. Lyttelton writes in the *Badminton Library*, ' there will probably be a coroner's inquest required.' Humphreys, of Kent, was another great mid-on.

## SHORT-LEG

When a right-hander is bowling on a sticky wicket I always like to have one of the best fielders on my side at short-leg, as he will have plenty of opportunities of distinguishing himself. It is a very difficult place to field well in, as it is hard to judge the exact pace of the ball. Short-leg's position varies with circumstances. On a hard, true wicket he may be as much as twelve yards from the bat; on a sticky one, and with a bowler who can be trusted not to bowl half-volleys, he may be only four yards from the bat, especially if the batsman is of the ' poky ' type. Hitch, of Surrey, stood very near in, and made many catches, but he rather overdid things, and was lucky, in my opinion, to have escaped accident. Major Wynyard, G. R. Hazlitt, of Australia, and Humphreys, of Kent, used to be very good in this position (as are G. O. Allen, Hendren, I. A. R. Peebles, R. S. Grant, J. W. A. Stephenson, R. W. V. Robins, and D. Compton to-day), and so were Rhodes and Braund, while A. O. Jones made a wonderful catch here in the England *v.* Australia match at Birmingham in May 1909. Hirst bowled a swerving ball which Noble got on the full pitch in the right part of the bat. Every one expected to see the ball travelling to the boundary when Jones caught it with his left hand about three inches above the ground. He was *facile princeps* in the slips; he could catch and return the ball from the country as well as Tyldesley, Denton, or Hutchings; there were few better mid-offs; and here he was at short-leg making a catch such as no other short-leg has surpassed.

## Some Rules for Fielding

1. Keep the legs together when the ball is hit straight to you.

2. Do not forget to back up. There should be at least ten yards between the men backing up, and also between the man nearest the wicket and the wicket.

3. Try for everything, but do not barge at the ball.

4. Keep on your toes.

5. Chase the ball as if you loved doing so; you ought to.

6. Use both hands, if possible, except for certain catches—especially in the slips.

7. It is a good thing to throw catches to one another between the fall of wickets.

8. Keep in the exact position your captain has assigned you; don't move about and be in your proper place one ball and five yards away the next. It is most annoying to both bowler and captain.

9. If you are third man, the best end to return the ball to nine times out of ten is the bowler's, because the non-striker, not being hampered in starting for the run by having just made a stroke, is more likely to get in.

10. If bowling, get behind your wicket when there is the least chance of a run out.

11. Keep your eye on your captain in case he may wish to move you without the batsman knowing.

12. Stick to it until the last ball of the day, no matter how tiring that day may have been.

13. Obtain as much practice as possible. Constantine tells us that he ' lived for hours on the slip machine.'

14. Balance is highly important, especially for a slip-fieldsman. Practise skipping; it gives added quickness.

I am greatly indebted to C. H. Taylor, the old Oxford and Leicestershire cricketer, whose insistence on the value of fielding earned for the Eton XI's of 1942-4 a good reputation, for the following remarks:

The notes which follow are based on my own experience of giving fielding practice and are not intended as instructions. I am sure that they can be improved on. They may be useful, however, as a starting point. If they appear to be didactic, they are not meant to be so: it saves space to put them in this form.

1. Time required is about one hour.

2. Satisfactory practice cannot be given to more than 12 boys.

3. 1st half-hour. Catching practice. The object is to instil confidence by giving as large a number of catches as possible. Obviously if a boy has caught 700 catches by June 1st, he is more likely to catch the 701st in a match on June 2nd than if he has merely caught and missed a few in club games in May.

Put 4 on slip cradle and keep 7. Change about at discretion. Keep wicket-keeper as collector of returned balls which should be thrown back gently. Watch carefully position of hands: no rat-trap catching. Fingers should be slightly spread and hands at right angles to course of ball (i.e. the tips of the fingers should never point towards the ball). Start gently at 10–15 yards: increase distance and difficulty (at all distances). Be careful on cold days as bruised hands and strained shoulders may result. Place boys in a line, well spaced, and always take them in order as they stand; random hitting wastes time and is dangerous. At all distances begin with stationary catches; go on with running ones, forward and back, left and right. Tell them before you start that bruised hands must be reported at once. Don't let a boy go on catching, if he is bruised.

4. 2nd half-hour. Ground fielding and throwing. The object is to combine speed with accuracy.

Place 10 men in positions as in a match; wicket-keeper (padded and gloved) in usual place; one boy (who should be varied) bowls or throws. It is impossible to snick intentionally to 1st or 2nd slip, but you can place two gullies close together and give them some warm cuts. Change positions of fielders from time to time, since off-side men obviously have the most interesting time. It is easy to fit in two extra-covers. Mainly ground fielding, but catches can be put in occasionally, especially for deep fielders.

Teach the fieldsman to have right foot behind ball (if he is right-handed) when possible, but not both feet. It is easy to demonstrate that if you have both feet together, it takes you much longer to gather the ball and throw it in and it is also much harder to stoop. Discourage one-handed work when two can be used. Insist upon over-shoulder throwing (the under-shoulder flick is wildly inaccurate unless the fielder has genius for it) and teach to throw three-quarter strength, not full force, or there will be inaccuracy. Show that much inaccurate ground fielding comes from looking up before ball is in hands. Keep an eye on moving in (but not more than 2 or 3 yards: a 10-yard walk is tiring and useless) except in the close positions. Teach all fielders, except wicket-keeper and 1st slip, to watch the batsman—not the bowler—so that they may anticipate his stroke and gain a yard or two. Backing up both of each other and the wicket-keeper. Full-pitch and first-bounce throwing according to distance and strength.

N.B. Good fielding makes weak bowling strong.

# CHAPTER V

## SOME THOUGHTS ON CAPTAINCY

APART from good batting, bowling, and fielding, matches are won by leadership, organization, and co-operation. A really good captain may make an otherwise weak eleven into a fair one, while, *per contra*, a bad captain may ruin the strongest eleven. The ideal captain must possess a sound knowledge of the game, a cool judgment, tact, and, above everything else, enthusiasm—for enthusiasm is a quality which enriches life and gives it zest, and the man who is enthusiastic about his eleven and their doings will, unless his influence and authority are sapped by disloyalty and want of co-operation, soon inspire the same feelings of zeal for the common cause in his followers. But a Napoleon amongst cricket captains can do nothing if the rank and file are disloyal, so that both leader and follower have their part to play. Neither can accomplish much without the other.

Cricket has become so scientific that the captain of to-day has to work hard. He must keep thoroughly up to date with all new ideas about placing the field, study carefully the methods of other captains, and work out in his own mind the why and the wherefore of every move on the cricket chess-board. The days have gone by for ever when a captain could change his bowling by the clock, or leave the field in the same position for every batsman. Different styles have to be studied, and the captain and the bowler between them must endeavour to set the field so that the batsman's favourite strokes are blocked. All these things are to be learnt only by experience—*experientia docet sapientiam*—and therefore take time. It is only natural that amateurs should make the best captains, though the Players were led for many years with conspicuous skill by Lilley, the famous Warwickshire wicket-keeper, whose advice, from his vantage position behind the sticks, a succession of English captains have not disdained to ask. But a captain would be a fool, if supposing he is not a wicket-keeper himself, and supposing the wicket-keeper knows something about the game, he did not occasionally consult his wicket-keeper, for the simple reason that he is in the best of all positions to see how the game is going.

When they first came over here the Australians were indifferently captained. A. G. Steel tells us in the *Badminton Library* that ' F. R. Spofforth bowled the greater part of the day on a fast Lord's wicket to the Hon. Edward Lyttelton, who was not dismissed until he had topped his hundred. Ball after ball was neatly cut on the hard true ground to the boundary, past the spot where third man ought to have been but was not.' In the last twenty years, however, the Australians have been blessed with six superb captains in H. Trott, Darling, Noble, Armstrong, Woodfull, and Bradman. Darling's judgment was sometimes at fault in 1905, but in 1899 and 1902 he was an admirable captain, while Trott earned great fame during the Australian season of 1897-8, and in England in 1896. But the greatest of the six probably was Noble, a most consummate ' shot blocker,' though he would be the first to admit that he was enormously helped in the accurate placing of the field by the fact that the bowlers bowled to their field—a most important factor and one in which many of the best English bowlers are perhaps wanting. When two batsmen were thoroughly well set, and likely to score fast if the field was set in a more or less orthodox manner, Noble's policy was to have an outer as well as an inner ring of fieldsmen, so that if the ball got past the in-fieldsmen there were men on the boundary to save the four. Occasionally the chance of a catch near in was missed by the wider distribution of the fieldsmen, but it was tantalizing to batsmen to see a four under ordinary circumstances turned into a single or at most a couple, and to get runs at anything like a fast rate was a matter of the greatest difficulty. Just as there are well-defined rules which a general should follow in war, so are there certain maxims for cricket captains, the chief of which are, don't fuss; don't tear your hair one minute and be dancing about with joy the next; don't be down on the man who has missed a catch—rather sympathise with him; don't take your mind off the game; don't be slack for even a minute; don't alter the field unnecessarily; don't fidget; don't be anything else but cheerful; and if beaten take your defeat in a cheerful, happy spirit. Cricket, after all, is only a game, and no moral disgrace can attach to failure. It is of vital importance to make your eleven believe in themselves. If a captain succeeds in doing so, he can almost persuade his men to make runs and take wickets. In times of failure exhort them, like Caesar of old, to remember their former prowess. Sound captaincy covers the dressing-room as well as the actual field of play. Don't forget occasionally to consult one of your side, if he is a judge of the game. Don't consult more than one, the bowler always excepted—this leads to confusion of ideas. Don't forget that it is you who have to make the final decision, therefore try to train your mind to take a calm view of circumstances and situations. Above all, encourage your men all the while, and never despair of victory. A fine determination to conquer at all costs is a great factor in success.

When a side has to bat for half an hour or so at the end of a day's play, the captain has to consider whether he should alter his order or not. Many things have to be taken into consideration, the state of the wicket, the light, and, above all, the temperament of the batsmen. A sound course to adopt is not to alter the order if half an hour remains. If one of the opening batsmen should be dismissed with only ten minutes to play, I should invariably keep until the next morning my number 3 batsman and send in a steady defensive batsman. A captain should insist on what may be called ' parade polish '—no pad straps hanging two or three inches down the legs, trousers unfolded and sticking out behind the pads—in fact no sort of slovenliness! A smartly turned out XI is generally a smart XI, and I have known a captain who sent off the field a man who had neglected to shave, and quite rightly too.

Remember that a change of ends often brings success. A captain should note the direction of the wind and any peculiarities in the ground, such as Lord's where the slope helps an off-break bowler at the pavilion end and conversely the nursery end helps a left-hander and a leg-break bowler, though that is no reason why they should not occasionally be tried at the opposite end. I have known J. T. Hearne take six wickets in an innings when on at the nursery end, and he, with his deadly off-break, must have bowled more overs from the pavilion end than any other man. Googly bowlers can bowl at either end. J. W. Hearne who could make his leg-break literally ' hum ' in the air invariably bowled from the pavilion end at Lord's, and it was from this end that K. Balaskas, the South African googly bowler, accomplished his great feat in the England v. South Africa Test Match in 1935.

Verity, too, a left-hander, obtained all his fifteen wickets v. Australia at Lord's in 1934 from the pavilion end, and to me, at any rate, Blythe was more difficult to play from this end.

Googly bowlers require careful management and the placing of their field is a special study; in this respect I am a great believer in a googly bowler always having third man back on a fast wicket. This saves many a boundary from the loose ball which nearly all bowlers of this type occasionally send down.

Organization naturally plays an important part in the winning of matches; and by organization I mean the choosing of the right kind of eleven for a particular match—e.g. don't on any account leave out your fast bowler, if you have one, on a hard wicket. This may be called the strategy of cricket—the disposition of your eleven before a ball has been bowled. As an instance of false strategy, the omission of a fast bowler from the England teams at Lord's and the Oval in 1909 may be cited. Organization of other kinds may be left to the committee of the club, who are responsible for discipline off the field, while the captain is responsible for discipline during the progress of a match. An undisciplined eleven is like an undisciplined army, untrustworthy, and disloyalty to a captain on or off the field is fatal to success.

An eleven playing together day after day has a great advantage. A regular order of going in is settled, the fieldsmen occupy the same positions in every innings, and a captain gets to know exactly what his bowlers are capable of under different circumstances. He finds out that so-and-so likes to go in No. 5, that another is a brilliant long-field but only fairly good at cover-point and vice versa, that Jones is your best bowler on a sticky wicket but only moderate on a true one, that Robinson is always anxious to go in ten minutes before the close of play. Then, again, each man knows that he is not playing for his place, and therefore does full justice to himself. All these things make up that almost indefinable but none the less real attribute which is called combination.

Lucky is the county which can depend on much the same eleven in match after match, for the individual becomes merged in the mass, and gives the tremendous power of unity to the efforts of the whole number. An eleven should be what its captain makes it; its character sooner or later should become the reflex of his own; his energy and his firmness are rapidly communicated, and his influence should be far-reaching. But loyalty and co-operation are, as I have said, absolutely essential. Without them he is terribly handicapped.

But if he can command these two essentials, the task of captaining a first-class eleven should be a never-ending delight to an enthusiastic cricketer. I have known men who hated captaining a side, but the majority have admitted that captaining gave a further interest in the game over and above the making of runs or the taking of wickets. They have said that the satisfaction felt when a well-thought-out method of attack and defence has come off has been intense, and as great as the making of a big score or a fine catch. Most men aspire to leadership in some form or other. The cricket field affords a delightful and fascinating opportunity.

The atmosphere of the dressing-room is most important. It should be happy and pleasant; there is no need for a feeling of undue tenseness. Courtesy to one's team and to one's opponents is essential. Cricket after all is only a game, though Test Matches are pretty 'grim' affairs nowadays.

One word more. Fight until the last ball. Remember three balls can take three wickets, e.g. the famous Cobden over in the University match of 1870, and the Eton v. Harrow match of 1910, 'Fowler's match.' No match is ever lost until the last ball has been bowled.

# CHAPTER VI

## CRICKET IN THE MAKING

CRICKET—cryce, Sax., a stick—*Dr. Johnson's Dictionary.*[1]

MR. HORACE HUTCHINSON thought that cricket began when first a monkey-man, instead of catching a coconut thrown him playfully by a fellow anthropoid, hit it away from him with a stick which he chanced to be holding in his hand, and Mr. Andrew Lang suggested that cricket dated back to B.C., when Cuchulainn, an Irish hero, played a game which consisted of the batsman defending with a bat, or club, a hole in the ground, into which his opponent tried to pitch a ball. At this kind of cricket, Cuchulainn, who was a kind of demi-god, defeated one hundred and fifty Colts of Ulster; the score was:

| | | | | |
|---|---|---|---|---|
| Colts, b. Cuchulainn | . | . | . | 0 |
| Cuchulainn, not out | . | . | . | 1 |

But cricket was not born, it ' just growed,' and it belongs to the British people. Its origin is involved in the mists of obscurity, and until the latter half of the seventeenth century it appears to be identified only with boys; but with the Restoration it seems to have leapt into popularity with men, though only some twenty years before Maidstone was described as ' a very profane town ' because ' crickets was played openly and publicly on the Lord's Day,' and the churchwardens of Eltham were fined two shillings each for playing cricket on the Sabbath.

[1] This is the usually accepted derivation, ' cricket ' being a diminutive form of ' cryce,' i.e. a little stick, or bat.

But, with the fall of Puritanism, cricket began to go ahead, and even abroad we hear of a match at ' Krickett ' played at Aleppo between a party from His Majesty's ships *Assistance, Bristol,* and *Royal Oak,* which were lying off Antioch, on 6th May, 1676. A naval chaplain, Henry Teonge, records this in his diary, and to him must be awarded the credit of being the first to plant the seed of our national game on foreign soil.

The first match on record is to be found advertised in *The Postboy* of March, 1700, taking place on Clapham Common. In 1744 we come across the first laws of the game, and on 18th June of that year the first recorded match—Kent *v.* All England, played on the Artillery Ground, Bunhill Fields, Finsbury Square, Kent winning by one wicket.

The diagram of the various changes in the height and width of the stumps will show that at this time there were only two stumps,[1]—and it was not out if the ball went *through!*

The shape of the bat has changed considerably from time to time, but nothing was laid down as to the width of the bat until the 1774 edition of the Laws, and it is interesting to note that the width is the same to-day—four and a quarter inches—though nothing is said of its length until 1835, the ball has been the same weight since 1774; before 1774 it was between five and six ounces.   Pads were invented in the 'thirties, but did not come into general use for twenty or thirty years.

In the original Laws of Cricket, 1744, there is no mention of l.b.w., but in 1774 we find this: ' The striker is out if he puts his leg before wicket with a *design* to stop the ball, and

[1] The two stumps are accounted for by an interesting little piece of cricket history.  Cricket was originally most popular in the Weald of Sussex and Kent, and there the tree *stumps* were the objective of the man who *bowled* the ball.  On the downlands, however, the lack of tree stumps forced the young shepherds to find an alternative.  This they found in the *wicket* or gate of the sheep pens, which consisted of two uprights and a detachable cross-bar called the *bail.*

actually prevents the ball from hitting his wicket.' In 1788 this law was altered, ' design ' was deleted, the word ' foot ' added, and the ball must pitch ' in straight line to the wicket and would have hit it.' Forty years later—1828— the law runs as to-day: ' If with any part of his *person*,

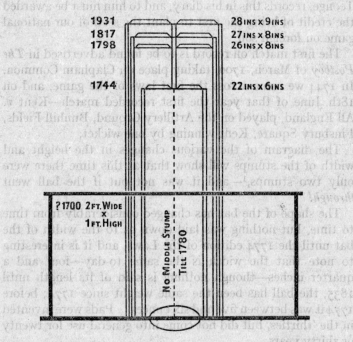

etc.,' so that the l.b.w. law has been the same, substantially, since 1788. This gave considerable food for thought, and was a strong point for those who would wish to see this law altered. The l.b.w. law was altered in 1937 after experimental trials in 1929 and 1930, so that a batsman may be out to a ball which ' shall have been pitched on the off-side of the striker's wicket and would have hit it.'

Originally, all bowling was under-hand, and it was so, of

course, in the days of the famous Hambledon Club, which was formed in 1750, and which broke up in, or about, 1791. The deeds of the Hambledon players and their opponents are told in John Nyren's cricket classic *The Young Cricketers' Tutor*.   Here we have a most interesting description of the form and characteristics of the cricketers of those days; men like David Harris, the famous bowler, whose bowling so impressed Nyren that he wrote that ' Harris would have made a beautiful study for the sculptor, and Phideas would certainly have taken him for a model.   First of all, he stood erect like a soldier at drill, then with a graceful curve of the arm, he raised the ball to his forehead, and drawing back his right foot, started off with his left.'

Then there was Beldham, ' whose cutting was as the speed of thought '; Richard Nyren himself, ' the chosen chief of all the matches, a fine specimen of the thoroughbred old English yeoman, and left-handed both as batsman and bowler,' and others whose names flit across these pages are Lambert, ' the little farmer,' who was the first off-break bowler, ' this deceitful and teasing style of delivering the ball,' as John Nyren puts it; ' Lumpy,' whose real name was Stevens, ' who would bowl the greatest number of length balls in succession '; Noah Mann, a fellow of extraordinary activity, ' who could perform clever feats of agility on horseback, a fine batter, a fine field, and the swiftest runner I ever remember,' and the first left-handed in-swinging bowler.   Noah was evidently a rare character, and his hitting at the crisis of a match between Hambledon and All England is historic.   ' Lumpy ' was bowling to him, and tossed one up a little too far, and begad! Noah was after it, and struck it for six.   ' Never,' says Nyren, ' shall I forget the roar that followed this hit.'

Further, there were those two ' annointed clod-stumpers,' Tom and Harry Walker.   ' Never, surely, came two such unadulterated rustics into a civilized community.'   But

Nyren must be read; I could go on quoting *ad infinitum* from this wonderful book, which should be a joy to all cricketers, for it gives a unique account of what may be called the 'Dawn of Cricket,' and of the men who 'made' the game.

The founding of the M.C.C. in 1787 was really the end of the Hambledon Club. The M.C.C. sprang from the old White Conduit Club, their first ground was where Dorset Square now stands, and was opened in 1787. The first match ever played at 'Lord's,' as it was called, after the owner of the ground,[1] was between Middlesex, with two of Berkshire and one of Kent, against Essex with two given men. The date was 31st May and Middlesex won by 93 runs.

In 1812, Lord moved from Dorset Square to North Bank, through which the Regent Canal now runs, and in 1814 he again moved, this time to the present ground. In each case he brought the turf with him, so that he who plays at Lord's to-day treads part of the same turf as the cricketers of one hundred and sixty years ago.

Since 1814, M.C.C. has grown from a small club to be the most mighty cricket organization the world has ever known. Its influence is world-wide, it is everywhere acknowledged as the lawgiver and the trustee of the game, and almost yearly it sends teams to every quarter of the globe.

One of the greatest figures in the history of M.C.C.—Lord Harris was, perhaps, the greatest—was the Rev. Lord Frederick Beauclerk. For well nigh sixty years he was a familiar figure at Lord's—in his prime he was an accurate slow bowler with pace from the pitch—and his word was law. But, unfortunately, he was as unscrupulous as he was accomplished, and he 'sold' more than one match.

> My Lord he comes next, and will make you all stare
> With his little tricks, a long way from fair.

---

[1] Thomas Lord, who came of a Jacobite family.

J. B. Hobbs

*G. W. Beldam*

C. B. FRY RUNNING OUT TO DRIVE

The famous Squire Osbaldeston and E. H. Budd were also prominent amateurs at this period, and Budd, like Albert Trott to come, used to go about armed with a three-pound bat, with which he once put a ball clean out of the first Lord's. This bat recently came into the possession of M.C.C. In July, 1817, William Lambert, the great Surrey player, scored the first 'double century'—107 and 157, for Sussex v. Epsom at Lord's.

In about 1820, round-arm bowling was introduced by John Willes, of Sutton Valence, and there was much argument over what was at that time called a revolutionary proposal, some people thinking it would ruin the game. However, the reformers eventually had their way, and the 'new' bowling had become firmly established some time before 1835, when M.C.C. gave it official sanction so as to admit of the hand being raised as high as the elbow, the back of it uppermost, and the arm to be extended horizontally. The mantle of Willes fell on William Lillywhite, 'The Nonpareil,' a little man of five feet four inches—but a most accurate bowler—and in a lesser degree on James Broadbridge, 'a fox-headed fellow,' both of Sussex. After the England v. Surrey match at the Oval, in 1862, the bowler was allowed to raise his arm above the shoulder, and bowl as is the universal practice nowadays, and ' liberty for the bowler was won.'

During the first quarter and middle half of the nineteenth century many arresting figures pass across the cricket stage, the two greatest of whom were, perhaps, Alfred Mynn and Fuller Pilch. Mynn was a tremendous fellow. Born at Goudhurst, Kent, in 1807, he is said to have been taught round-arm bowling by John Willes, and in course of time he acquired great pace. Until W. G. Grace appeared, Mynn was the greatest personality in cricket. Standing six feet one inch and weighing some seventeen or eighteen stone, he took a short and deliberate run to the wicket, and bringing his arm over in a swing 'as smooth as a piston rod,' as Major H. S. Altham puts it in his *History of Cricket*, he kept a perfect length on the leg-stump, and made the ball go with his arm. He was also a powerful hitter, and a magnificent short-slip, his hands being enormous. He was extremely popular, and when not batting or bowling was generally surrounded by a crowd of admirers, as he walked, bat in hand, round his beloved Kentish grounds in much the same way as I saw Dr. Grace arrive on the Clifton College ground in August 1894. Like Grace, he was a national institution.

Mynn lived for many years at Bearsted, near Maidstone, and his house on the edge of the green is still shown to cricket pilgrims. He is buried at Thurnham, two miles from Bearsted. He was called the 'Lion of Kent,' 'Alfred the Great,' and the 'Monarch of all Bowlers,' and in some verses by Mr. W. J. Prowse, of Tottenham, which were published in *Bell's Life* on 10th November, 1861, we read these lines:

With his tall and stately presence, with his nobly moulded form,
His broad hand was ever open, his brave heart was ever warm;
All were proud of him, all loved him as the changing seasons pass,
As our Champion lies asleeping underneath the Kentish grass;
Proudly, sadly, we will name him, to forget him were a sin,
Lightly lie the turf upon thee, kind and manly Alfred Mynn.

Fuller Pilch must have been the Lionel Palairet of his day. He was a Norfolk man by birth, but afterwards played for Kent. He was the first forward player, and he not only drove the half-volley through the covers, but forced the good-length ball on the off-side. In this way he, to a very great extent, mastered the new school of round-arm bowling, and it is written of him that he had a terrific hit between mid-off and cover which gained him many a four or five runs.

He was one of the great masters of the art of batting, and at the other end, more often than not, was 'Felix,' whose real name was Nicholas Wanostrocht, author of the famous *Felix on the Bat*, and the Felix mentioned in *Tom Brown's Schooldays*—'Felix, 56 not out, and without a chance.' He was left-handed, knew the whole science of the game, and used to throw his right foot forward and hit the half-volley outside the off-stump, almost like Woolley of to-day.

Kent were a great side in those days; and it was no idle boast when the poet wrote:

And with five such mighty cricketers 'twas but natural to win
As Felix, Wenman, Hillyer, Fuller Pilch and Alfred Mynn.

Another arresting personality was William Clarke, of Nottinghamshire, captain and manager of the All England XI which travelled about the length and breadth of the country. He bowled under-arm, the ball being delivered about the level of his hip, with a consistent spin from leg and a consistent length. His name is one that lives, and will live, in cricket history—as will that of John Wisden—'very fast and ripping' a true round-arm action, very straight and accurate in length. In 1864 he published the first *Wisden*—'The Cricketers' Bible'—of which I am the fortunate possessor of every issue.

One could write much about the cricket of this period, but space forbids, and one must curb one's enthusiasm and mention but a few names, such as Jackson, of Nottinghamshire, whose pace was described as 'very fearful,' and who alone amongst cricketers before W. G. Grace, appeared in the pages of *Punch*. Alfred Shaw, most accurate of slow-medium bowlers, who round about the year 1862 suggested that the popping-crease, instead of being cut with a knife in the turf, should be marked in chalk. Other names are George Parr and Richard Daft, of Nottinghamshire, F. P. Miller and C. G. Lane, of the Oval, where the first match was played in June 1846, Surrey beating Kent by ten wickets—H. H. Stephenson who took the first English team to Australia, and William Caffyn. Then came Hayward and Carpenter, of Cambridgeshire; Hayward, uncle of Tom, who played so fine a part both for Surrey and for England, and Carpenter, father of Herbert Carpenter, an Essex stalwart in the early days of this century.

In 1864 there arrived the greatest personality the game has ever known in the person of W. G. Grace, the ever famous Champion. He revolutionized the art of batting and made modern cricket. Before his day a batsman was either a back player or a forward player, 'W. G.' combined both styles, and for nearly forty years dominated the cricket world.

W. G. first played for the Gentlemen in 1865, at the age of sixteen, and he was playing for them when he was well over fifty. Apart from his supreme batting, he was a very clever slow round-arm bowler, and a wonderful field; indeed, a fine athlete, good enough to win a 440-yard hurdle race over twenty flights of hurdles, in one minute ten seconds, at the Crystal Palace, on 31st July, 1866, *on the same day* on which playing for England *v.* Surrey, at the Oval, he scored 224 not out. He also threw the cricket ball 122 yards at some sports at Eastbourne.

In the course of his career, he made 54,896 runs and obtained 2,864 wickets. He bestrode the cricket world like a Colossus, and in estimating his performances it must not be forgotten that the great majority of wickets in his day were nothing like so true as they are now. He simply 'murdered' fast bowling. I once had the temerity, at the end of his career, to ask him whether there was any type of bowling which he disliked, and his answer was characteristic: 'I did not mind what they bowled, if I was in form, but the faster they bowled, the better I liked them.' I, who had the honour of going in first with him on more than one occasion, can well realize what he must have been like in his prime, for even when he was over fifty he could play the terrific fast bowling of Jones, the Australian, as well as, if not better than, any of his contemporaries.

Cricketers may come, and cricketers may go, but there will never again be such a personality as the Champion. With his giant figure, black beard, and M.C.C. cap, he was the outstanding figure on every cricket ground, and it was said of him, and with truth, that he was as well known by sight as any man in England. His two brothers, 'E. M.' and 'G. F.' were also fine cricketers, but it is no disparagement to them to say that W. G. stood head and shoulders above them both. The three of them played for England, at the Oval, in September 1880, in the first Test Match ever played between England and Australia in England.

Round about the time that W. G. was killing fast bowling, there were two great Yorkshiremen, George Freeman and Tom Emmett. W. G. had a tremendous opinion of Freeman, stating that he thought him the best of all the fast bowlers he ever played, but Freeman played comparatively little cricket, and retired after the end of the season of 1871.

Yorkshire has produced many great cricketing characters, but there will never be a greater one than Emmett. He was a man of inexhaustible good humour and spirit, and a fast to fast-medium left-handed bowler who could occasionally pitch the ball on the leg-stump, and hit the top of the off. I never, of course, played in first-class cricket with him, but he coached me at Rugby, and I can recall with delight, even after all these years, his cheery: 'See here, Mr. Warner,' as he took the stump out at the bowlers' wicket in the net, and taught me some stroke. He was a most encouraging coach, and I shall never forget two of his maxims: 'Smell her, sir, smell her,' and 'If you come to her, come.' Every Rugby boy who knew him, loved him, and I can see him now, as though it were yesterday, striding across the Close, with his grey and well-shaped head, crowned by a Yorkshire cap, held high, and his body as straight as the most ramrod sergeant on parade could desire. Many are the stories told of him, and his name will ever be associated with the greatest of all our cricketing counties.

With W. G. at his best, round about the year 1873, the year in which the County Championship in something like its present form first started, and in which, incidentally, I was born, I may well close this chapter, and come to more modern days, dealing with what has become at once the most notable and the most characteristic feature of first-class cricket—Test Match Cricket.

# CHAPTER VII

## ENGLAND AND AUSTRALIA

IT was not against Australia that England played what may be called the first international match at cricket, but against America and Canada, as far back as 1859—before the North and South War—during the tour of George Parr's team, a tour so well described in *Kings of Cricket*, by Richard Daft. George Parr, a great personality, was called 'The Lion of the North,' and to this day there is a tree standing just beyond the boundary on the Trent Bridge ground, which is always referred to as George Parr's Tree—tradition asserting that he once hit a ball to square-leg over it. The first visit to Australia was in 1861. H. H. Stephenson, Surrey cricketer and huntsman, and afterwards the mentor of many a famous Uppingham cricketer, being in command of a side which was, as in the case of Parr's team, composed entirely of professionals. There followed other English teams—in 1864, under Parr, and in 1873 'W. G.' himself, the Colossus of Cricket, was seen in Australia. But the first what is now called 'Test' Match between England and Australia did not take place until March 1877, when Australia defeated J. Lillywhite's team by 45 runs, at Melbourne; Charles Bannerman scoring 165, retired hurt, for Australia. In the following year the Australians paid their first visit to England under the captaincy of D. W. Gregory—an illustrious name in Australian cricket, the Gregorys being to Australia what the Graces were to England. This team arrived unheralded and unsung—and lost their first match *v.* Notts, by an innings and 14 runs, but a few days later, on 27th May, the fame of Australian cricket was established for all time; for on that date, in the short space of four and a half hours, they defeated, on a very difficult wicket at Lord's, a powerful M.C.C. team, by nine wickets. M.C.C. made 33 and 19, Australia 41 and 12 for one wicket. 'W. G.' scored 4 and 0, and as *Punch* put it:

> Our Grace before dinner was very soon done,
> And Grace after dinner did not get a run.

The bowling of F. R. Spofforth, 'The Demon'—so called not only because of the fear which his bowling inspired, but also because of a certain Mephistophelian cast of countenance—and of H. F. Boyle, and the fielding of the Australians, was something of a revelation. That night all England was talking of them, and their hotel, the old Tavistock, in Covent Garden, was surrounded by an enthusiastic and congratulatory crowd. There was no fixture with England that season, but two years later they met and were beaten by five wickets at the Oval by England, captained by Lord Harris, who in the winter of 1878–9 had taken out almost an entirely amateur side to Australia. It is only fair to state, however, that owing to an injury, Spofforth was unable to play at the Oval, and the absence of their famous bowler was, of course, a tremendous handicap.

Two years later, on 28th and 29th August, followed the most famous of all Test Matches, at the Oval—when England was beaten by 7 runs. That defeat came as a heavy blow to our cricketing pride. England literally went into mourning. It was after this game that the phrase 'The Ashes' came into being. *The Sporting Times* published the following epitaph:

In affectionate remembrance
of
English cricket
which died at the Oval on
29th August 1882
Deeply lamented by a large circle of
sorrowing friends and
acquaintances
R.I.P.

N.B.   The body will be cremated and the ashes taken to Australia.

This 1882 Australian team was a fine side—with bowlers like Spofforth, Palmer, Garrett, Boyle, and Giffen—the last but a mere boy, but destined to develop into so great an all-rounder as to be called the 'Grace of Australia'—and with a splendid and stylish batsman in W. L. Murdoch, the captain, hitters in H. H. Massie and G. J. Bonnor, who could win a match on a bad wicket—T. Horan, and the prince of wicket-keepers in the immortal J. McC. Blackham. The fielding, too, was splendid, and altogether it was a well-balanced eleven, if not really strong in batting. Some critics rate it as the best of all Australian elevens, but a majority of opinion would probably award the palm in this respect to the teams of 1899, 1902, and 1921, which were far superior in batting strength, and had as bowlers men like H. Trumble, M. A. Noble, E. Jones, W. Howell, J. M. Gregory, E. A. Macdonald, A. A. Mailey, and W. W. Armstrong.

After the conclusion of Murdoch's tour the Hon. Ivo Bligh—'St. Ivo,' as he was called in Australia—set forth on a pilgrimage to recover the Ashes, and winning two out of three matches against Murdoch's men was presented with an urn containing some ashes, which stands in the Pavilion at Lord's to-day, 'plain for all men to see.'   Unfortunately, in a sense, 'St. Ivo' was persuaded to play a fourth match—Murdoch's team being altered in two or three instances—

which he lost, and the historians still argue as to whether he did in point of fact regain the Ashes.

The Australians had no doubt taught us much about bowling, fielding, and wicket-keeping, and they had learnt a great deal about batting from us, and at the time, and for several years afterwards, uncommon prestige, and something of romance, surrounded their cricket. This continued for some years, but from about 1886 onwards there was a marked decline in their general form, though the 1888 side had two outstanding bowlers in C. T. B. Turner and J. J. Ferris. For six weeks they went through England, bowling out side after side for small totals on the sticky wickets of that year; and moreover, they defeated England at Lord's by 61 runs, though England had full revenge by winning the other two matches by an innings each.

The revival of Australian cricket may be said to have been due to the visit of Lord Sheffield's team to Australia in the winter of 1891-2, Australia winning two of the three Test Matches and over a hundred thousand spectators watching the game at Melbourne.

'W. G.' after an interval of eighteen years, revisited Australia. Many people were doubtful of the wisdom of his going at his age, forty-three, but the Champion played splendidly and headed the batting averages, proving himself still without a peer amongst the world's batsmen.

The 1893 Australian eleven to England were easily beaten in the Test Matches, and then came one of the most interesting of all English tours in Australia, the visit of A. E. Stoddart's team in 1894-5.

This tour is well described in George Giffen's book *With Bat and Ball,* and the games aroused tremendous interest, not only in Australia, but here. At the conclusion of the fourth match the result was two-all, and the fifth Test Match, at Melbourne, was won by Stoddart's eleven by six wickets, Richardson bowling superbly, and J. T. Brown and

Albert Ward taking part in an heroic stand in the second innings. A. E. Stoddart was one of the most popular English captains that ever visited Australia and his name is held in honour there to this day. It was during this tour that the word 'Test' was first applied to these matches, and I believe I am correct in saying that the *Pall Mall Gazette* was the first to coin the word.

We won in England in 1896, but only just won, the Australians being a very fine side, and they were an even finer side when Stoddart went back to Australia in 1897, and was defeated in the Test Matches by four games to one. Ranji and MacLaren batted superbly, as did Hill and Darling for Australia, but our bowling was far below that of Australia.

In 1899 in England, four of the Test Matches were drawn and Australia won the match at Lord's in overwhelming fashion by ten wickets. A. C. MacLaren's visit to Australia a couple of years later saw Australia again successful by four games to one.

Again in 1902 Australia won the rubber in England, but though unsuccessful during these years England had a very fine side. As it happened, however, Australia were a little stronger all round.

Great names at this period pass across the stage: MacLaren, Ranjitsinhji, Jessop, Rhodes, Jackson, Fry, Lockwood, J. T. Hearne, and Lilley, one side, and Darling, Noble, Hill, H. Trott, H. Trumble, S. E. Gregory, and Victor Trumper on the other. All these men were stars of the first magnitude, and it may well be that although we lost the rubber in 1902, the eleven which played at Birmingham was, probably, the strongest that has ever represented England. Here are the names: MacLaren (capt.), Fry, Ranji, Jackson, Jessop, Lilley, J. T. Tyldesley, Rhodes, Hirst, Braund, and Lockwood. This was indeed the Golden Age of cricket, and much glamour and, indeed, glory surrounded the Test Matches.

In 1903 occurred a departure from precedent. Hitherto teams to Australia had been taken out by private individuals; now the Marylebone Club undertook the conduct of these tours, and they honoured me with the captaincy of their first team. I was in a peculiar position, never before having played for England, and yet finding myself captain of an English team in these great matches.

Pessimists abounded—they often do—but the result of the tour was a victory for England by three matches to two. We had a fine side which worked together in perfect unison, both on and off the field, and so long as I live I shall never forget the afternoon of 3rd March, 1904, when at twenty minutes to six Hirst bowled down Cotter's wicket and the Ashes were ours. The great men of the side were R. E. Foster, who made the then record score in Test Matches of 287, at Sydney, in the first Test Match; Rhodes, Hirst, Hayward, Braund, J. T. Tyldesley, and B. J. T. Bosanquet, the inventor of the googly, whose bowling definitely won us the fourth game at Sydney.

England had not beaten Australia since 1896, and we had a tremendous welcome when we returned. The M.C.C. gave a dinner in our honour, when I was put up to speak before Lord Alverstone, the Lord Chief Justice of England, who as president of the M.C.C. was in the chair. I am by courtesy 'my learned friend,' but never before had I appeared before a Lord Chief Justice or addressed a jury of so many eminent men.

The Australians in 1905 were no match for England in England, but in 1907 they again won the Ashes, the M.C.C. team under the captaincy of A. O. Jones being beaten by four matches to one, though many of the games were exceedingly closely fought. In 1909 things went all wrong in England, and although many were convinced that the best English eleven was superior to the Australians, yet we were beaten, the Australians winning two matches to our one, and the critics said some hard things of the selection committee.

In 1911 I was once again in Australia as captain, but owing to a serious illness I played no cricket after the opening match of the tour, J. W. H. T. Douglas leading the side on the field, and leading it so well that we once again returned with the Ashes, having beaten the Australians four—one.

I owe Douglas a deep debt of gratitude. There has been no more determined or energetic cricketer; a keener or finer fighter never lived, and his bravery and stout heart were, and are still, proverbial. Mr. Douglas's tragic death in the North Sea in December 1930 when, in a collision between two ships, he undoubtedly sacrificed his own life in an attempt to save his father's, was but typical of a rare character. Father and son were devoted to each other—it was a really beautiful relationship—and they perished together. 'Johnnie' is always spoken of amongst cricketers with rare affection. He was a good friend, stout-hearted, good-tempered, and loyal; he did much for England, and more for Essex. Douglas's bowling, together with that of F. R. Foster and Barnes, coupled with the superb batting of Hobbs and Rhodes, were the chief factors in our success. But the team, if it did possess something of a tail, was a strong and well-balanced side. Barnes and Foster bowled as no pair of bowlers have ever bowled before, or since, on Australian wickets. To this day Australians maintain this, and it was indeed a fine sight to see these two men in action. Foster's fast-medium to fast left-hand, with immaculate length and great speed off the pitch, was a rare foil to Barnes, and Douglas in the fourth and deciding Test Match obtained five wickets for 46 runs. In regard to Barnes, he was the best bowler on all wickets that I have met, having every good quality—spin, break both ways, flight, and accuracy. The Australians have no doubt at all that he is the greatest bowler England has ever sent to Australia. Hobbs and Rhodes were a wonderful first-wicket pair, Hobbs at this time being at his best. His beautiful style and variety of stroke roused the enthusiasm of the Australian crowds, and he had a rare first-wicket partner in Wilfred Rhodes, who thus achieved the unique distinction of having bowled and batted first for England. Other men who did well were Woolley, Gunn, and J. W. Hearne, who made a century in the second Test Match before he was twenty-one, and who the Australian critics described as a 'young Arthur Shrewsbury'; and I am convinced that had Hearne enjoyed good health he would have been second to none as an all-round cricketer. The wicket-keeping of Smith and Strud-wick was very good, and altogether it was a great side.

As I had been fortunate on my first tour in having Mr. J. A. Murdoch, a fine-looking and very courteous man, who looked like a diplomat of the old school, as manager, so was I equally fortunate on this tour in having Mr. Tom Pawley in a similar capacity. Of boundless energy and imbued with a fine patriotic spirit, Mr. Pawley's able administration, readiness to oblige, good temper, and care for our every comfort, contributed in a marked manner to the happy results obtained.

On our return to England we met the Rest of England at Lord's, and beat them by an innings and 10 runs. To my great joy the doctors allowed me to play and I was fortunate enough to score 126. That day, 23rd May, 1912, was one of the happiest days of my cricketing life. Tom Pawley was so delighted at my coming off that he shed tears of joy. It was during this match that while we were in the field Lord Harris remarked to Mr. Russell Walker, 'Russie, I believe this is about the best side I have ever seen.' This may possibly have been an exaggeration, but opinion in Australia was unanimous that up to that time we were just about the strongest side England had ever sent them.

With that tour ended my actual playing connection with cricket in Australia. It was written in the Book of Destiny that some twenty-one years later I was to return to Australia, when a great controversy, which led to intense feeling arose, but for myself I would say this, that my personal recollections of Australia and Australian cricketers are of the happiest; and that I carry away the most delightful reminiscences of my cricketing days in Australia.

In 1912 in England there occurred the Triangular Tournament, when Australia, South Africa, and England met each other in Test Matches. It was a very wet and cold summer and the experiment did not turn out a success. In the first place the weather ruined match after match; secondly the South Africans were far inferior to both England and Australia, and thirdly the Australians, owing to a domestic disagreement, were deprived of five or six of their greatest cricketers. I do not think that the Triangular Tournament will ever be repeated. England under the captaincy of C. B. Fry came out top, Barnes bowling in wonderful form on the very difficult wickets, and Hobbs and R. H. Spooner making most of the runs.

Then came the Great War, and there were no Test Matches until the winter of 1920–21, when the M.C.C. sent a side to Australia under the captaincy of J. W. H. T. Douglas. The M.C.C. were reluctant to send a team at this time, saying, and with truth, that we had not recovered from the war, but the Australians were very anxious to have a team. They had had no visiting eleven since the M.C.C. team of 1911–12 and they were desirous of getting the game going once more in their country. The Australians started with this advantage, that the Australian Imperial Forces had played a series of matches in this country during the summer of 1919 and had proved themselves a good and interesting side. It was really good training for men with such natural ability as J. M. Gregory, H. L. Collins, W. A. Oldfield, C. E.

Pellew, J. M. Taylor, and others; and there can be no doubt that the A.I.F. team formed the nucleus, and a very strong one, for the subsequent splendid Australian elevens.

Australia, under W. W. Armstrong, won the rubber by five–love, Douglas and his team battling against tremendously superior forces. Douglas himself did well, both with bat and ball, and Hobbs's batting was up to his finest standard. The Australians, although the opposition to them was not formidable, showed themselves a very fine all-round side, and they emphasized their superiority when they came to England in 1921, winning three matches out of five and drawing the other two, so that Australia had now won eight Test Matches in succession.

England, still in process of building an eleven, found 'the slings and arrows of outrageous fortune' raining on her, for very early in the season the great Hobbs was injured and did not play in the first three Test Matches. He was selected for the fourth but on the first day of it he was smitten with appendicitis, and had to be operated on immediately. Through this, and other misfortunes, our selectors were so much at their wits' end that the eleven was changed in match after match. The fast bowling of Gregory and McDonald for the Australians was very fine indeed. They both had great pace, great energy, and great determination and as a foil to them were A. A. Mailey, one of the greatest and cleverest of googly bowlers, and Armstrong himself who was so accurate that he could pitch a ball with his slow to medium leg-breaks on the proverbial sixpence.

After the first three Test Matches, Douglas who had led England, retired in favour of the Hon. L. H. Tennyson, Douglas serving under the new captain with complete loyalty as was only to be expected from one of his character. It was thought that, possibly, Tennyson might change the luck, and he certainly batted very well, playing the fast bowling with confidence. His innings at Leeds, when with a very badly damaged hand he scored 63, was a courageous effort, and one which his grandfather, had he been alive, would no doubt have commemorated in an ode.

In 1924 A. E. R. Gilligan was selected by the M.C.C. to lead their team in Australia. He had a good side with Hobbs, and Sutcliffe of Yorkshire, as an opening pair of batsmen, who were destined to make the world ring with their feats for the first wicket for many a long year, and Tate, a superb bowler. But though the matches were keenly fought, Australia winning at Adelaide by only 11 runs, once again we had to bow the knee to Australia, who won four of the five Test Matches.

There were some great cricketers in this English side, for apart from Hobbs, Sutcliffe, and Tate, there were Woolley, Hendren, and others, and it was very evident that English cricket was on the up grade. Gilligan's fielding at mid-off was one of the features of the tour.

In 1926 Australia was again here, with England determined to beat her. We had now recovered from the war, and there were many fine cricketers, and though we had been beaten in Australia there was a feeling of quiet confidence. The first four Test Matches, owing to weather and high scoring, were drawn, and the fifth match, at the Oval, was therefore the deciding one. What a match it was. The wonderful batting of Hobbs and Sutcliffe on a really difficult wicket will be talked of as long as there is a history of cricket, and in the end, England, under her young captain, A. P. F. Chapman, won by 289 runs. It was a great day for English cricket, for after many long years of waiting and disappointment its prestige had been restored. The Australians were the first to congratulate us, and speaking dispassionately, I think that even the Australians will agree that in the general interests of the cricket of both countries it was high time England achieved success; it would never do for one side to be 'on top' for long periods.

K

In 1928-9 England, under A. P. F. Chapman, was again successful, winning the rubber in Australia by four matches to one. Again Hobbs and Sutcliffe were very much to the fore; but here a new figure comes to overshadow their performances—Hammond. He actually scored 905 runs in nine Test Match innings, with an average of 113 and including scores of 251, 200, 177, and 119—the last two being made in one match. D. R. Jardine and Hendren also batted well and the fielding, headed by Chapman himself, to whose fielding the word 'magnificent' is appropriate, has never been surpassed. Added to this, Larwood, Tate, Geary, White, and Hammond were an ideal bowling combination. It was a great triumph for a great team, and Chapman's happy personality had much to do with the successful result.

Australia checked England's run of success in 1930 when they beat us here in England, winning both at Lord's and the Oval, the matches at Nottingham, Leeds, and Manchester being drawn. D. G. Bradman was the outstanding figure in the Australian eleven with scores of 8, 131, 254, 1, 334, 14, and 232 in the Test Matches. His batting was amazing; he seemed to be completely master of every type of bowling. His stroke play was magnificent and he was regarded, and rightly regarded, as the greatest batsman in the world, but he was not the only great Australian batsman, for W. M. Woodfull the captain, and a very much liked one too, W. H. Ponsford, A. F. Kippax, A. Jackson, V. Richardson, and others, were all good men, and Grimmett, assisted by Wall and Fairfax, bowled well. Grimmett's figures in the Test Matches are not very impressive, but he was none too lucky, and he always seemed to be dominating the batsmen. He and Bradman were the great match-winning factors.

England had a good side with great individual players, but it was not such a strong combination all round as that of Australia, though the difference between the two elevens was little. Bradman was England's trouble; had he been content with scores of 120 or 150, all would have been well, but he smashed through our defences with his stupendous two hundreds and three hundreds.

This was one of the happiest tours in England, and Australian cricketers have assured me that they enjoyed every moment of it. They went back to Australia, not only with the Ashes of victory, but, I am certain, with the pleasantest remembrances of the old country.

In the early months of 1931 the Board of Control appointed a selection committee consisting of Mr. P. Perrin, Mr. T. A. Higson, and myself, as chairman, to hold office for two years. Our ostensible duty was to select the teams for the Test Matches v. New Zealand and India, and for the trial matches in 1931 and 1932, but the real object was to build up a side for the Australian tour.

I have always found selecting teams interesting and, indeed, fascinating work. One must expect criticism, but criticism, if constructive, is helpful, and here I may say that we had every possible encouragement both from the Press and from individuals. It would be hard indeed for any chairman to have better colleagues than Mr. Perrin and Mr. Higson. They went about the country seeing a great deal of cricket, and their knowledge of the game, their capacity for taking pains, and their zeal were of the greatest possible help.

It is really quite easy to select the first ten or eleven men for a tour abroad; it is the last four, or five, that are difficult, but I think one may fairly say that we evolved a very good side, in spite of the fact that neither K. S. Duleepsinhji nor R. W. V. Robins were able to accept the invitations sent them by M.C.C. We recommended to the M.C.C., who of course had the final say in the matter, D. R. Jardine as captain. He had shown qualities of leadership in the matches against New Zealand and India and he worked with us with great keenness and enthusiasm. He was co-opted to help us in the choice of the various elevens, and towards the end, Lord Hawke, as Chairman of the M.C.C. Cricket Committee, was added to our number, and was, of course, in the chair.

The tour which followed was destined to prove one of the most memorable in the history of English cricket, but this is not the place to discuss the vexed question of the method of bowling adopted by Larwood, and in a lesser degree by Voce, which led to such a storm. As in 1928-9, England won the rubber by four matches to one. We lost the second Test Match, at Melbourne, by 111 runs, but won the others easily (on paper), though the fourth Test Match at Brisbane, which was played in extremely hot weather, was a grim struggle almost to the last ball.

The outstanding figures in the team were Larwood as a bowler, and Sutcliffe and Hammond as batsmen, but many another did right well, notably G. O. Allen, as an all-rounder, R. E. S. Wyatt, Leyland, and Paynter, who, coming straight from a sick-bed, played a heroic innings at Brisbane.

In Larwood England undoubtedly had a truly magnificent fast bowler, and Allen, Verity, and Voce gave him most able support. Ames kept wicket remarkably well, and the fielding, except in the first innings of the last Test Match, was up to a very high standard. Hammond was magnificent in the slips; G. O. Allen made a great name for himself at 'short leg,' and the captain himself brought off many a fine catch.

Australia lacked all-round men and—in order to ensure a full complement of bowling—a long tail was unavoidable. Never before, indeed, had Australia had such a long tail. Bradman, McCabe, and Woodfull were their most reliable batsmen, but Bradman made only one century. W. J. O'Reilly, a really fine medium-paced right-handed bowler, came to the front. Accurate in length and with plenty of spin, our men held him in high respect.

To Jardine's captaincy England owed a great deal.  His capacity for taking pains amounts to genius; he is a skilful manager of bowling and he never spares himself.  Relentless of purpose, he is full of courage and would never ask any one to do anything which he would not do himself; and he welded the side into a very efficient all-round combination. He met with tremendous criticism from the whole of Australia in regard to what the Australians called 'the body-line' bowling of Larwood, but he never swerved from his purpose. It should be added that during a time of storm and stress and in a very intense atmosphere, no body of men could have behaved better and with more loyalty, discretion, good temper, and sound sense than this M.C.C. side.

It is safe to say that for intensity of feeling no previous tour can compare with the visit of this team.  It was certainly 'a first-class row,' but when individuals quarrel, they are often better friends afterwards than they were before; and we may hope that it may be so in this case.  Like Tom Brown and Slogger Williams after their famous fight at Rugby, England and Australia have shaken hands, and we may expect the bitterness of this tour to be forgotten amidst mutual respect and admiration, and in the glamour of the finest skill.

The tour of the Australians in 1934 was not the happy affair of four years earlier.  The body-line controversy was still seething, and it is impossible to regard the season as otherwise than unpleasant.  D. R. Jardine, who at the time was captaining the M.C.C. team in India, stated on the eve of the arrival of the Australian team in this country 'that he had neither the desire nor the intention of playing cricket against the Australians this season'; Larwood refused to play for England, and a certain section of the press seemed anxious to promote strife rather than to allay it. The match between the Australians and Nottinghamshire was a tragic affair, and when the Australians took the field for the last innings they were received with a storm of booing. Subsequently there was much trouble for Nottinghamshire, and the committee of the county club resigned *en bloc*. In such an atmosphere the selection committee, Sir Stanley Jackson, P. A. Perrin, and T. A. Higson, had a most difficult and unenviable task, and it was not surprising that Australia won the rubber by two games to one. Australia won at Nottingham, on the stroke of time, by 238 runs, O'Reilly (eleven wickets for 129 runs) bowling magnificently—and at the Oval by no less than 562 runs. At Lord's England won by an innings and 38 runs. The games at Leeds—a moral victory for Australia—and at Manchester were drawn.

England had a strong batting side with Sutcliffe, Leyland, C. F. Walters, Ames, R. E. S. Wyatt (captain), and Hammond, though the last two failed, Wyatt's highest being 44 and Hammond's 43. Our bowling, however, with Larwood and Voce absent and G. O. Allen only available at the end of the season because of an operation—the three most successful bowlers on the 1932-3 tour in Australia—was not comparable to that of W. J. O'Reilly and C. V. Grimmett, who between them obtained no fewer than 53 of the 71 wickets that fell.

D. G. Bradman and W. H. Ponsford batted magnificently for Australia, as did S. J. McCabe, but it was the bowling of O'Reilly and Grimmett which laid the foundation of Australia's success. They were of immense value to their captain, W. M. Woodfull.

Australia's fielding was also superior to that of England, who in the final match at the Oval missed several catches. It was altogether an annoying season for us, and especially because of all the trouble behind the scenes. Bradman after the first six weeks or so was as great a batsman as ever, scoring 304 at Leeds and 244 at the Oval, while Ponsford made 181 at Leeds and 266 at the Oval, the two batsmen having partnerships of 388 at Leeds and 451 at the Oval. At Lord's, England catching the Australians on a bowler's wicket, Verity returned an analysis of 15 wickets for 104 runs, equalling Rhodes's 15 wickets for 124 at Melbourne in 1904. England totalled 440 (Leyland 109, Ames 120, and Walters 82); Australia 284 (Brown 105) and 118.

At Manchester on a heart-breaking wicket for bowlers the scoring was quite abnormal, England making 627 (Hendren 132, Leyland 153) and 123 for no wicket, and Australia 491 (McCabe 137) and 66 for one wicket, an aggregate of 1,307 runs, and only 20 wickets fell. At the Oval Australia's innings totalled 701 runs.

In Australia in 1936–7, England, under the leadership of G. O. Allen, lost the rubber by 3–2, but Allen restored the good feeling between the rival teams, and a happy atmosphere prevailed. The old courtesy of combat was restored, and the body-line controversy disappeared into the limbo of forgotten things. Allen worked tremendously hard, and his batting, bowling, and fielding went a long way towards winning the first two Test Matches, but did he not make a mistake in having no match practice for three weeks before the final and deciding Test? After so long an absence from the middle one is apt to lose the atmosphere of the field. All the critics on the spot—and the *Evening Standard* had no less than three: C. B. Fry, Neville Cardus, and Bruce Harris—were unanimous in praising his leadership, and he enjoyed a well-deserved popularity. Only one Test—the fourth—was played without interruption by rain. England won the first two Test Matches, and lost the last three, chiefly because of Bradman's wonderful batting and O'Reilly's and Fleetwood-Smith's—a left-hand googly bowler —bowling. England suffered from an incredible number of injuries—the most serious of which was to R. E. S. Wyatt, which kept him out of the first three Test Matches. Wyatt had been selected as one of the opening batsmen, but when he was again fit to play he never occupied that position; and in the fourth Test Match Verity actually went in first with Barnett. Perhaps the answer to this is that with the middle of the batting order failing badly Wyatt was preferred at No. 5 or 6 to supply 'concrete' to the side. But though it is easy to be wise after the event, the omission of Paynter, one of the successes of the 1932-3 tour, was a mistake. The English batting was very uneven, only Hammond, Leyland, and Barnett doing themselves justice, and nearly half of Hammond's aggregate of 468 runs came from a great innings of 231 not out in the second Test at Sydney. England lost a rare chance in the fourth Test, at Adelaide, when, after dismissing Australia for 288 on a perfect wicket, they could only obtain a lead of 42 runs, the batting falling to pieces after Barnett, 129, had given us a great start. In the last three matches Bradman scored 690 runs in five innings—13, 270, 26, 212, and 169. The English team was rather overloaded with fast bowlers—Allen himself, K. Farnes, Voce, and Copson—and Copson did not find a place in any of the Tests. A medium-paced bowler with the energy and stamina of, say, Captain J. W. A. Stephenson, might well have been very valuable, especially as his fielding would have been something of an inspiration.

The Australian side which visited England in 1938 was under the captaincy of D. G. Bradman, who was making his third tour in this country. He soon proved himself to be an admirable captain, both on and off the field, and played cricket in the finest possible manner. Unhappily he injured himself during the final Test Match at the Oval, and took no further part in the tour. At Scarborough, for the first time since 1921, the Australians lost a match in this country other than a Test Match, when H. D. G. Leveson-Gower's XI beat them by 10 wickets.

The Australian team of 1938 was one of the weakest bowling sides which has visited this country, and it was a grave error to leave C. V. Grimmett behind, for since this tour he continued to take a large number of wickets in Sheffield Shield cricket in Australia.

W. J. O'Reilly was still the best bowler in the world. His length was accuracy itself, he spun the ball, and changed his pace with great cleverness. He did not, however, receive adequate support. L. O'B. Fleetwood-Smith, except in England's second innings at Leeds, was a failure. E. L. McCormick, who had great difficulty with his run-up to the wicket, and consequently delivered an abnormal number of no-balls, caused England a very anxious half-hour on the first day of the Lord's Test and was sometimes dangerous with the new ball. The rest of the bowling was negligible.

England's batting was far sounder all round than Australia's. Four young players made their début against Australia: Hutton, D. Compton, Wright, and Edrich. The last-named failed, but Hutton and Compton both played some magnificent innings; and Wright, if his analyses were not outstanding, was a distinct bowling find. Of the established batsmen W. R. Hammond, Paynter, Ames, Hardstaff, and Barnett all batted very finely. In addition to Wright the bowling was chiefly in the hands of Bowes (unfit for the first three Tests), Verity, and K. Farnes. Much of it was of a high standard, Bowes bowling particularly well in Australia's first innings at Leeds and at the Oval, but occasionally it was wanting in length.

W. R. Hammond, now an amateur, led England, and played the innings of his life—240—in the second Test Match at Lord's.

Except in the fourth Test Match at Leeds, when the conditions undoubtedly favoured the bowlers, the run-getting for the series was abnormally high.

In the opening Test at Trent Bridge England scored 658 for eight declared against Australia's 411 and 427 for six. Hutton, 100, and Barnett, 126, began with an opening stand of 219, while D. Compton, 102, and Paynter, 216 not out, made 206 for the fifth wicket. Australia began by losing six wickets for 194, but S. J. McCabe rose to the occasion in magnificent style, and actually made 213 out of the last 273, his final 72 being scored in 28 minutes. Bradman and Brown both made 100's in Australia's second innings. The second Test at Lord's, which also ended in a draw, was notable for Hammond's wonderful innings of 240. Paynter, 99, helping him to add 222 for the fourth wicket. After leading by 494 to 422 on the first innings England were in danger with five wickets down for 76, but D. Compton came to the rescue with 76 not out, at a crisis, and scored for the most part on a difficult wicket. Bradman made yet another century, and W. A. Brown distinguished himself by playing through Australia's first innings for 206 not out.

Injuries kept Ames and Hutton out of the England team at Leeds, and this completely upset the balance of the England XI (after the third Test had been abandoned without a ball being bowled), and on a wicket which assisted O'Reilly and Fleetwood-Smith, Australia won by five wickets, though England, whose batting failed badly, might conceivably have pulled the game out of the fire if more use had been made of Wright in the Australians' last innings. Once again Bradman batted superbly, this time making 103 out of Australia's first innings total of 242.

The final Test Match, which was to be played to a finish, provided England with an overwhelming win by an innings and 579 runs, and the Tests thus finished ' all square.' It was a thousand pities that injuries prevented Bradman and Fingleton from batting in this game. England's mammoth and record score of 903 for seven, declared, included Hutton's 364, the highest and longest (it lasted 13 hours and 20 minutes) innings ever played in Test cricket, a stand of 382 between Hutton and Leyland, 187, and 169 not out by Hardstaff. Fleetwood-Smith's one wicket cost 298 runs!

Bradman, of course, was the outstanding batsman for Australia, but W. A. Brown made a great impression, scoring 512 runs with an average of 73·14. A beautiful player off his legs, his back play was particularly strong.

England were the better side, but in Bradman and O'Reilly Australia had the greatest batsman and the greatest bowler in the world.

# CHAPTER VIII

## ENGLAND v. SOUTH AFRICA

South African cricket had no such sensational beginning as Australian, for several visits had been exchanged between English and South African cricketers before the public came to realize that a new power had arisen in the world of cricket. It was not until 1904 that South African cricket was regarded seriously, and then, probably, only by a few. It needed the splendid form shown by P. W. Sherwell's 1906 and 1907 elevens to convince the world that here, indeed, were opponents worthy of our best men. English teams under the captaincy of C. A., now Sir Aubrey, Smith, the world-famous film actor, and W. W. Read visited South Africa during the winters of 1888–9 and 1891–2, and in 1894 H. H. Castens brought over a side to this country, but it attracted little attention, their form being only moderate, though E. A. Halliwell, a superb wicket-keeper, and C. O. H. Sewell, who afterwards played for Gloucestershire, were destined to make names for themselves. Lord Hawke took strong sides to South Africa in 1895–6 and in 1898–9, and in 1901 J. D. Logan was responsible for a South African team that came here under the captaincy of M., afterwards Sir Murray, Bisset, Chief Justice of Rhodesia. This was a good side and a visit by the powerful Australian team of 1902 to South Africa stimulated interest in the game. J. H. Sinclair, who is referred to in greater detail in another part of this book, was the outstanding figure amongst the South Africans, and C. B. Llewellyn was a fine all-rounder—a dashing left-handed batsman, a capital slow

left-handed bowler, and a wonderful field at mid-off.
Llewellyn had a curious career.   He played for South Africa,
the country of his birth, for Hampshire, for which he became
qualified, and he was a reserve man for England *v.* Australia,
at Birmingham, in 1902, so that he can claim a unique
record.   In the three Test Matches against the 1902 Australia
side, he took 25 wickets for 18 runs each.   The first Test
Match was drawn, and Australia won the second and third,
but South Africa made quite a good fight.

Frank Mitchell, the former Cambridge and Yorkshire
cricketer, was captain of the 1904 side, and this team lost
only three matches and, at Lord's, defeated by 189 runs an
England XI, a strong side which included Ranji, Jessop,
MacGregor, and other good men.   Schwarz puzzled all the
batsmen and as he also scored 102, he was the hero of the
match.   J. J. Kotze, a man of fine physique, showed himself
almost as fast a bowler as Kortright, and he could bowl for
long spells, keep a length and bring the ball back from the
off by body swing rather than by finger spin.   There were
some good batsmen in this eleven—Mitchell, Hathorn,
Llewellyn and Tancred; and Halliwell's wicket-keeping was
superb.

The result of the M.C.C.'s tour in South Africa in 1905–6,
the first occasion on which M.C.C. had sent a side to South
Africa, came as something of a surprise to the cricketing
public in England, South Africa winning the rubber of Test
Matches by 4–1.   The first of these matches is described in
the chapter 'The Greatest Game I Ever Played In,' and
though we won the fourth by four wickets, we were out-
played in the second, third and fifth matches.   The South
African googly bowlers were something of a nightmare on
the matting wicket, only F. L. Fane and J. N. Crawford
making runs, and when they came here in 1907, C. B. Fry,
whose 129 in the third Test at the Oval was, perhaps, the
finest innings that accomplished batsmen ever played, alone

met with any consistent success against them. It was a wet season and sticky wickets were frequent, and many a fine batsman was put to it. This team will long be remembered, spectators flocking to see them bowl; and not since the days of the earlier Australian elevens have any bowlers been more talked about. People used to say, 'Let's go and see the South Africans bowl.' England won the second of the three Tests by 35 runs after a tremendous fight, at Leeds, the other two being drawn, that at Lord's being memorable for a splendid innings of 115 by Sherwell, the man who had gone in last in the famous game at Johannesburg. The batting of the South Africans, viewed as a whole, was disappointing, but the fielding could scarcely have been bettered and Sherwell was an extraordinarily good wicket-keeper.

In 1909-10, South Africa won the rubber by 3–2. Faulkner, now a great all-round cricketer, averaged 60·55, and took 29 wickets for 21·89 each, but he and Vogler, 36 wickets for 21·75 each, had to do practically all the bowling, for White and Schwarz had lost their form, as had Sinclair. There were some close games, the first, at Johannesburg, which the South Africans won by 19 runs, almost equalling in interest and excitement that of January 1906. H. D. G. Leveson-Gower led a strong English side, for which Hobbs batted magnificently, and Simpson Hayward's lobs 'fizzed off' the matting wicket at Johannesburg.

The South Africans paid their first visit to Australia in 1910-11 and were defeated 4–1. They met a very powerful array of batsmen—Trumper, Bardsley, Hill, Armstrong, Macartney, Kelleway, and Ransford—and on the cast-iron wickets, the googly lost its terror. Vogler was so completely off colour that he was left out of three matches, but Schwarz made a return to his old self and bowled consistently well. Faulkner batted with rare skill averaging 73·20 with a highest score of 204, and Nourse and J. W. Zulch also did well, but they did not receive much support. Sherwell, who had played no cricket since his tour to England in 1907, returned to captain the side, and the Australian critics placed him in the same class as Blackham as a wicket-keeper, and this high estimate of his skill was thoroughly deserved.

The Triangular Tournament in 1912 was the idea of Sir Abe Bailey, a great and generous supporter of South African cricket, but it was something of a failure due largely to the abominable weather and to the unrepresentative character of the Australian team. The South Africans were beaten three times by England, and twice by Australia, the game at Nottingham being drawn. Their batting was not good enough on the sticky wickets against bowlers like Barnes, Woolley, F. R. Foster, and Dean, and their bowling fell away from the high standard of 1907, though Faulkner and Pegler bowled very well, the former taking 163 wickets for 15 runs each, and Pegler 189 at the same cost during the tour.

M.C.C. sent out a powerful side to South Africa in 1913–14 under the captaincy of J. W. H. T. Douglas which won four of the five Test Matches and drew the other. South Africa were building up a new side and future promise was there. H. W. Taylor batted magnificently and the Englishmen could not say too much in praise of him. Barnes was a terror on the matting wickets, but Taylor in the Test Matches made scores of 109, 8, 28, 19, 40, 70, 16, 93, 42 and 87, while for Natal, he scored 83 not out, 42 not out, 91 and 100.

The Australian Imperial Forces team on their way back to Australia played two matches against a South African XI at Johannesburg and won both of them, but these games are not officially regarded as Test Matches, and F. T. Mann's 1922–3 M.C.C. team were South Africa's next visitors. This was a great tour, England winning two matches and South Africa one, the other two being drawn. South Africa won the first by 168 runs, Taylor playing a glorious second innings of 176, and J. M. Blanckenberg and E. P. Nupen bowling finely, and they only just lost the second by one wicket. The third and fourth games were drawn and England won the deciding game by 111 runs, Russell scoring 140 and 111 for England and Taylor 102 in the second innings of South Africa. Kennedy and Macaulay were the outstanding bowlers for England and Hall, a left-hander, and a good one too, and Blanckenberg for South Africa. Mann won the admiration of all as a captain both on and off the field.

In 1924, South Africa lost three of the five Test Matches here, the other two being drawn. Totals of 390, 341, and 323 proved that their batting was strong, and it was the bowling which failed. Nupen who commanded respect on the matting wickets was a failure, and it was a great misfortune to lose the services of G. F. Bisset who early in the tour broke a bone in his ankle. He was a very fast righthanded bowler, who bowled with marked success against Captain R. T. Stanyforth's M.C.C. team on our next visit to South Africa in 1927-8. In the final Test of this tour, his bowling with a strong wind behind him was said to have been 'the fastest ever.' Honours were even, each side winning two matches, and one, the third, being drawn. In H. G. Deane, South Africa had an inspiring captain, who winning the toss in every match, was not afraid to put his opponents in first on no fewer than three occasions. The South Africans were a strong batting side with no tail, and fought all the way, and it was clear that they were recovering their former prowess. Taylor was almost as great as ever, R. H. Catterall, an attractive forcing player, scored well, and Deane apart from his able leadership made runs when they were wanted and fielded magnificently. We had five tip-top batsmen in the Yorkshiremen Sutcliffe and Holmes, E. Tyldesley, Hammond and Wyatt; and I believe we should have won the rubber had Geary, an uncommonly good bowler on the matting, not been injured after the first Test in which he took twelve wickets for 130 runs.   One of the features of the tour was the wicket-keeping of H. B. Cameron.

The South Africans did not win a match here in 1929, but they ran us hard at Lord's, Leeds, the Oval and Birmingham, and they might have gained actual victory but for a succession of accidents to some of their best men.   Although they lost the last two matches, they left the impression that they would be a difficult side to beat in the near future. The bowling was not as strong as the batting, but Quinn and Vincent, left-handers, and Bell were good bowlers, and at times more than that, and Owen Smith and Morkel capital all-rounders.   A most attractive side with many fine fieldsmen amongst whom Owen Smith was outstanding.

During the winter of 1930–1, M.C.C. sent out a side to South Africa, under the captaincy of Chapman, which, with batsmen like Hammond, Hendren, Leyland, Wyatt, Sandham, Turnbull, and Chapman himself, and bowlers like White, Peebles, Tate, Voce, Goddard, and Allom—with Duckworth and Farrimond to share the wicket-keeping— looked good enough to win the rubber.   The result, however, was contrary to general anticipation, South Africa winning the only one, the first, of the Tests which was brought to a definite conclusion.   Without wishing to make excuses, it should, in fairness, and as a matter of record, be stated that we were very unlucky in the matter of illness and accidents. Sandham met with a motor accident before the first Test which kept him off the field for the rest of the tour, and further, Hammond, Hendren and Tate at different times were overtaken by illness.   The first Test was a tremendous fight, South Africa winning by 28 runs, the totals being South Africa 126 and 304, and England 193 and 211.   Nupen again showed that whatever his shortcomings on turf he was a formidable bowler on matting, and his eleven wickets for 150 runs was the chief factor in this victory.   On the

L

turf wicket at Cape Town for the laying of which Kotze was responsible—he, though a bowler, must in his heart of hearts have been a genuine friend of batsmen!—South Africa scored 513 for eight wickets, declared, and England 350 and 252, but at Durban, on turf again, England had the better of another drawn game. The fourth Test at Johannesburg was a prolonged and most interesting struggle. South Africa needed 37 to win with three wickets to fall, and as Cameron was 69 not out, the draw was rather in favour of South Africa. The final game at Durban, once more on turf, was also unfinished, with no particular advantage to either side, and was memorable for a queer incident. The state of the field and the weather influenced Chapman to put South Africa in to bat. 'A difficult wicket was certain,' writes *Wisden*, 'but bails of the size to fit the stumps could not be found, and the umpires had to make a set before the game could begin.' It was a preposterous situation and reflected little credit on the ground organization. That South Africa were a good side is certain. B. Mitchell, greatly improved after his tour in England, Taylor, Siedle, Cameron, McMillan, Catterall, and Nupen formed a strong group of batsmen, but the bowling, with the exception of Nupen—and then only on the 'mat'—and Vincent, was not exceptional. Hammond, Hendren, and Leyland batted finely for England, and the bowling was good, if nothing more, but the side were handicapped by the accidents which befell them, and for that reason never settled down into a smooth working combination.

July 2nd, 1935, was a red-letter day in the history of South African cricket for on that day, at Lord's, South Africa, by 157 runs, won a Test Match in England for the first time  We were fairly and squarely beaten, and the crowd gave the winners an enthusiastic reception, gathering in front of the pavilion and cheering for a quarter of an hour. This was the second match of the series, and the only one that was finished. The first, at Trent Bridge, was drawn very much in England's favour, rain preventing any cricket on the third day. The third, at Leeds, was also unfinished, rather in our favour after we had declared, the fourth, after another declaration by England, ended in an even draw, and the fifth, at the Oval, was also without a definite result, England again declaring after scoring 534 for six wickets in reply to South Africa's first innings total of 476.

Whether the South Africans were a better side than Sherwell's famous team of 1907 is doubtful, but they had a better record, winning 17 and losing only 2 of their 31 first-class games, as against the 17 wins and 4 defeats in 27 matches of their predecessors. Sherwell's team were stronger in bowling, but they were not so good a batting side. In H. F. Wade this 1935 side had a first-class and popular captain, who managed his bowling excellently, fielded smartly near the wicket, and played some useful defensive innings, particularly in the Tests at Leeds and Old Trafford. Mitchell was the best batsman and his 164 not out at Lord's was a great innings. He was also a fine slip fieldsman. The South Africans were a difficult side to get out with practically no tail. In a dry summer and on the beautiful wickets which prevailed—except at Lord's where the 'leather jacket' had devastated the ground— their bowling analyses do not read well, but Bell, Vincent, Crisp, Langton and Balaskas made up a varied attack. I do not think I have ever seen better googly bowling than that, at Lord's, by Balaskas, whose analysis was O.—59, M.—16, R.—103, and W.—9, and his subsequent absence from the side owing to an injury made all the difference to the strength of their attack. Cameron's wicket-keeping was on a par with that of any wicket-keeper of any age, and he was a beautiful and consistent hitter.

Hammond's 1938-9 M.C.C. side in South Africa won one match, the third, by an innings and 13 runs, the other four being drawn.  The wickets—now of grass at Johannesburg, as well as at Cape Town and Durban—were preposterously perfect, absolutely 'plumb' with no life in them, and the batting averages on both sides were fantastically high.  The fifth Test at Durban was to have been played to a finish, but it was drawn, although it lasted ten days, the eighth being a blank owing to rain.  Ten weekdays and two Sundays!  So heavy was the scoring that in the Tests Hammond and Paynter averaged 87·00 and 81·62 respectively, Valentine 68·75, Ames 67·80, Gibb 59·12, Hutton 44·16, and Edrich 40·00, while A. D. Nourse, a son of D. Nourse, Mitchell, Grieveson, Van der Byl averaged between 60 and 51, and Melville, Rowan and Dalton between 47 and 44.  One can imagine what the bowlers' analyses looked like!  The fame of Hammond and his men attracted greater crowds than ever before, but it is sincerely to be hoped that in future the South Africans will see to it that some 'dope' to help the bowlers rather than the batsmen is introduced into the preparation of their wickets.

South Africa from small beginnings has now taken a sure place amongst the cricketing powers, and she has every right to be proud of her achievements.  Moreover, she has universally 'played cricket' both on and off the field—as have her famous Springboks—in the finest possible manner and spirit.  There is no need to emphasize their great popularity in this country; it is known to all.  He who takes part in a cricket tour to South Africa is a fortunate man, for he will find himself in a country brimful of interest, with a glorious climate, and inhabited by charming people.  Who can forget, as Kipling put it, 'the silence, the shine and the size of the 'igh inexpressible skies?'  Cricket has no concern with politics, it welcomes all to its fold, and the more often South Africa and England meet on the cricket and football fields the better for both countries.  Cricket is a great brotherhood, a Freemasonry, a spell binder.

# CHAPTER IX

## CRICKET IN MANY CLIMES

THE combination of Britisher and Sunshine spells cricket— or so, at least, it seems to one who has travelled many thousands of miles. Not only do Englishmen themselves play in sunny lands they have made their homes, but they infuse the cricketing spirit in those around them. Cricket could hardly be called the Dutchman's national game, and yet in the representative South African team and in the Colony elevens we find more than one Dutch name; while it is a common sight in the West Indies to see black boys in the airiest of costumes playing in any odd corner with an old tin pan for a wicket, a piece of wood for a bat, and a ball of very queer shape indeed. Up-country in Australia, where the stations are often miles apart, the great thing on Saturday afternoons is the cricket match. 'Saltbush Bill' thinks nothing of riding thirty or forty miles to play on a matting wicket, cut out of the middle of the bush, the tall and melancholy gum-trees standing up like giant spectators on every side. All over the empire we find the same enthusiasm for the game. When Lord Hawke's team played at Graaff-Reinet, in the Cape Colony, many of the opposing side had ridden over forty miles that morning to take part in the match, and four or five of the Rhodesian XV that we played at Bulawayo had come by coach from Salisbury, over 300 miles away. The rivers were swollen, the roads a swamp, and the journey took seven days!

It seems but yesterday that Lord Hawke's team started for the West Indies; and what a tour that was! Fresh from Oxford one enjoyed every single moment; it was all so new.

The cricket was good, if not exactly first-class, and we had many close finishes.  Lord Hawke was regarded as a sort of god who descended from some glorified Government House to play cricket.  He was always called 'De Lord' by the natives, and the bowlers were invariably urged to 'Give de Lord a duck!'  Once or twice the Yorkshire captain did ' get a duck,' and the scene which followed was, I venture to think, unique in the history of cricket, the natives turning somersaults, dancing, beating the ground with their sticks, and yelling and shrieking like a lot of parrots.  The West Indian native is 'mad' on cricket.  He climbs the trees outside the ground, from the branches of which he keeps up an amusing and running comment. Occasionally a branch breaks, and some 'black gentleman' is deposited on the earth, to the intense delight of those who have secured a stronger perch.

Philadelphia[1] was the only town in the United States where cricket had taken anything like a firm hold.  Here baseball was almost a secondary consideration.  The grounds were excellent, though the wickets might have been improved, the hospitality unlimited, and our cousins good sportsmen.  The newspapers afforded us great amusement. We were called 'British lions,' and were told that the 'hearts of Baltimore girls are going pit-a-pat,' while, when the Gentlemen of Philadelphia beat us in the first match, 'Waterloo for Englishmen' was the heading in one newspaper.  There was a splendid 'poet,' R. D. Paine, a rival of poor Craig's, to whom Jessop was:

> The human catapult
> Who wrecks the roof of distant towns
> When set in his assault.
> His mate was that perplexing man
> We know as ' Looshun-Gore,'
> It isn't spelt at all that way,
> We don't know what it's for.

[1] There is, alas, little cricket in Philadelphia to-day.

Bosanquet's name, too, puzzled people—'the gentleman whose name sounds like a bunch of roses!'

He that went to Oporto with T. Westray cannot in this world forget the delights of that delightful city; while my return visit to America and Canada was, if possible, even more enjoyable than the first.

When I first went to South Africa cricket there was just becoming first-class. J. H. Sinclair was in his prime, he was a magnificent all-round cricketer, and there were three or four other good men as well, including Llewellyn. Lord Hawke had a fairly strong eleven, including Trott, then at his best, Tyldesley, Haigh, Cuttell, and F. Mitchell; and we won both Test Matches, the first only by 30 odd runs after being 100 runs behind on the first innings, and it was obvious that very shortly South Africa would have to be reckoned with.

Lord Hawke was to have captained the team which toured New Zealand and Australia in 1902–3, but at the last moment he was unable to come with us. He did me the honour of appointing me captain in his stead, but we were everywhere known as 'Lord Hawke's team'; and we flew his colours—light blue, dark blue, and yellow, so well known in almost every quarter of the globe. We travelled via New York, San Francisco, and Honolulu to New Zealand, and then, via Australia, home again, through the Suez Canal. In the course of the tour we played cricket from the Golden West to the most southerly town in the world, and in the three principal cities in Australia. For pure interest this was one of the best of all my tours. In New Zealand we won all our eighteen matches, being far too strong for our opponents; but we were beaten both by Victoria and South Australia, and drew with New South Wales. New Zealand has been modestly called 'God's own country' by the late Mr. Seddon; and though one is diffident about going so far as the man who did so much for his adopted country, one can well say that New Zealand is possessed of every variety of scenery and that the climate is excellent. The three weeks we spent in Australia were, in the light of what happened subsequently, interesting for the fact that the first googly Bosanquet sent down on the Sydney ground clean bowled Trumper. I remember Charles Bannerman, the crack Australian batsman of the 1878 team and the first man to score a hundred in an England v. Australia match, was much impressed with the possibilities of Bosanquet's googlies, saying that on the perfect wickets his was the type of bowling to win matches.

Within seven months I was back in Australia with the M.C.C. team, the first tour abroad for which the M.C.C. were responsible, two years later the team the M.C.C. sent out was fairly surprised by the rapid progress the South Africans had made. That team was to find that the South African bowlers were about the best in the world, especially on their own matting wickets. The tour established once and for all time the reputation of South African cricket, though when we returned to England and told people that we had knocked up against the most difficult type of bowling —the googly of accurate length on a matting wicket—it was thought that we were either exaggerating the facts or making excuses for defeat. The visit of the South Africans to England in 1907 showed that we had made no mistake.

Since 1903, the M.C.C. have undertaken the control of all tours to Australia, South Africa, India, West Indies, and New Zealand, while they have also sent sides to Canada, Denmark, Holland, Egypt, and South America. Lord Tennyson and Sir Julien Cahn, too, have captained sides abroad, the former in Jamaica, and the latter in South America as well as in Canada, United States, Bermuda, Jamaica, Singapore, New Zealand, Denmark, Ceylon and Malaya.

I was back in Australia in 1911–12, and I also had the good fortune to captain M.C.C. sides in South America

(1926-7), and Holland (1928), and of all my tours abroad, I think I enjoyed that to America more than any other. From Monte Video, on the Atlantic, to Lima, on the Pacific, the M.C.C. flag was seen and it was remarked at the time that we were 'not only ambassadors of cricket, but of Empire.' Surely no cricket team ever saw so many 'cities and men' in the course of three months. This tour was unique in that not a single game was played within the British Empire—another proof that cricket has set a girdle round the earth, and that it has become the interest not only of the British race but of half the world. As we steamed into the harbour of Monte Video, Captain Parker, of the *Andes*, paid us unique honour by flying the M.C.C. flag at the yardarm, a compliment afterwards repeated at Callao, the port of Lima, by Captain Splatt, of the *Orita*. Never before had a cricket flag been hoisted on any ship on any sea. That flag is now tattered and torn, for it has braved the elements in many parts of the world, and it remains an emblem of good fortune and of victory, and to me, and I believe to some others, an inspiration.[1]

The M.C.C. are ever ready to do all in their power to encourage cricket in our Dominions and abroad; but with five countries—Australia, South Africa, India, West Indies, and New Zealand—all asking for a visit from English teams, the strain on our cricketers is intense. New Zealand could possibly be combined with the visit to Australia, but unless some of the Dominions are willing to accept teams which are not fully representative it would seem as if a longer interval will have to elapse between visits, except in the case of the Australians, who are far and away our strongest

[1] This flag was given to the author after the M.C.C. tour in Australia in 1903-4. It has flown on three tours in Australia, 1903-4, 1911-12, and 1932-3, in South Africa, South America, Holland, and in the Test Matches at Lord's, the Oval, and Old Trafford, in 1926. It has never yet been hauled down in a rubber of Test Matches, and some noted cricketers regard it with almost superstitious reverence. It is, at any rate, the author's most valued, and proudest, cricketing possession.

opponents and with whom we have been playing cricket for over seventy years. What is called, by many, an 'unrepresentative' team is often a very good side, for we have so many excellent cricketers in this country that there are always good men ready and willing to take the place, and fill it ably, of a player with, at the moment, a greater name.

By these means, too, we should be giving a chance to younger men, and affording them the immense experience and educational value which such tours bring in their train.

Australia, because of her great prowess and renown, and because of the longest cricketing tradition, must have, so far as is humanly calculable, the best possible England team sent to her every four years; but it does appear likely that the other Dominions may have to be content with something rather less than this.

Canada, our oldest Dominion, saw the first official M.C.C. side in 1937 under the captaincy of G. C. Newman. The success of the Hon. R. C. *Mathews'* team in England in 1936 had given a big fillip to the game in Canada which had previously been encouraged by the tours of a strong Australian XI captained by V. Richardson (during which Bradman scored 3,782 runs with an average of 102·21), and by a good English team under the late Sir Julien Cahn, a devoted lover of the game. Newman had a good all-round lot of amateurs with him and of the 19 matches played 12 were won, 6 drawn and only 1 lost to R. C. Mathews' XI. From every point of view the tour was a great success.

# CHAPTER X

## SOME CRICKETERS OF MY TIME: ENGLISH

For skill pure and simple no batsman has ever surpassed K. S. Ranjitsinhji, Victor Trumper, Hobbs, or Don Bradman. This may sound like heresy when one thinks of *W. G. Grace*, but in actual execution I do not believe that even he was their superior. 'W. G.', however, will always remain the Champion. He created modern batting. Never has there been such an all-round cricketer, and never has any cricketer kept up his form over so long a period of years. At sixteen he was playing for the Gentlemen, and at fifty he was still going in first for them at Lord's and scoring 43 and 31 not out on a difficult wicket against Lockwood, J. T. Hearne, and Haigh. The first time I played cricket with him was on the Clifton College ground in August 1894, and well I remember his arrival on the ground, and his cheery greeting of: 'It's down the well, Webbie; eight o'clock to-night, don't forget'; for he invariably invited the amateurs of the Middlesex eleven to dine with him during the match at Clifton, and ' it ' was the champagne.

One of the finest innings I ever saw him play was in his Jubilee match at Lord's in 1898. The M.C.C. Committee had happily arranged for Gentlemen *v.* Players in that year to start on July 18th, his fiftieth birthday, and what a welcome he met with when, on losing the toss, he led the Gentlemen into the field! Every one on the ground, including even the sternest pavilion critic, rose at him and cheered him with a spontaneous enthusiasm that is seldom seen at Lord's. Two splendid elevens had been chosen, though it was not easy to understand why L. C. H. Palairet was omitted from the Gentlemen's team, and Richardson from the Players'. It may be interesting to give the names:

*Gentlemen:* W. G. Grace, A. E. Stoddart, F. S. Jackson, C. L. Townsend, A. C. MacLaren, J. R. Mason, J. A. Dixon, S. M. J. Woods, Capt. E. G. Wynyard, G. MacGregor, and C. J. Kortright.

*Players:* Shrewsbury, Abel, Gunn, Storer, Tunnicliffe, Brockwell, Alec Hearne, Lilley, Lockwood, Haigh, and J. T. Hearne.

The Jam of Nawanagar was abroad that season.

The cricket was worthy of the occasion, the Players winning just on time by 137 runs, W. G., who had gone in late in the second innings owing to a bruised hand, and was also lame, batting splendidly for 31 not out. The match excited great interest, and W. G. is said to have smiled from the beginning to the end, so delighted was he with the reception the public gave him. Apart from being the greatest cricketer of all time, W. G. was the greatest personality the game has as yet produced. That massive figure with the huge black beard and swarthy face crowned with an M.C.C. cap represented power and sheer driving force, and his mere presence on a side inspired confidence in his own ranks and something akin to fear in those of the enemy. He was invariably very nice and sympathetic to young players, though he was, it is said, rather prone to appeal for l.b.w., and as a captain he was a bit of a martinet. Slackness in any shape or form he could not stand; but he occasionally dropped on the wrong person, and I remember his making a most energetic and hard-working professional field at long-on to J. T. Hearne, and long-off to C. L. Townsend, who was bowling at the other end, in a match between M.C.C. and the Australians at Lord's. When someone suggested that he should save

—— by going long-off to Townsend, W. G. replied: 'No, no; Harry is lazy, it will do him good!'

Mr. Henry Perkins, the late secretary of M.C.C., thinks that the two best innings he saw W. G. play were his 165 for the Gentlemen *v.* the Australians at Lord's in 1888, and a 98 for M.C.C. *v.* Yorkshire in the seventies.

W. G.'s physique was phenomenal, and the greatest feat he ever accomplished was for Gloucestershire *v.* Kent at Gravesend in May 1895, when he scored 257 and 73 not out, besides bowling forty-three overs, and *was on the field during every ball of the game*, Gloucestershire winning by nine wickets, in spite of the fact that Kent made 470 in their first innings. A member of the Kent team of those days tells me that 'He (W. G.) dashed off at the end of the match to catch a train, running most of the way to the station, a crowd of small boys following, anxious to be near the hem of his garment.'

W. G. thought that Spofforth was the finest bowler—his variation of pace and flight being most deceptive—and that G. Freeman was the best *fast* bowler he ever played against, though he placed both Lockwood and Richardson very near to Freeman. He had a particular partiality for fast bowling, as I have already mentioned on page 116.

In his prime W. G. was the best change bowler in the world, bowling round-arm slow with his hand barely above the shoulder. He kept an accurate length on or just off the leg-stump, and imparted a peculiar flight to the ball. He put a lot of top spin on the ball, and nearly always got out a batsman who had never played him before. He was a wonderful field anywhere in his youth, and in later days a good point, many a hard hit finding a safe resting-place in those enormous hands.

In any attempt to estimate the merits of cricketers, *K. S. Ranjitsinhji*—the late Jam Sahib of Nawanagar—would certainly be placed in the front rank. I am often asked: 'Who is the best batsman you have ever seen?' and he would be a rash man indeed who would venture to answer that question definitely. Rather would one say that where several are pre-eminent it is wise to place them all in the same category. Ranjitsinhji would be found in Class I in any honours list, together with Grace, Hobbs, Trumper, Bradman, Macartney, Fry, Clem Hill, and Woolley.

There seems to be a general idea that batting came easily to Ranjitsinhji. That he was a natural cricketer, with an exceptionally keen eye, lissom wrists, a quick brain, and a peculiarly beautiful balance, there is no question, but few have worked harder at the game to improve their natural abilities. He would engage the best professional bowlers—men like Richardson, Lockwood, and J. T. Hearne—for a month or more, in April and September, and bat to them for hours every day, acquiring stamina—he was always rather delicate—as well as skill.

Ranjitsinhji did not get into the Cambridge XI until his last year, 1893, and then he probably owed his Blue more to his fine slip-fielding—where he and A. O. Jones made an almost incomparable pair—than to his merits as a batsman.

After he came down from Cambridge, he qualified for Sussex, and made his first appearance for that county, at Lord's, in May 1895, scoring 77 in his first innings, and 150 in the second v. M.C.C., and it was immediately recognized that he was the coming batsman.

In the following year, he broke 'W. G.'s' record aggregate with 2,780 runs, and an average of 57, and in 1899 and 1900 he scored over 3,000 runs. An average of 60, 70, or even 80 was not uncommon to him, and in the season of 1900 he scored over 200 on five occasions.

To some extent, he revolutionized the art of batting. He found that, with his wonderful eye and wrists, he could play back to almost any ball, however good a length, and however fast. Like Bradman, he seldom played a genuine forward stroke, for, again like Bradman, he found that balls to which he could not play back he could, with his quickness of foot, get to and drive. Very few batsmen possess this exceptional quickness of eye, and it would be a very false and fatal doctrine indeed to lay down that forward play should be discarded.

Ranjitsinhji was a master of every stroke, but his two best strokes were, perhaps, the late cut, at which he has never been excelled, and his play on the on-side. He did not merely glance the ball to leg; he did that, of course, but he also forced it at a tremendous pace to every quarter of the on-side, from wide of mid-on to long-leg. He played his famous leg glance with a dead straight bat, merely turning his wrist over at the last possible second, and flicking the ball away.

Ranjitsinhji was also a very powerful driver, and, when he chose, could play a hitting game on the lines of a genuine driver, like Lyons or Jessop. He was, indeed, a master batsman, but he was a law unto himself. His phenomenal quickness of eye permitted him to do things which were impossible for others. 'He could play back,' as Major H. S. Altham writes in his *History of Cricket*, 'to the fastest bowlers on the fastest wicket, and never had to hurry his stroke.' On a fiery wicket he was quite wonderful, and on this type of wicket he has never been surpassed, and probably equalled only by 'W. G.' and, perhaps, C. B. Fry.

Ranjitsinhji was also a fine fielder in the slips, and, indeed, anywhere, and a very fair medium-paced bowler, for he could turn the ball from the off, and flight it cleverly.

The Jam Sahib was a great personality, and tremendously popular with his charming manners, sense of humour, and gift of hospitality. His slim active figure, with his silk shirt flapping in the breeze, was welcome on every cricket ground, and I think it may be said that no county has ever, at one and the same time, possessed two such batsmen as Ranjit-sinhji and C. B. Fry. They drew enormous crowds wherever they played, and it was seldom indeed that they both failed.

Perhaps the finest of the many fine innings that Ranjit-sinhji played was his 154 not out for England against Australia on a lively wicket, at Old Trafford, in 1896. Clem Hill, H. Trumble, and Ernest Jones, who played for Australia in that match, were always talking of that innings. For A. E. Stoddart's second team in Australia, he averaged 60·89 in eleven-a-side matches, including a brilliant century in the first Test, though handicapped by a bad throat. Ranjitsinhji was a fine shot and fisherman, and a remarkably good racquets and lawn-tennis player. He once remarked that 'lawn-tennis was really his game, not cricket.' Ranjit-sinhji was a very well-read man with a quick nimble brain. He played a big part in Indian life and politics, and his sudden death in March 1933 was a great blow to his many friends and admirers. At the time of his death he was Chancellor of the Chamber of Princes.

*Arthur Shrewsbury* at his best ranked second only to W. G. as a batsman, and on difficult wickets he had no superior. He was sometimes very slow, but his cricket was so correct and scientific that he was always interesting to watch. His back play was perfection, he was a beautiful late cutter, though he left many off balls alone, and he excelled in all the scoring strokes on the leg-side. He had great command over his stroke, especially in a favourite lofting drive over mid-off's head, for which he often got two runs, and which one might compare with an approach shot at golf. Some of his innings will never be forgotten, and among them may be mentioned his 164 and his 113 for England against Australia at Lord's in 1886 and 1893, both of them when the pitch helped the bowlers. He was some-

G. W. Beldam

FINISH OF RANJITSINHJI'S FAMOUS LEG-GLANCE

*G. W. Beldam*

J. TUNNICLIFFE BRINGING OFF A RIGHT-HANDED CATCH
HIGH UP AT SLIP

thing of a genius in the masterly grace of his style. Henry Kirk, for years the dressing-room attendant at Trent Bridge, and so well known to those who have travelled with Lord Hawke's teams, had a great admiration for Shrewsbury, and used to tell us that often on going out to bat after luncheon he would say to him: ' Kirk, a cup of tea at half-past four, please' (this was before the days of tea intervals); 'and,' added Kirk, 'if they didn't run him out he was generally there.'

*William Gunn*, Shrewsbury's partner in many a long stand and the finest bat-maker in Christendom, was a beautiful player. Exceptionally tall, he had an enormous reach, and his style was very graceful. He and Shrewsbury year after year used to get a hundred—occasionally two hundred—each against Sussex at Brighton, and this was taken so much as a matter of course that half the Notts eleven used, it is said, to go away from the ground and bathe in the sea when their side were batting. As the Hon. R. H. Lyttelton writes in *Giants of the Game*: 'The Sussex team ought all to be scientific batsmen, for they have fielded out to so many thousands of runs made by Shrewsbury and Gunn that they ought to have become permeated through and through with their methods.'

Gunn played for England on innumerable occasions, and he was such a superb long-field that when he was in Australia he had twenty-one catches in 'the country' and bagged them all. Even through the lapse of years how clearly do the figures and accents of these two men come back to one— 'Sta' back, Arthur.' 'Sta' back, Billy.'

So long as there is a history of cricket, the names of Shrewsbury and Gunn will be found in its pages.

*Sir Stanley Jackson* has had no superior, except Hobbs and Sutcliffe, as a run-getter in England in Test Matches against Australia. His record is amazing. Five times he

M

scored an innings of over a hundred, besides making such minor (!) scores as 93, 86 not out, 82, etc., *and he was never able to go to Australia.* Of all the famous innings he has played, I think his 144 not out, at Leeds, in 1905 was the best. His cutting on that occasion on a somewhat slow wicket was a model of timing, and he made a number of hard drives; and his success, apart from his actual skill, was in great measure due to the fact that he took great pains to play himself in. He never underrated bowlers, nor did he overrate them; he merely played each ball on its merits. Sir Stanley Jackson had a beautiful style, and though thoroughly orthodox, possessed all the strokes. He was a fine cutter and on-driver, excelled especially on soft wickets, and his supreme confidence was an enormous asset both to himself and to his side. The reputation he gained as '*The* man for a big occasion' was indeed thoroughly deserved. It has been suggested that he was nervous while waiting to go in to bat. That may or may not have been so, but he was very much of a lion in the middle. Sir Stanley was also a capital medium-paced bowler with a nice easy action, and his over in the Test Match at Nottingham in 1905 is historic. Noble and Hill looked set for the day when he went on to bowl. Off his first ball Noble was caught at the wicket; the fourth clean bowled Hill; and the sixth saw Darling caught at slip.

From his earliest days at Harrow 'Jacker' always possessed great natural skill as a cricketer, and to his inborn ability he brought much intelligence to bear. He will go down to posterity as one of the very finest players that ever lived. 'Jacker' was a highly successful captain of England —a position for which he had to wait some time—for he was tactful and diplomatic and understood men. And he was a good tosser. He virtually retired after his great year in 1905, but played two matches in 1906, and in David Denton's benefit match at Lord's in 1907. He was President of the M.C.C. in 1921, and is now a Trustee of the Club and an important figure in the world of cricket.

Here is a good story from Leeds. Yorkshire were playing the Australians in 1902 and in Australia's second innings six wickets had fallen for 23 runs of which Hirst had taken five and Jackson one. A voice in the crowd shouted, 'Here, Lordie (Lord Hawke), take off F. S. and put on Scof (Haigh).' Lord Hawke took no notice of this and in his next over Jackson obtained four wickets, two bowled, one l.b.w., and one caught at the wicket, without a run being scored off him. As the players were returning to the pavilion with an excited crowd round them, a little man in a big bowler hat and none too small boots came up to Jackson and said, 'F. S., t'was me who said take off F. S.' Jackson looked a bit embarrassed but stroking his moustache replied, 'Well, I don't think you are a very good judge.' The bowler-hatted one replied, 'Maybe, but bah gum they did bat bad!' Jackson's analysis was: O.—7, M.—1, R.—12, W.—5, and Hirst's O.—7, M.—4, R.—9, W.—5. Yorkshire won by five wickets, the scores on a very treacherous pitch at Leeds were Australians 131 and 23, Yorkshire 107 and 50 for five wickets.

Many Australians aver that *A. C. MacLaren* is the finest batsman we have ever sent them. Certainly MacLaren's record in Test Matches in Australia is as good as that of his fellow Harrovian in England, and so highly was he thought of that there were to be found men who would lay even money that he would get a hundred every time he went in at Sydney! But MacLaren has made his hundreds for England not only in Australia, but in this country as well, and the best innings I ever saw him play was an 88 not out in the Test Match at Lord's in 1899. It was a sad day for England, Australia winning by ten wickets, but MacLaren's batting was something to console us. The Australians were very strong in bowling that year, with Jones, Trumble, Noble, and Howell all in their prime, and MacLaren, leading a forlorn hope, played magnificently. His batting possessed something akin to the grand manner. He appeared to be saying to the bowler: 'I am here to hit you, and I mean to lose no time about it'; and this forcing style was the very essence of his batting. When in form he played every stroke so beautifully and so naturally that one wondered why he ever got out. He was a perfect master in forcing good-length balls to the boundary. MacLaren captained England in no fewer than twenty-two Test Matches. He was un-doubtedly a very able tactician, being a master in the placing of the field. A very good-looking man, he was a most attractive character with a great sense of humour. Possibly he was a bit of a pessimist, but he was a good-natured one.

No one has studied cricket more thoroughly than *C. B. Fry*, who has brought a great brain to bear on the game, with the result that he has reduced theory to a fine art. His powers of observation are immense, and just as Sandow developed every muscle in the body by a carefully thought-out plan of action, so did Fry develop every stroke in the batsman's art, and brought run-getting almost to a certainty. The list of his big scores is amazing. On four occasions has he made two separate hundreds in a match, and on three occasions has he just missed this distinction by a single run, while in the course of his career he has scored 26,382 runs with an average of 49·68. There are some who think that Fry could not cut, but I saw him play his great innings of 144 for England *v.* Australia at the Oval in 1905, and on that occasion his cutting was superb. There is no greater judge of cricket; he knows it from A to Z. Magnificently built, every inch of him a superb figure of a man, Fry, as all the world is aware, has been as great an athlete as ever lived. At Oxford he was captain not only of cricket, but of the athletic club, and the Association football XI, and would undoubtedly have won a Blue for Rugby football as a three-quarter back but for an injury to his ankle. He was one of the greatest all-round athletes the world has ever known—and a veritable Admirable Crichton. Fry has done some very fine things in representative cricket—his innings, for instance, against the South Africans at the Oval stands out as one of the masterpieces of batting—and he ranks with the greatest players of modern times. His defence was superb, his back play being equal to that of K. S. Ranjitsinhji himself, and his driving magnificent both for its strength and for its remarkable accuracy. What he would have done in Australia, had he been able to go there, no one can say for certain, but opinion is agreed that he would have distinguished himself greatly.

It was at Repton that Fry learnt the A B C of the game, and it is to Ranjitsinhji that he attributes the vast improvement he made after going down from Oxford. There are many cricketers, myself among them, who owe much to the delightful and thoughtful articles he has written on cricket. My tutor, at Oriel, the Rev. A. G. Butler, used to admire him greatly, and declare that he was like a Greek god. Fry was a scholar of Wadham. He was placed at the top of the Scholarship List—above 'F. E.' (Lord Birkenhead), who was fourth—and obtained a First in Classical Mods.

Many years ago I was dining with Ranji at his house near Staines and the talk not surprisingly turned to cricket. I asked our host, 'Who is the best batsman in your opinion, leaving out yourself?' I remember the reply, typical of his modesty, 'My dear Plum, I was not really very good—I was lucky.' We all laughed and told him he was non-suited. He then went on, 'I judge a batsman on his ability on every type of wicket and against every type of bowling, and taking this into consideration, I put "Charlo" (Fry) first. He was almost as good as W. G. on a lively wicket against fast bowling, on a sticky wicket he was as good as anyone, on a slow wicket he was better than anyone else, and on a perfect wicket he was as likely to make a big score as anyone.' This is indeed high praise coming from such a master of the art of batting, and who shall say that it was not deserved? For myself, great admirer as I am of Fry, I put Hobbs first of the English batsmen of my time. He never failed England and on every sort of wicket, including the then matting wickets in South Africa against the great googly bowlers, a severe test this, he was supreme.

*Hayward* shared with Hobbs and Tyldesley the distinction of being the finest professional batsman of his day. There is no need to dwell on his many great performances in every kind of match, for England, for the Players, for Surrey; it would take too long, and mere figures are often boring. I always think of Hayward as a solid rock against which many a bowler has dashed in vain. There never was a more imperturbable batsman—so sound and so watchful, and so strong when he did make up his mind to have a 'go.' The straightest of bats was the foundation of his defence, and he was an ideal No. 1 in any eleven. He was a great player of fast bowling. In 1906 he scored 3,518 runs in first-class cricket, a record.

Before Hayward, *Robert Abel* was the great Surrey batsman. 'The Guvnor,' as Abel was popularly called, was accused of not playing with a straight bat, but I fancy the bat was about in the perpendicular when it actually met the ball; and in any case it did not appear to hurt his defence. It seems to me that if one possesses a wonderful eye one can play as one chooses. Abel was very short in height, and was reputed to dislike fast bowlers like Kortright and Woods, but in his time he certainly made a good many runs off fast bowling, on one occasion scoring over 200 against Kortright at the Oval. His asking for his sun hat was a sure sign that he felt like batting, and I remember C. M. Wells saying to me, in a Surrey *v.* Middlesex match at the Oval, 'How awful! The Guvnor has sent for his sun hat; that means he will be here all day'; and he was.

Abel once played an innings of 350 against Somerset at the Oval. In those days the usual talent-money for a professional was £1 for every fifty runs. No one had ever before, for Surrey, made such a big score, and the committee thought that £5 would be a fitting sum to give Abel. The latter, however, was a bit of a jester, and is reported to have said that there would not be much point in his making more than 250 in the future!

*G. L. Jessop* was described by a Philadelphian newspaper as 'the human catapult who wrecks the roofs of distant towns when set in his assault.' Bending low over his bat, he either drove the ball into the long-field, or swept it round to square-leg, while if the ball was at all short he could cut magnificently. It was in this wonderful cut of his that Jessop was the superior of all other hitters. C. I. Thornton, and the Australians, Bonnor and Lyons, drove, in all probability, a longer ball, but none of them could cut like Jessop, whose ability to score with this stroke, added to his power in the drive and the pull, made it so difficult to place the field for him. He was the essence of unorthodoxy; indeed it was once said of him that he had 'raised rustic batting to a science,' but there was the stamp of genius about everything he did; and strange as it may appear to say so, few batsmen watched the ball more carefully. He possessed, of course, a wonderful eye, and he made use of every ounce of weight in his body.

I have seen Jessop bat often, and splendidly, but I do not remember having ever seen him play quite so well as he did in the England *v.* South Africa match at Lord's in 1907, and I am not forgetting his great innings of 104 against the Australians at the Oval. In this innings against the googly bowlers, whom he was meeting for the first time, he received but 63 balls, and yet in an hour and a quarter he scored 93 out of 145 runs.

Jessop's remarkable qualities as a field are referred to in another part of this book, and when he first came out he was a very fast bowler, and a good one too.

*Major E. G. Wynyard* was one of the best natural batsmen ever seen and had he been able to play regularly there is no saying what he might have done. Even as it was he seemed able to come straight into first-class cricket and make heaps of runs. He was a very enterprising batsman with plenty of strokes, and a marked individuality of his own. He could drive well, delighted in hitting a left-handed bowler over cover-point or extra-cover's head, and rejoiced in a pull, to accomplish which he used to go down on his right knee and hit at the pitch of the ball. He was a magnificent field in almost any position, but excelled chiefly in the slips and at short-leg, and was by no means a bad lob bowler. Major Wynyard played for England *v.* Australia at the Oval in 1896, and appeared for the Gentlemen at Lord's and in representative M.C.C. matches. He was also invited by Stoddart to go to Australia, but was unable to obtain the necessary leave from the military authorities. He was a wonderful all-round athlete, playing for England at Association football, winning the international toboganning prize, and excelling at every kind of game and sport. He won the D.S.O. in Burma, while he gained the Humane Society's medal for saving life in circumstances of exceptional bravery.

He was the finest cricketer the Army has produced.

*Hirst* ranks as one of the very best all-round cricketers England has ever had, his performances with bat, ball, and in the field being marvels of skill and consistency.[1] For years no England eleven was complete without him, and he was the backbone—and more—of Yorkshire. He was most dangerous when at bay, many of his finest efforts having been achieved when his side were in desperate straits. He was a born fighter, but with a spirit so generous and gentle that he was ever ready with an excuse or an explanation for the failures of others. He shared with Jack Hearne the distinction of being the most popular and respected professional of the day, and those who have never heard the welcome he received from a Sheffield crowd when he went out to bat to set right the failure of half the side have missed something. I am not going to liken 'his beaming face to a harvest moon in seasons of glory and plenty!' as a professional cricketer once wrote of him, but this I know, that it did one good to see him laugh. In many ways he was the ideal cricketer, so straight, so strong, so honest. He preferred knur and spell to football, though he played for the M.C.C. team at Fremantle and Adelaide, when he appalled his opponents, for he simply ploughed his way through them like a battle cruiser doing her twenty-six knots!

It is hard to single out the best innings he ever played, for the simple reason that he played so many, but there are two I always think of in connection with him. The first was for Yorkshire *v.* Surrey at the Oval in 1906, and the second for Yorkshire *v.* Middlesex at Lord's in 1910. On the first occasion the fast bowling of N. A. Knox and P. R. May was, on a more than usually fiery Oval wicket, flying about in a very awkward manner, and on the second Yorkshire looked a beaten side when he came in to bat. His

[1] In fourteen out of seventeen seasons Hirst performed the 'double,' and in 1906 scored 2,385 and obtained 208 wickets.

magnificent effort at the Oval could not prevent Surrey winning, but his great innings of 137—curiously enough the first hundred he had made at Lord's—enabled Yorkshire to gain a glorious victory within half a minute of time. So plucky, so full of resource, and so cheerful, he had no superiors, and scarcely an equal, when things were going wrong. Occasionally on fast wickets he overdid his famous 'pull,' but he made scores of runs with it in his time, and it was far from being his only stroke; for he was one of the best of cutters, and he could drive very hard and cleanly both to the on and to the off. His bowling and fielding at mid-off are referred to in other chapters.

*Hallam* and *Wass* won the Championship for Nottingham-shire in 1907. Between them, they obtained 298 wickets—Hallam 153, Wass 145—no one else taking more than 25 wickets. They did literally all the bowling, sending down 1,565 overs between them. It was a very wet summer and the many sticky wickets suited their styles exactly. Hallam had a quick lively run-up to the crease, kept a wonderful length, at a slow-medium pace, right hand, and was always doing something with the ball both in the air and off the pitch. Wass was fast medium right and one of the most difficult of bowlers on false turf when he relied on a quick leg-break—not so much contrived by finger spin as by a turn of the wrist. He first attracted attention by bowling Arthur Shrewsbury twice in the nets at Trent Bridge. No one, it was said, had done that until Tom came along. He was one of the characters of the cricket field. He used to mutter when one stopped a particularly good ball, with a sort of 'How the H——l did you play that one' look in his eyes. Once when an umpire decided against a l.b.w. appeal of his he raised both hands in the air and called on his Maker to witness what an injustice had been done!

After my playing days were over, I was often at Trent

Bridge for some of the great matches and invariably Tom
Oates used to say to me, 'Your old friend Tom is here; I
know he would like to see you,' and in 1938 I sat next to
him during a part of the Test Match, and we fought our
battles over again. He made me laugh a lot!

He and Hallam were certainly a fine pair of bowlers.

If not such a fine batsman as his brother R. E., *H. K.
Foster* was a remarkably good player. He made a brilliant
century in the 'Varsity match, cutting, off-driving, and
'slashing' in a manner which almost took one's breath
away, and he was captain of Worcestershire for fourteen or
fifteen years. In his earlier days he was almost entirely an
off-side player, facing squarely to the bowler—a 'one-eyed
batsman,' as Spofforth might say; but Alfred Shaw came
down to Worcester one spring and persuaded him to alter
his stance, with the happiest results. As became the finest
amateur racquets player England ever had—he won the
championship eight times—Foster was a beautiful timer of
the ball. He was the sheet-anchor of Worcestershire cricket
for twenty years and more. He had the right appreciation
towards the game, was an admirable captain, and a delightful
companion. He captained the Gentlemen both at Lord's
and the Oval, and in 1921 was Chairman of the Selection
Committee.

I had the good fortune to see *R. E. Foster's* record innings
of 287 for England *v.* Australia at Sydney in December
1903. He was at the wickets seven hours and ten minutes.
On the Saturday, 12th December, he was in three hours for
71 runs; on the Monday, four and a quarter hours for 216
runs. In the last hour he actually scored 80 runs. He gave
a difficult one-handed chance to S. E. Gregory at 49, otherwise his cricket was faultless. The Australian critics
criticized the first half of his innings rather severely, I

remember, but the wicket during part of this period was not quite easy, and his batting on the Monday was as good as anything I have ever seen. When he beat W. L. Murdoch's 211 for Australia v. England at the Oval, the cheering was tremendous, but it was nothing to the ovation he received at the end of his innings. It was Foster's first innings in a Test Match. Hirst and I got 'ducks' in this innings, and our scores were up on the board from Saturday to the following Wednesday! ! ! I can see them now.

Many batsmen seem unable to combine effectiveness with a graceful and easy style; but if Foster were to remain at the wickets for an hour without making a run, one could not help admiring the beautiful way in which he used his bat. Style in cricket counts for less than it did, but it is always delightful to behold, especially when it is so natural and unforced as Foster's. And then, with all his grace of movement, he had as great a variety of stroke as any batsman in the world—Trumper and K. S. Ranjitsinhji not excepted. A wonderful late cutter, with the strongest of wrists, he has been known to drive the best bowlers of the age as if they were merely local club bowlers. He seemed to be able to make the bowling dance to his own pleasure and whim, and to place it exactly where he liked, irrespective of his opponents' endeavour to circumscribe his hitting to any one particular area. He was a magnificent fielder in the slips—and, indeed, anywhere; if he had played regularly it would have been impossible to leave him out of an England eleven. The Walkers, the Studds, the Lytteltons, the Fords, the Steels, and the Ashtons are the great cricketing families, but none were greater than the Fosters.

Foster was a brilliant 'Soccer' forward, and played frequently for England. He was also a great racquets player and golfer. Indeed, there was no game at which he did not excel.

The best innings I ever saw *B. J. T. Bosanquet* play was for England *v.* New South Wales at Sydney in February 1904. In a little over an hour he made 114 runs. The ball was turning a bit, W. P. Howell especially got a good deal of work on from the off; but Bosanquet preferred the ball to turn in to him than to come straight on, and he banged this breaking ball to all quarters of the on-side. Three balls in succession would he flick round on the on-side; the field would gather in that direction and then the next ball would be sent rattling against the off-side boundary. Other very fine innings of this great and original cricketer were his 214 for England *v.* Yorkshire at the Oval in 1908, and his 50 on a difficult Lord's wicket *v.* Kent in the same season. Bosanquet combined great skill with great confidence, and he had every physical attribute for a batsman. His forearm was immensely strong, and though he seldom cut late, he used his wrists with effect in his forcing strokes on the on-side. He was a wonderful player to a left-handed bowler like Rhodes, appearing on a good wicket to have almost two strokes for every ball. This was strongly emphasized in a great innings of 214 *v.* Yorkshire, when he seemed able to hit the ball which pitched outside the off-stump either through the covers or round on the on-side. His bowling has already been mentioned; but it may be mentioned that to this day the googly is always referred to in Australia as the 'Bosey,' in honour of its inventor.

No batsman ever made his runs in a more attractive way than *R. H. Spooner*, and from his first appearance in county cricket it was obvious that a really great batsman had arisen. I remember Watson, the Lancashire bowler of the seventies and eighties, saying that Spooner was the finest schoolboy batsman he had seen since A. G. Steel, and a successful début against Middlesex at Lord's fully confirmed that opinion. On that occasion Spooner scored 44 and 83 (within three weeks of his leaving Marlborough) against J. T. Hearne, Trott, and C. M. Wells, and though I have seen him play many fine innings since, I do not believe he has ever batted much better than he did on that day at Lord's.

So beautifully did Spooner time the ball that to the onlooker he appeared to put no 'wood' behind his strokes —an impression rapidly altered as one saw the pace at which the ball went to the ring. At Scarborough he once drove a ball of Haigh's out of the ground, and to me, at the other end, he seemed merely to play forward at it. Had he been but a fair or even a moderate field, his batting by itself would have been enough to have given Spooner a strong claim to play for England, but his value to a side was greatly increased by his perfect fielding; for as a cover-point he was inferior only to Jessop, S. H. Saville and Hobbs. As Jessop and Saville were, strictly speaking, extra-covers rather than cover-points, Spooner may be said to have been the best cover-point in England after Hobbs. Moving very quickly to the ball, he had a lightning-like return—picking up and throwing in the ball after the manner of S. E. Gregory, the Australian. As George Hirst remarked when he first saw Spooner play, 'That lad will have to have bad luck if he doesn't play for England one of these days.' Spooner was asked to captain the 1920–1 M.C.C. team to Australia, but was compelled to decline. No more charming personality ever stepped on to a cricket field.

It may safely be said that *J. T. Tyldesley* was without a superior on a bad wicket, and the best innings I ever saw him play was at Melbourne in January 1904, for the M.C.C. team against Australia, on a pitch of this kind. In England when a wicket is sticky the ball turns quickly enough in all conscience, but it does not get up straight in your face as is its habit under similar conditions at Melbourne. M.C.C. were all out for 103, of which Tyldesley made 62. A better innings has surely never been played on a bad wicket than this. If a cricketer keeps his figure and keeps fit there is no reason why he should not go on getting runs for years after he has passed half the allotted span; 'W. G.', Shrewsbury, William Gunn, Hobbs, and Abel did not attain their best until they were over thirty. The first thing that goes in a batsman is not his quickness of eyesight but his quickness of foot, and Tyldesley attributed much of his success to dancing in the winter. Wherefore his advice to 'get into the ballroom in the winter' is worthy of consideration. Besides dancing, Swedish exercises, skipping, squash racquets, any exercise, indeed, which makes one quick on one's feet is, therefore, to be recommended. Tyldesley was a great long-fielder.

In the days when Somerset delighted to humble the strongest, they numbered no better fighting man in their ranks than *Braund*. This admirable all-round cricketer was the very essence of energy; indeed, he would willingly have bowled all day at one end, and fielded in the country at the other. At his best no England eleven was complete without him, for he was a great field at slip, a sound and reliable batsman, and a difficult leg-break bowler. He made hundreds for England against both Australia and South Africa, and his name is to be found in the century list of Gentlemen *v.* Players at Lord's. His singing of 'The Blind Boy' was a feature of my first tour in Australia, and he was a very companionable traveller.

Another great Somerset player was *L. C. H. Palairet*, possibly the most beautiful batsman, so far as pure style goes, that ever lived. His batting, indeed, was 'a thing of joy'—the minimum of exertion and the maximum of power, and every stroke played with perfect swing and balance. One could not imagine him making an ugly or ungainly stroke. He was a magnificent player on the off-side, his treatment of good-length balls outside the off-stump being masterly. He was, too, a fine driver, and has hit as many balls into the river at Taunton as anyone. On sticky wickets he used to play forward more than most great players usually do, but he got his bat well up to his left leg, and the off-breaking ball did not have much chance of getting through. I have seen him play some fine innings when the turf was false. It was a pity he was never able to go to Australia. He would have made thousands of runs there.

The first match I played for Middlesex was v. Somerset at Taunton on 6th August, 1894. A. J. Webbe was then captain, and Stoddart, F. G. J. Ford, and Sir T. C. O'Brien were in their prime. I was delighted when any of them spoke to me!

What fine batsmen those four were; they made Middlesex cricket popular all over the country. *Webbe* was a great cutter, but he was past his best when I first knew him, though no one could have played a better innings than he did on his last appearance for the county. This was v. Worcestershire at Worcester in July 1900. The wicket was very nasty for a time, and Arnold in those days could bowl on a sticky wicket. We were apparently 'in the cart,' six wickets being down for 75 runs, but Webbe showed great defence, and ably assisted by a fellow Harrovian, Robertson, who batted superbly for 118, saved the match for us.

The Walkers created Middlesex cricket, and Webbe continued to build well on the sure foundation they laid; and it was only in the fitness of things that 'Webbie,' to know whom was to love, should have retired from the scene of so many triumphs with yet another laurel in his wreath. He was the soul of Middlesex cricket.

G. W. Beldam

R. E. FOSTER
Finish of off-drive

G. W. Beldam

A. C. MacLaren's Secondary Position

*A. E. Stoddart* was a grand all-round athlete, excelling at Rugby football—as well as at cricket and golf. He was a beautiful bat, free and aggressive, who used to take the bowler by the scruff of the neck and knock the stuffing out of him. He went four times to Australia, twice as captain, and he played for years for England, the Gentlemen, and Middlesex. His greatest innings were probably 215 not out for Middlesex *v.* Lancashire at Old Trafford, 195 not out and 124 for Middlesex *v.* Notts at Lord's, while he twice made over a hundred in Test Matches in Australia. Stoddart was a splendid field, in his earlier days in 'the country' and at mid-off, and later in his career at extra-slip. He had a peculiar habit of dropping on his right knee when stopping a hot drive. He was one of the best captains I have ever played under, with an infinite capacity for taking pains, and an eye to the smallest detail. A great personality, he was immensely liked both here and in Australia.

*Sir Timothy O'Brien* was a great batsman. Powerfully built, he was a fine driver and a beautiful late-cutter, who was very fond of the 'chop' stroke to the ball that keeps low outside the off-stump. Two of his innings will go down to posterity. The first was against Yorkshire at Lord's in 1889, when he scored 100 *not out in eighty minutes*, Middlesex, who had been set 280 runs to get to win in three hours and thirty-five minutes, winning by four wickets ten minutes before time; and the second against Surrey at the Oval seven years later, when on a difficult wicket he made 137 against Lohmann, Richardson, Lockwood, and Hayward, who was at that time in the habit of getting 100 wickets in a season. Sir Timothy was a particularly fine player when the turf was sticky, and a clever point. On the few occasions he captained the Middlesex eleven he showed marked ability as a leader. On a sticky wicket he had no superiors. 'W. G.' had a great opinion of him.

N

*F. G. J. Ford* has been described as 'six foot two of don't care.' Left-handers may come and go, but only Woolley surpasses Ford in point of grace and style. So easily and with so little apparent effort did he bat that he gave the impression of caring little whether he got out or not. As a fact he was a very keen cricketer, who suffered from rather indifferent health. He had rare swing and reach, and so hard did he drive the ball back that the bowler used often to jump out of the way. I have seen Johnny Briggs skip behind the umpire half in fun and half in all seriousness. Ford liked fast bowling, and used to have great duels with Mold. If Mold did not get him out in the first over or two he used to punish him tremendously, and Lockwood and Richardson, too, have often had good cause to remember him. Ford was rather wanting in defence, and cannot, therefore, be compared with Clement Hill, J. Darling, W. Bardsley, or Woolley as a left-handed batsman, but he was a lovely player to watch. When he, Stoddart, and Sir Timothy were in the eleven, Middlesex were worth going a long way to see.

*C. M. Wells's* bowling and fielding were even more valuable to Middlesex than his free and determined batting. His score of 244 against Notts at Trent Bridge was to the general public his greatest feat; but to me his greatest performance was his thirteen wickets for 68 runs against Yorkshire at Leeds in 1900. From the ring Wells was probably rather a simple-looking bowler, but there was nothing simple about him when one faced him at the wickets. He bowled slow, with a long and rather quick run, while he possessed that inestimable virtue of making the ball look to be farther up than it really was. Wells's best ball was the one on which he put an apparent big break, but which came straight and quick off the pitch; he has had many a l.b.w. with it.

But if he failed to make runs or get wickets, Wells could

be counted on to save heaps of runs in the field, at extra-cover especially, but indeed anywhere on the off-side. I have heard Palairet complain that Wells stopped all his drives between cover and extra-cover. A keener cricketer never lived. Wells was in his day one of the finest half-backs at Rugby football in England. That position requires exceptional quickness of foot, and this extreme readiness to start made him the magnificent extra-cover he was; for though a man of heavy build, Wells could cover the ground and move to a ball like lightning. His versatility was extraordinary. He excelled in everything he took up, from the classics to fishing. As a master at Eton, he did a great deal for the cricket there.

*Albert Trott* was a most original and enterprising bowler. He was dangerous on any pitch; but if in form it was on a perfect one he was seen to most advantage, for he relied on niceties and variations of pace, rather than length and break, to get the enemy out of the way. When he first came to England, and for three or four years subsequently, he had that 'curl-in-the-air ball' to a very marked degree; and during the years he was qualifying for Middlesex he had great fun with this ball. When he was not playing cricket in Australia Trott shone as a baseball pitcher, and it is to this that he owed his power of curling a ball. He not only curled it from leg, but he made it drop in the air after the manner of the baseball pitcher, and over and over again have I seen an apparent full pitch to leg land on the batsman's toe. Then he had a wonderfully good fast ball—which he was far too modest with, and which he was apt to forget for hours at a time. He was the sort of bowler who required supervision, for if left to himself he might work a theory to death and lose a match in four overs. On the other hand, he could win—and often did win—a match in a quarter of an hour.

On a sticky wicket he could be very difficult, and yet I have known occasions when on such a wicket, when the odds were two to one on his bowling the batsman neck and crop, he has tried to get him caught in the long-field. A certain perversity of genius prevented him from being the best all-round cricketer in the world.

As a fielder, especially at extra-slip and to his own bowling, Trott had scarcely a superior, and those huge hands of his afforded a safe resting-place for the hottest return.

And then he hit a ball over the pavilion at Lord's—a feat no one else has accomplished;[1] and he once drove a ball clean out of the Trent Bridge ground, which damaged severely the spokes of a hansom cab, and which I really believe would have given him twenty-five runs had he been playing on the veldt.

But the best innings he ever played was his 164 for Middlesex against Yorkshire at Lord's in 1899. On that occasion he hit with terrific power, one drive striking the pavilion rails with such force that it rolled back within a few yards of mid-on. He might have been caught deep on the on-side towards the end of his innings by Moorhouse (fielding substitute for Denton), whose explanation for not getting to the catch was amusing, to say the least of it. Trott hit the ball so high that Moorhouse had plenty of time to get under it, but in the end it fell at his feet, and when one of his colleagues asked: 'Why didn't you try to catch her, Bob?' he replied: 'At first I didn't see her up against that —— blackboard [the big scoring-board], and then when I sees her up there and acoming to me, I says, "Oh —— it!" and I leaves it'!!!

*F. L. Fane* captained England against Australia, played for the Gentlemen *v.* Players at Lord's, and

[1] M. A. Noble was the bowler, and the match was M.C.C. *v.* Australia, at Lord's, on July 31, 1899.

made many long scores for Essex. He was a great
traveller, having played cricket in Australia, New Zealand,
South Africa, and the West Indies, and on his first tour to
South Africa he stood head and shoulders above everyone
else on the M.C.C. side. His 143 in one of the Test Matches
at Johannesburg was a remarkably fine innings. Fane was
a fine off-side player, his strong forward strokes and quickness of foot being very effective, and on his day he was very
attractive to watch. He was a good field at third man and
in the country, and a safe catch.

In point of method the nearest approach among English
cricketers to Trumper was *K. L. Hutchings.* Hutchings had
not Trumper's ease and general grace of style, but at his
best he was extraordinarily brilliant. Possessed of enormously strong forearms and wrists, he hit the ball hard,
while his back and on-side play was superb. He seemed to
make his stroke at the last moment, but so powerful was
his wrist, and so excellent his timing, that he could force
good-length balls to the boundary. One of his finest strokes
was when, by a quick flick of his wrists, he would hit—*not
play*—a good-length ball on the middle and leg-stump from
a fast bowler round on the on-side. Hutchings had also a
hard square cut. His fielding was magnificent—indeed, all
round he was about the best fielder in England; for he was
equally good in any position—slips, long-field, or off-side,
and he was a superb thrower. He was the idol of Kent
grounds.

*Denton* was one of those unlucky people of whom some
irresponsible who was suffering from verborrhœa once said
that 'he had not a Test Match temperament'—whatever
that may mean—and this narrow-minded dictum helped to
keep him out of England elevens. More people are talked
into and talked out of teams than the world knows of.

Denton was the hardest hitter of his size and weight I have ever seen, and no one timed the ball better. He possessed very supple wrists. He was always going for the bowling, and being possessed of plenty of strokes, generally got his runs at a great pace. He had a lovely stroke over extra-cover's head, pushed the good-length ball between point and cover, and on a slow wicket was a fine puller and hooker. He played some extremely good innings against Middlesex. His fielding in the long-field and at third man has never been surpassed.

Nine times out of ten a left-hander is a batsman's greatest foe on a sticky wicket, but *Haigh*, in his prime, was as difficult a bowler on a sticky wicket as any left-hander. He possessed an enormous and very quick off-break, he had a capital fast yorker, and his flight was very deceptive, for he used 'to pull the ball back in the air' without any apparent change of action. His run up to the wicket was peculiar, for in his final stride his body was very near the ground, his left leg being shot out in front of him with a very long reach. He dragged his right foot along the ground as his arm came up, and for this reason wore an armour-plate of brass on the toe of his right boot. On a hard, true wicket Haigh was never a really difficult bowler, probably because his length was not accurate enough, an occasional failing of his on sticky wickets. He was a useful bat, and caught many catches at cover-point off Rhodes. Always happy and smiling, there was no nicer professional cricketer.

Wherever the game is played *Lord Hawke's* name is known. He was the first to preach the gospel of cricket throughout the empire, and for five and twenty years he was captain of Yorkshire. It is no secret that when he took over the leadership of that famous county things were not as they should have been. There was little discipline, and prac-

tically no *esprit de corps*; but by wise and tactful management he soon altered that, and under his guidance the
Yorkshire eleven were looked on as the model of what a
county side should be, well disciplined, well drilled and
efficient. Of course, he had able cricketers under his command, but in the first instance he created the spirit and
organization out of which that splendid team arose. He
has been a good friend to the professional. Lord Hawke
was an unrivalled manager on tours abroad. He thought
first of others and last of himself, and never spared any
trouble or pains to make his men happy and comfortable.
The natural result was that he was regarded with great
affection. He was the ideal leader of a touring team. He
knew well how to maintain discipline, but he was kind and
considerate to a degree, and he ruled by love rather than
by fear. To gain his colours was a high distinction. He
took me on my first tour abroad and I owe much to him.
He was an uncertain starter as a batsman, but he could
drive very hard and late cut well, and when he got runs he
got them in such good style that one wondered why he was
not more often successful. More than once he pulled Yorkshire out of a tight place. He was President of M.C.C. in
1914 and throughout the Great War. He was called the
Odysseus of Cricket, for he travelled far and wide, having
taken teams to Australia, New Zealand, South Africa, West
Indies, South America, the United States, and Canada.

*N. A. Knox*, of Surrey, in his best form, was very nearly
as fine a fast bowler as Lockwood or Richardson. He was
faster than any English bowler since Kortright, except Larwood, and was always likely, even on the truest wickets, to
get up to an awkward height. But he was far from depend-
ing on pace and the ugly rise of the ball, for at times he
broke back almost as much as Richardson. He was a great
match-winner, and his bowling for Surrey in the summer of

1906 was superb in spite of the fact that he was often at a disadvantage owing to a strained leg. In that season he took 117 wickets in county matches for eighteen runs each, bowling only 593 overs, so that he obtained, on an average, a *wicket every five overs*—a remarkable performance. In the Gentlemen *v.* Players match at Lord's that year he obtained twelve wickets—eight of them clean bowled—in *forty-four overs and one ball*, for 183 runs. His pace was really intimidating, and only three or four of the professional batsmen faced him with any confidence. Finer fast bowling has seldom been shown by an amateur.

Knox was a fine bowler from the time he first appeared in the Dulwich eleven, when year after year he used to knock out for a small score the strong eleven I used to take there. On one occasion I was three short on the evening before the match, but I obtained as substitutes the Jam of Nawanagar, Bosanquet, and F. Mitchell, of Cambridge and Yorkshire, and captain of the South Africans, at the time, 1904.

*A. O. Jones*, the Nottinghamshire captain, was energy personified; one could see that in his walk. He was a magnificent fielder, a dashing, daring bat, and there were few, if any, better captains. His performances for Notts would fill a volume, while he played frequently for England. As far back as 1896 he was in the Gentlemen eleven at Lord's, when the amateurs were represented by what I believe to be one of the strongest Gentlemen elevens that ever took the field. Here was the team in the order of going in—W. G. Grace (captain), A. E. Stoddart, K. S. Ranjitsinhji, L. C. H. Palairet, F. S. Jackson, A. C. MacLaren, Sir T. C. O'Brien, S. M. J. Woods, A. O. Jones, E. Smith, and G. MacGregor. Jones went in No. 10 in the Cambridge eleven of 1893, his slip-fielding, and not his batting, getting him his blue. Later, however, he developed into a fine batsman who, though bending low over his bat with bent knees in his preliminary position, stood up very straight to play the ball. Jones hit well all round, but his best stroke was a terrifically hard half-drive half-cut past point. No other batsman that I know of played this stroke with such certainty. Some of his catches live in one's memory, and are referred to in greater detail in the chapter on 'Fielding.' Jones captained the M.C.C. team in Australia in the winter of 1907–8, but had poor luck. He started off splendidly, and he seemed to have worked his team up to a high pitch of enthusiasm and efficiency, when on the eve of the first Test Match he was struck down by a serious illness. His loss was immense both as leader and player, and though he took part in the fourth and fifth Test Matches, he was far from fit. Nottinghamshire owed much to Jones. It would be impossible to imagine any side of which he was in command being slack in the field. He was the prince of Rugby referees.

*E. R. Wilson* was one of those bowlers who could literally pitch a ball on a sixpence, and he was a master in varying the flight of his deliveries. Slow in pace, Wilson had a very easy action, and Yorkshire made a great mistake in forgetting him for so many years. He was one of those bowlers who the pavilion critic is always saying 'ought to be hit into the ring,' but the batsman who could do so was never discovered.

Wilson had a distinguished record as a cricketer both at Rugby and Cambridge, being captain of both teams, and his knowledge of scores and all that appertains to the history and literature of the game is profound. He has been called a 'walking *Wisden*,' and he is an uncommonly able writer. His chapter on bowling in the *Badminton Cricket*, 1920 edition, is a classic.

Oxford have never had a finer all-round cricketer than *W. H. B. Evans*, who met with such a tragic death when flying with Col. Cody some years ago. Had he been able to keep up the game regularly after leaving Oxford, it is quite likely that he would have had the distinction of playing for England. He was a beautiful bat who had, to some extent, modelled his style on Ranjitsinhji, for he seldom played forward, relying for defence almost entirely on his back stroke. He possessed an easy, natural style, quick footwork, and his off-driving was particularly fine.

Evans was a fast-medium bowler of moods, but on his day he could make the ball turn back quickly, although his length was not always accurate. He was a first-class slip and possessed a great knowledge of the game.

*A. J. Evans* is a son of A. H. Evans, the famous Oxford cricketer of the early eighties, and a cousin of W. H. B. Evans. A natural player, Evans could go into a first-class match, as he often did, and make runs without having previously had a bat in his hand. He had a really good style, getting well forward to fast bowling and driving hard on the off-side.

It was very unfortunate that he failed in the Test Match at Lord's in 1921, for his method of batting was the right one to meet the Australian bowlers, and he was a really fine slip. Unfortunately he missed two catches, neither of them by any means easy, in the Test Match at Lord's, and the Selection Committee did not again consider his claims. I am not saying that they were wrong, but what I mean to say is, that despite his failure as a batsman and in the field in that match, Evans was an England cricketer. Evans distinguished himself greatly in the 1914–18 war in the Flying Corps, and his book—*The Escaping Club*—is one of the most thrilling narratives I have ever read.

No one ever played fast bowling better than *P. A. Perrin*. His record for Essex is splendid, but for some reason or other, he over and over again declined the invitation of the M.C.C. committee to play for the Gentlemen *v.* Players at Lord's, though he did actually appear in one match, in 1906.

Very tall, Perrin had a beautiful style, and so superb was his back play that he used to play the fastest bowlers—and it should be remembered that in his prime there were many great fast bowlers in England—with ease.

Perrin was accounted a slow field, and so he was, if placed in the long-field or cover-point, but at short third man, or in 'the gully,' as it is called, he has brought off many fine catches. Perrin never played for England, but as a batsman pure and simple he was quite good enough to do so. He is a fine judge of the game and in recent years has been an invaluable member of the Selection Committee in Test Matches.

*Russell*, of Essex, is a son of Tom Russell, the old Essex wicket-keeper, and was a batsman for whom I had considerable admiration. He scored a hundred in the fourth and fifth Test Matches in England in 1921, though the last hundred cannot be placed in the ordinary category of Test Match hundreds, as the greater part of it was made not even against the change bowlers of the Australian XI. He also scored a century in the third Test Match at Adelaide in January 1921, and in the six Test Matches in which he took part he scored over 100 in three of them, in addition to a double century *v.* South Africa, at Durban.

Russell obtained most of his runs on the on-side, but he could, when he liked, drive very swiftly past extra-cover, and many critics thought that he did not develop the off-side part of his game as much as he might have done.

There have been few better hitters than *F. T. Mann*, the old Middlesex captain. Not even Thornton or Lyons, Bonnor or Jessop could have driven a longer ball than some of Mann's longest drives.

He once hit a ball on to the top of the covered seats opposite to the pavilion at Lord's, the ball bouncing some twenty yards into the practice ground, and this against something of a breeze. This great hit was made off a ball from Macaulay in the Middlesex and Yorkshire match at Lord's in 1920. I have also seen Mann hit a ball into the St. John's Wood Road, while he has bombarded the pavilion seats at Lord's on several occasions, and against Yorkshire, he once drove Rhodes three times in one over on to the top of the pavilion at Lord's.

By no means was he a hitter purely and simply, for he possessed a good defence, and some of his innings can well be described as great.

Mann had something of the quality of George Hirst at mid-off, where he was a veritable sand-bank, no drive being too hard for him to hold. He led Middlesex to the championship in 1921.

Mann was thrice wounded, severely, during the 1914–18 war.

*George Gunn*, a nephew of William Gunn, batted extremely well in Australia, scoring over a hundred in two of the Test Matches in the winter of 1907–8, and playing almost equally well in 1911–12. He was, at his best, one of the finest batsmen in England, but his play varied owing to indifferent health. It was easy for anybody to see that he was naturally a very fine player, with an easy, graceful style, great quickness of foot, and plenty of strokes. At his best there was something verging on genius about his play. He made bowling look very easy, and he was a fine slip.

There was assuredly no better all-round cricketer in England between 1907 and 1914 than *Tarrant*. Born in Australia, he is related to a great English cricketer of bygone days, Tarrant, the famous fast bowler of the sixties, and he was little over twenty years of age when he decided to come to the land of his ancestors and try his luck. For years he was the mainstay of Middlesex. Season after season he scored his thousand runs and took his hundred wickets, and he was the man an England eleven was in want of at the time. But the rules regarding qualification were not altogether logical, and Tarrant was a sort of No Man's Lander. He might not play for Australia, and he might not play for England, though he was good enough for any eleven in the world.

Tarrant was a most determined and resourceful, if not a pretty, batsman. He played back splendidly with his bat well up against his right leg, and watched the ball like a cat does a mouse. He seldom played right forward, indulging in a sort of half-cock stroke which, though ungainly, was very effective. He was a remarkably good hitter on the on-side, and played off his legs beautifully, but when all is said and done his glory was the cut. At this stroke he had no superior. Tarrant was, in a sense, a curious bowler. On a good wicket he would keep a perfect length, and yet more than once on a sticky wicket, when he had only to bowl a length to get the other side out as fast as they could come in, he would send down full pitches and long hops. This failing probably arose from an endeavour to spin the ball too much, but if he did happen to hit off his length when the ground was helping him, it was fairly safe to assume that his opponents would not bat for long. Tarrant is about the only Australian I know who could not throw, but he was an excellent and very keen field at mid-off, or at short-leg, or in the slips.

I saw *Rhodes* play his first match for Yorkshire, *v.* M.C.C., at Lord's, in May 1898. On that occasion he went in to bat last. Thirteen years later he was going in first with Hobbs for England *v.* Australia, at Melbourne, and helping to break the record for the first wicket in Test matches. In an earlier chapter an attempt has been made to give some idea of the beauty and greatness of his bowling, but though his name will no doubt be remembered more as a bowler than as a batsman, his record as an all-round cricketer surpasses even that of Hirst. On sixteen occasions he scored over 1,000 runs and obtained over a 100 wickets in an English summer; making over 2,000 runs in 1909 and 1911. Rhodes was a very great cricketer from the beginning to the end of his career. Mr. Neville Cardus calls him 'the legendary Rhodes. History hangs about the man.'

His bowling was a thing of joy, a delight to the eye, all grace and ease and effortless rhythm, and if his batsmanship was not really distinguished for style, he was an extremely sound player, with two or three effective strokes, who knew exactly how much to essay. His was a rare cricket brain, and he made use of it. There have scarcely ever been two better runners between wickets than Hobbs and Rhodes. The understanding between them was so perfect that seldom did they call for a run. His first Test Match, in 1899, was W. G.'s last, and when he was recalled to the colours for the final Test at the Oval in 1926 there were three men— Chapman, Stevens, and Larwood—in the England XI who were not born in 1899! What a welcome the crowd gave him, and the young generation gazed upon a slow bowler whose peer the world has seldom seen.

*C. L. Townsend* began playing for Gloucestershire when he was a schoolboy at Clifton. As he grew he developed his batting immensely, but, as so often happens, to the detriment of his bowling. F. G. J. Ford, at his best, ran him close, and H. T. Hewett (for a season or two about 1892) and the late F. M. Lucas were very fine left-handers, but I do not think that any of these were quite the equal of Townsend. Townsend was very tall, and made the most of his height, and while retaining all his old powers of defence was an extremely fine hitter as well. When he played regularly he was in the habit of making his thousand runs and taking his hundred wickets a season. His father, Frank Townsend, was a great Gloucestershire player in the seventies and early eighties, and his son's record at cricket and 'Soccer' at Oxford is an interesting continuation of the story.

*J. R. Mason* was captain of the Winchester eleven in 1893, and in August of that year he made his first appearance in the Kent eleven. For years he was the most interesting personality of that famous team, and his popularity was immense. From Catford to Dover and from Tunbridge Wells to Canterbury, Men of Kent and Kentish Men—and ladies too—united in praising 'Jack' Mason. Mason was the finest all-round cricketer Kent have ever had, with the one exception of Woolley. As a slip-fielder he was in the very front rank; indeed, it would be hard to name a better. He had a great reach, big hands, a sure eye, and was quick in moving to the ball. He took his chances without the least fuss, and I put him in the same class as R. E. Foster, A. O. Jones, Tunnicliffe, K. L. Hutchings, Hammond, and Braund as a slip-fielder.

Mason was the best cricketer who has never played for England in England, though he was 'in reserve' on one occasion. He went to Australia with Stoddart's second team, and if his batting, after a good start, was disappointing, he bowled well, and his fielding was greatly admired. Mason was an admirable captain, and a sound judge of the game. His modesty was proverbial.

*J. T. Brown* was a very fine batsman.   He and Tunnicliffe, the one short and thick-set, the other exceptionally tall, used to go in first for Yorkshire, and many a big score did they put up.   Their first-wicket record stood for thirty-four years— they put on 551 runs before they were parted for Yorkshire *v.* Derbyshire at Chesterfield in August 1898.   Brown excelled at the late cut and the 'chop,' and made great use of a forcing stroke just in front of point, while he was very fond of what may be called a half-arm hook stroke, which he frequently brought into use on sticky wickets.   He seldom drove straight or past mid-off, and was, perhaps, apt to fall to a catch at the wicket or in the slips on first going in, but on his day he was brilliant in the power and variety of his cutting.   When he was first seen in the nets in Australia, Major Wardill, the secretary of the Melbourne Club, to whom many generations of English cricketers are indebted for much kindness, remarked that 'Brown won't make ten runs on the tour'; but he was utterly wrong, and it shows how deceptive form in a net may be, for Brown was very near the top of the averages of Stoddart's first team, and played a great innings of 140 at a critical point in the final Test Match, when the score stood at 'two all.'   Brown used to lisp, and his repeated 'Steathdy, John, steathdy,' when either he or John Tunnicliffe was nearing his 50, was a feature of a Yorkshire match.   He died, to the regret of all, at the early age of thirty-five.

I have never seen a cricketer at the age of nineteen quite so good as *J. N. Crawford* was.   He went straight from Repton into the Surrey eleven, and at once established himself as an invaluable all-rounder, scoring in his first season of county cricket over a thousand runs and taking a hundred wickets.   Standing straight up to his work, Craw-ford had an attractive style of batting, and delighted in straight driving.   Many a ball has he put on to the top of, or into, the Oval pavilion, and he made one of the biggest hits I have ever seen at Lord's, the ball pitching on the top balcony of the pavilion. On a wicket that did anything he was a dangerous bowler, and even on the best of wickets he generally managed to get some work on the ball. He did very well both in Australia and in South Africa for M.C.C., and was in the England eleven here against the South Africans in the summer of 1907. Subsequently he went to Australia, and did great things for South Australia.

Born in Cambridgeshire, *Hobbs* was recommended to the Surrey authorities by Hayward, and from the moment he appeared in the county eleven in the summer of 1905 it was obvious that here indeed was a player of high class. He stood forth a batsman splendidly equipped at every point. Always on the look-out to score, his quickness of foot enabled him to get into position in plenty of time for his stroke, and he was exceptionally strong on the on-side, in playing off his legs, hooking, and pulling, while he had a neat and effective late cut, and drove well past cover-point. He invariably batted magnificently in Australia, while his batting in South Africa was described as 'wonderful.' 'Over and over again he started off with three fours in the first over, and the South African bowlers seemed unable to bowl a length to him. It was like Trumper in 1902.' Hobbs was a fine field at cover-point, with a safe pair of hands and a very smart return. He was crisp and neat in all his movements, and gave one the impression of thoroughly enjoying every ball of a match. His record in Test Matches, both here and in Australia, is outstanding, and from about 1910 to 1928 he was the best batsman in the world. He won many matches for England and was always at his best on the big occasion. His style was the acme of ease and perfection, and he excelled on every sort of wicket and against every type of bowling. A charming character, he

o

is as popular in Australia as he is in England. To hear him talk one would think that he had never made a run in his life. He, if any one, represents 'the straight bat and a modest mind.' He has beaten many records, and has been an example and an inspiration to many. If 'W. G.' was the Champion, Hobbs is the Master.

*Woolley* is very tall, and makes the most glorious strokes, his long swing and power of timing enabling him to drive a long ball. His driving and back play being extraordinary, and his off-driving and cutting are equally fine. He was, in the opinion of many, the greatest of all left-handed batsmen—I would rather see him bat than any one. He remains one of the big figures of cricket, and his batting has given sheer delight to thousands both here and in Australia. He can hit the ball straight over the bowler's head with great power, and he has a very fine forcing stroke past mid-on off a ball just short of a good length. When bowling Woolley had a nice action after the manner of Blythe, but he was faster through the air, and brought the ball down from a greater height. He could be very difficult on a sticky wicket, but he has bowled little in recent years. He was a fine field either in the slips or at short leg, and was about the best all-round cricketer in England twenty years ago. He has been called 'The Pride of Kent.'

*Mead* (of Hampshire) was a left-handed batsman. His position at the wicket was rather ungainly, as there was a somewhat awkward bending of the knees, but in actual playing the ball his style was good and his defence sound. Like most left-handers he was very strong in all the leg-side strokes, and he drove well on both sides of the wicket. He was quick on his feet, frequently jumping in to slow or medium bowling, and he was one of the best players of googly bowling. His record for Hampshire is extremely good, and he has made centuries for England *v.* Australia and South Africa, and for the Players *v.* Gentlemen. He was a fine slip.

*J. W. Hearne* kept up, and more than kept up, the reputation of a famous cricketing family, for apart from his skill as a googly bowler, referred to in a previous chapter, he was—at one time—on a hard true wicket and against the highest class of bowling, the second best batsman, next to Hobbs, in England. His style of batting was remarkably sound in method. On a sticky, difficult wicket he was not so good, perhaps, as several others; but in fine weather, and on a good wicket, he was as likely as not to make a century against any bowling in the world. Before he was twenty-one he had scored a hundred for England *v.* Australia, and for Players *v.* Gentlemen, and on the M.C.C. tours in Australia in 1911–12 he was called, by the Australian critics, 'the young Arthur Shrewsbury'—a high compliment indeed. With good health and freedom from accident he would have been second to none as an all-rounder.

The name of *Hendren* was closely associated with that of J. W. Hearne in the Middlesex eleven, but he was a different type of player. He was a far more brilliant batsman, and when he was going there were few cricketers better worth watching. He was an extraordinarily powerful driver, and a master of the hook shot.

A fine fieldsman, he excelled in any position, and he played the game with a *joie de vivre* which was a tonic to his colleagues. He began disappointingly in the two Test Matches in which he played in 1921, but subsequently he did very well on tours in Australia, and on occasions in England. It is the fashion to say that his record in Test Matches is only moderate; but figures show the contrary. In his career he made 57,610 runs and scored 170 centuries with an average of 50·81. He also made 725 catches. He was a great favourite wherever he played and he deserved his immense popularity. An Irishman, he had a ready, but never an unkind, wit. He left the cricket field in a blaze of glory and affection, for when he came out to bat in his last match at Lord's, the large crowd sang 'For he's a jolly good fellow' and cheered for several minutes. His reply was a splendid innings of 103. I regard Hendren and Hearne as my 'children' for I 'brought them up.' I am very proud of them.

*J. W. H. T. Douglas* played a very big part in cricket. A better man at the crisis of a match I have never known. He was determination and perseverance incarnate, and his coolness was remarkable. He was never ruffled. When he began he was but a moderate cricketer, but he developed into one of the best all-round men of his time, and his record between 1910–21 was extremely good. A very sound batsman with a superb defence, his bowling, on his best days, was even more remarkable. For years he bore the brunt of the bowling for the Gentlemen *v.* Players, and the Gentlemen never possessed two finer bowlers on hard wickets than he and F. R. Foster. Fast-medium, he could swing the ball either way, he kept a length, and his deliveries came quickly off the ground. He never tired, and he put his whole soul in every ball he bow'ed. His bowling in the Gentlemen *v.* Players matches at Lord's in 1911 and 1914 will never be forgotten, and his name will live in the history of cricket. Hobbs held his bowling in high repute, saying, 'He always has a good one for me.' His deeds for Essex would fill a volume, and he has been a fine Test Match player. His death by drowning in the North Sea in December 1930, was a great blow to his many friends—and he had friends amongst both young and old cricketers.

*P. G. H. Fender* was for many seasons one of the best all-round cricketers of the day. No one would call him an orthodox batsman, but he was a very dangerous one, having something of the 'Jessopian' quality about him. He was the sort of cricketer who could win a match for his side by half an hour's daring hitting.

Fender was a clever bowler who could turn the ball both ways, though the real difficulty of his bowling lay in the fact that he so often deceived the batsman in the flight of the ball. A fine fieldsman in the slips, Fender was an admirable captain. He possessed tremendous enthusiasm, had a fine knowledge of tactics, could get the best out of the men under him, and always lived in the game. He is a fine judge of cricket.

*Lord Tennyson* is a grandson of the poet, and his cricket comes from his mother's side, whose brother, Cecil Boyle, was a great bowler at Oxford. He was two years in the Eton XI, getting his place in the first year as a fast bowler, and though he scored 38 and 51 not out in the Freshmen's match in 1909, he was not thought good enough for a trial in any of the Cambridge fixtures.

Soon after he went into the army, and little was heard of him until July 1913, when, playing for M.C.C. against Oxford, he scored a brilliant 100. Soon after that he was asked to play for Hampshire, and in successive matches played innings of 28, 36, 116, 111, and 4, also 96 and 19, and within a month of his first appearance at Lord's he was quite a celebrity.

He went out to South Africa in the winter of 1913–14 with the M.C.C. team, but met with little success on the matting wickets. In 1914 he was disappointing, and neither in 1919 nor 1920 did he do anything out of the ordinary, but in 1921 he batted in fine form, and had the distinction of captaining England in the last three Test Matches. His innings at Leeds will never be forgotten, for badly handi-capped as he was by an injured hand, he rose superior to all difficulties. Very powerfully built, he hit the ball hard in front of the wicket, relying chiefly on hard driving for his runs. He could also hit a short ball very hard on the off-side, and he had a very good pulled-drive.

A most enthusiastic cricketer, under his captaincy Hamp-shire in one season, 1921, obtained a finer record than ever before in their history. He is one of those men of whom it may well be said that he loves cricket.

*E. Tyldesley* is a brother of J. T. Tyldesley. He was not, perhaps, a very good starter, there being a certain hesitancy in his play when he first went in, but let him remain at the wickets for twenty minutes or so and he became a brilliant batsman. Many of his strokes were reminiscent of his famous brother, one of the greatest batsmen England has ever had, and without a superior on a soft wicket. Tyldesley was a fine hooker and could also drive straight, and was a fine player of fast bowling. He was a great success on the matting wickets in South Africa, and no captain could wish for a better and more loyal chief of staff.

*V. W. C. Jupp* distinguished himself greatly as an all-round cricketer. He bowled medium-slow right-hand, varied with an occasional slower one and his deliveries came off quickly. If the wicket was at all worn he could be very effective, spinning the ball a great deal from the off. Jupp was an attractive batsman, for he cut and drove well.

He was an excellent field, particularly on the off-side, and altogether an all-round cricketer who should, perhaps, have gone even farther than he did. In ten out of thirteen seasons after the war he completed the 'double.' He was asked to go to Australia in 1920, but was compelled to decline.

*N. Haig*, who succeeded F. T. Mann in the captaincy of Middlesex, is a nephew of the late Lord Harris, and one of the keenest and most enthusiastic cricketers living. Though by no means physically strong he had tremendous vitality, and he could bowl half the day and bat the other half.

He bowled fast-medium, made the ball come quickly off the ground, and swerved the new ball in rather awkward fashion for the batsman in the first few overs. For many seasons he did great work for Middlesex. He was a natural ball-game player.

*Sandham's* batting was built on the soundest lines. Very painstaking and keen, he learned a great deal from going in first with Hobbs, though he did not resemble that batsman in any degree. The keynote of Sandham's batting was soundness, but he had plenty of strokes. His many partnerships with Hobbs have delighted the Surrey crowd, and, like Holmes, only Sutcliffe's outstanding success prevented him opening regularly for England. In the long-field and at deep third man he was a fast runner and accurate thrower.

*Holmes*, of Yorkshire, played for England in the first Test Match at Nottingham in 1921, and played very well in the first innings, and although he was twelfth man in the second Test Match at Lord's he did not again actually figure in the English XI until 1932, when he played *v.* India at Lord's.

Holmes's performances for Yorkshire have been very noteworthy. He did not drive very much, but was a master of the square cut and the hook stroke, and a most difficult man to get out. Some Yorkshiremen believe that he was an even better batsman than Sutcliffe; but this is surely an exaggeration. Holmes was no doubt unlucky in not being more often selected for England, but it was impossible to alter the famous first-wicket combination of Hobbs and Sutcliffe, which proved so tremendously successful in match after match. But Holmes on his part can point to in-numerable great first-wicket partnerships with Sutcliffe, including the record, 555 *v.* Essex at Leyton in 1932. Holmes was also a fine long-fielder with a safe pair of hands.

*Brown*, of Hampshire, was in some respects the best all-round cricketer in England, for he fielded superbly at mid-off, was an able wicket-keeper, a determined and good, if not a great, batsman, and a fair bowler. At one period he was a fast bowler, but time lessened his pace. A beautifully built man, he was extraordinarily active and strong, and played the game with great enthusiasm and zest.

*A. P. F. Chapman* was one of the personalities of the cricket field, and has been a great and happy figure. He was a glorious field anywhere, and especially in the slips, at short third man, or at silly-point. He brought off many amazing catches, and for England *v.* the West Indies at the Oval he made the best catch I have ever seen at third slip. The ball was going fast, and feet wide of Chapman, but he got to it, and held the ball low down with his right hand, lying full-length on the ground. A dashing left-handed batsman with tremendously strong wrists and forearms, he achieved many a triumph, including centuries for Cambridge *v.* Oxford, for Gentlemen *v.* Players, and for England *v.* Australia. He led England to victory over Australia at the Oval in the famous match of 1926, and won the rubber 4–1 in Australia in 1928–9. He was also captain of England in four matches in 1930. He was captain of Kent for some years, and a very successful one. Built on ample lines, Chapman was none the less very active.

*A. E. R. Gilligan* learnt his cricket at Dulwich and developed it at Cambridge. Later he captained Sussex, and the revival of that county was very largely due to his enthusiastic and cheerful leadership. His fielding at mid-off was one of the sights of the game, for he was quick on his feet, brilliant with either hand, and he had a smart return. He was also a clean hitter and a more than useful fast bowler who, if his arm was rather too low to satisfy the canons of style, could do something with the ball in the air. At all events he was a good enough bowler, with Tate, to dismiss South Africa on a *perfect wicket*, at Edgbaston, in 1924, for a total of 30, eleven of which were extras. He captained England against South Africa in 1924—and the M.C.C. team in Australia at the end of that year. He did little as a bowler or batsman in Australia, but his fielding is still remembered, and he was a popular captain. Perhaps he was too easy-going and too ready to concede a point, but men liked playing under him, for he was encouraging and his fielding an inspiration. He was also selected by M.C.C. to captain their team in India in 1926–7. Altogether he played a big part in the game, and Sussex, especially, owe much to him. He never was quite the same cricketer as before after a terrible blow under the heart in a Gentlemen *v.* Players match at the Oval.

*A. W. Carr* led Nottinghamshire for many years with distinction, his captaincy being well-balanced, enthusiastic, and courageous. I first met him on the cricket field when, as a boy of seventeen, he made some thirty or forty runs *v.* Middlesex, hitting the ball very hard even at that early age. Subsequently he became very prominent amongst English cricketers—a powerful batsman with a smashing drive, who hit more with his shoulders than with shoulder and wrist combined, and a fine field in the slips or at short-leg, and a captain to whom the Nottinghamshire bowlers, and especially Larwood, were greatly indebted for careful working. Never did he bowl Larwood one over too many. Nottinghamshire have had such admirable captains in the past as J. A. Dixon and A. O. Jones, and Carr who led England *v.* Australia in

1926 in four matches out of five was not the least admirable of them, for he was a thoroughly sound judge of a cricketer. Carr is a good man across country, but whether, like Noah Mann of old, he can pick up a handkerchief off the ground while galloping I do not know.

*I. A. R. Peebles* is a natural bowler with a beautiful action. Very tall, he brings the ball down from a great height, flights it—Woolley once remarked of him: 'He is a fine bowler before he pitches'—and can turn it both ways, though in recent years his leg-break has lost much of its former spin. There can be no doubt that he has been over-bowled. He began young and too much work was thrown on him. His best years were 1929, 1930, and 1931, but an injured shoulder caused a temporary set-back. Few bowlers have had greater command of the googly. He can bowl it at will, make it turn very quickly, and withal keep a length, but he possibly overdoes it. To a left-handed batsman he is particularly dangerous. Peebles is an ardent bowler. He always has a ball in his hand, and if he is not in a match he is generally at the nets. He is a fine fieldsman at short-leg or at short third man with a safe pair of hands, and fields his own bowling extremely well.

*R. W. V. Robins* is one of those cricketers who galvanize a side. Batting, bowling, or fielding, he is full of life and energy, and so obviously enjoying every ball. The first time I saw him bowl was for Cambridge *v.* The West Indies in 1928. His going on at all was treated as an experiment, which was regarded with something akin to mirth on the top of the pavilion at Fenners; but he bowled his leg-breaks and googlies extremely well and with great success, and from that time his bowling has been of great value to any side. With a short run up to the crease he imparts tremendous spin to the ball, and on his day can win a match in half an hour; but, for some unaccountable reason, he is only a moderate bowler to left-handed batsmen. There are few finer fieldsmen, for he excels in any position, and as a batsman, being very quick on his feet, he is always attacking the bowler. He was asked to go to Australia with the M.C.C. team in 1932, but was compelled to decline. Short in height, he is the essence of activity and keenness—the sort of cricketer who is always interesting to watch. He was an excellent and most inspiring captain of Middlesex, and was also a fine Association footballer.

*H. Sutcliffe* is a cricketer for whom I have a great admiration. At the end of a Test Match, at Leeds, I congratulated him on a splendid innings, and he replied: 'I love a fight' —which is the keynote of his cricket. There may be other batsmen who are greater in pure technique, but Sutcliffe was essentially a big match player. Nothing upset him, nothing destroyed his equanimity. He could be beaten three balls in succession, and yet he went on his way just as if he had hit those three balls for four each. He was a great player. His deeds for Yorkshire would fill many a page, and in Test Matches he has a glorious record. In his first two games for England *v.* Australia he scored 59 and 115 at Sydney, followed by 176 and 127 at Melbourne. On that tour (1924-5) he scored four centuries in the Test Matches. His two finest innings *v.* Australia have been, I think, his 135 on a sticky wicket at Melbourne, and his 161 at the Oval in the memorable 1926 match, seven-eighths of it on a pitch which gave the bowler every assistance, heavy rain in the night having been followed by hot August sunshine. Finer cricket than he and Hobbs played I have never seen. Indeed, England never possessed a finer first-wicket pair than Hobbs and Sutcliffe. Eleven times have they shared in a partnership of over a hundred runs *v.* Australia. Sutcliffe's defence was perfect and his judgment rarely, if ever, at fault, he knew exactly how much to attempt. He was a superb hooker of any ball the least short, a good leg hitter—often sweeping a bowler like Grimmett to long-leg—and, indeed, exceptionally strong in all on-side strokes. His off-driving was, occasionally, very good, and he could cut square effectively and safely. On the short side, but so neatly built that he looked taller than he was, Sutcliffe nearly always played without a hat, or cap, and his beautifully brushed hair which never seems to become ruffled even during the longest innings is as well known at Sydney, Johannesburg, or Bombay, as at Lord's, the Oval, or Headingley.

Like A. P. F. Chapman, the *Nawab of Pataudi* has made centuries for England *v*. Australia, for Gentlemen *v*. Players, at Lord's, and in the University matches—in this last instance 238 not out, the record individual score in this contest. Coming to England when a boy of fifteen or sixteen he owed a great deal to the coaching of Woolley. His method has been developed on the soundest lines, he has a wonderful eye, lissome wrists and plenty of strokes; but he must allow no one to persuade him to curb his natural style, which is an almost ideal combination of defence and attack. His innings of 165 for the Gentlemen, in 1932, was a masterly effort against such bowlers as Larwood, Tate, Voce, Freeman, and Hammond, which made a lasting impression on those who saw it.

*Ames* is undoubtedly the best wicket-keeping batsman England has had. Very quick on his feet he is a great lover of a half-volley, and his stroke play is both varied and strong. At one time he was not at all certain against the highest class of bowling, but constant practice in the best company has brought vast improvement in this respect. His performances in recent years have been conspicuously good. He made over 3,000 runs in 1933, over 2,000 in 1932, '34, and '37, and over 1,000 eight times. A century *v.* Australia, at Lord's, in 1934, three against the West Indies and two against South Africa are also to his credit.

The critics have been at variance as to his exact ability as a wicket-keeper, but figures speak for themselves, and he has three times dismissed 100 men in a season. In Australia in 1932–3 and in 1936–7 he kept very finely and his missed chances in the many Test Matches in which he has taken part can be counted on the fingers of one hand.

Whatever his lack of success on Australian wickets, *Freeman* is the best googly bowler England has ever had. He obtained 304 wickets in 1928, and in seven other seasons he took over 200 wickets. Between 1927–31—that is five seasons—his 'bag' amounted to 1,303 wickets! Twice he has taken 17 wickets in a match, thrice 16, five times 15, ten times 14—these figures speak for themselves. Freeman will surely rank amongst the great bowlers of history. His accuracy of length and direction are amazing—he flights and spins the ball—and he could, and often did, bowl most of the day for Kent. There was great economy of effort in his action, for he took a very short run, and always appeared to be bowling well within himself.

It is said that Essex, for whom his brother did useful work as a batsman, failed to appreciate his merits, but he was not only half, but three-quarters of Kent's bowling for many years. One of the smallest men who every played first-class cricket, Freeman rejoiced in the nickname of 'Little Tich,' and he and the six-foot-three Woolley were the idols of every cricket ground in Kent.

I first met *D. R. Jardine* in the summer of 1919 during a match, at Lord's, between a public schools' eleven and a team which the M.C.C. had asked me to get together.

Jardine had that year been captain at Winchester, and according to H. S. Altham, 'about the best boy captain I have ever seen.' Previous to that I had known his father—the hero of a great hundred in the University match of 1892. He used to come down to Rugby to play for Balliol against the school, and gave a small boy kindly encouragement which was much appreciated.

When in 1931 I came into closer contact with the son, I realized—it was easy to do so—that here was a man who was a thorough student of the game of cricket, keen and competent, one who had thought much and pondered deeply over the tactics and strategy of the game and, incidentally, a stern critic of his own cricketing abilities. The coming tour to Australia appeared to him in the light of a crusade, and it was certain that he would put his whole soul and endeavour into the work in front of him. Backed by my colleagues, I recommended him to the M.C.C. committee in an appreciation of the situation which is, no doubt, in the archives of Lord's.

It appears that on his previous visit to Australia with Chapman's M.C.C. team, Jardine had neither understood nor been understood by the Australians. Unfortunately he was not *sympatica* to them, nor they to him, and the actual result of the 1932-3 tour, though it brought us a great triumph, was at a great price, and left many people wondering whether cricket was really a game.

Jardine, through a storm of controversy which is quite unparalleled in the history of cricket, refused to bow his head and his courage and determination are not to be gainsaid.

In regard to his abilities as a cricketer, Jardine is undoubtedly a fine and stylish batsman. With his great height he is a remarkably good player of fast and fast-medium bowling, but he is not quick on his feet and is far less at home to slow spin bowling. There have been few better batsmen at a crisis, and over and over again he has set right the failure of half his side. He gave convincing evidence of this in the Test Match against the Indians at Lord's in 1932, when after England had made a disastrous start in both innings he came to the rescue with superb innings of 79 and 85 not out. There is, indeed, no one whom I would rather see going in to bat when things are desperate. Nevertheless, it is to be wished that he would pay more attention to his off-side strokes, for he undoubtedly has the capacity to score more freely in that direction. At present an opposing side is able to pin down his rate of scoring to little more than 20 runs an hour. He plays too much off his back foot and does not make enough use of his left shoulder. As a fieldsman he developed into a very safe catch in 'the gulley,' and some of the catches which he made in that position were really splendid. Jardine is a many-sided man. He is versed in the law, he has read a good deal, and he is an ardent shot and fisherman. He is, too, a good racquets and squash racquets player.

*W. R. Hammond* stands out as the best all-rounder in the world to-day. He is, indeed, a glorious cricketer, who is at his best when playing a forcing game which is his natural bent. To an exact sense of timing he adds great physical strength, and when he makes up his mind to hit, the ball literally flies off his bat. A beautiful off-side player, his back strokes are as hard and as clean as his forward or driving strokes—and when he is in, cover-point, mid-off, and extra-cover are kept very busy indeed. On the on-side his stroke play is far stronger and more varied than it was. An easy style, quickness of foot and wrists like steel make him most attractive to watch even when he is scoring slowly.

One of the most dramatic moments in the Test Matches in Australia in 1932–3 was when Wall sent his off-stump flying yards in the first innings of the second game at Melbourne.  He had begun with a couple of fours, and looked about to play a big innings, and on his dismissal a shout went up such as I have never heard on any cricket ground in the world.   There were 63,000 spectators present, and for several minutes they yelled and cheered and waved their hats and handkerchiefs.   The almost frantic rejoicing was a rare compliment to a great batsman.

Hammond is a valuable fast-medium bowler with a perfect action, and his fielding, too, in the slips reaches something like perfection.   Everything Hammond does on the cricket field bears the hall-mark of natural genius.   The ideal cricketer.

One of my most vivid memories of Hammond is his batting at Sydney with Grimmett bowling, Richardson at mid-off, Bradman at extra-cover and Fingleton at cover.   At one moment he would be moving down the pitch, at another moving back for his famous 'back' stroke, while the fieldsmen picked up these 'red hot' strokes with amazing speed and accuracy.   It was indeed the game of cricket at its highest level.

In all first-class cricket, Hammond has scored 47,145 runs with an average of 55·72.   In Test cricket he has played 125 innings, scored 6,883 runs, made 101 catches, and taken 83 wickets.

One of his finest innings was 32 on an absolute 'glue pot' at Melbourne in 1937.   The ball, even a half volley, was kicking up, and the bowlers could turn the ball feet, but even in these adverse conditions, 'Hammond made strokes and played an innings which I shall never forget' as one of the England eleven put it.   Those who have played on or seen a sticky Melbourne wicket will appreciate the greatness of the performance.

One interesting feature about Hammond's cricket is that he seldom, if ever, hooks.   He forces the ball that others would attempt to hook past the bowler or through the

D. R. JARDINE

M. W. TATE

A good action—notice the use he is making of his left arm

cover-point region. And in this connection, I would recommend an article by Major C. H. B. Pridham in the *Cricketer Spring Annual* of 1937 in which he points out how often the greatest batsmen have been dismissed in attempting to hook.

His record *v.* Australia is very fine indeed. He has scored eight centuries against them, including a double one—119 not out and 177 at Adelaide in 1929, 251 at Sydney, and 200 at Melbourne on the same tour. He may well equal Hobbs's record of twelve centuries. He has also made three centuries *v.* South Africa, and three *v.* New Zealand, including 336, a record in Test Matches, at Auckland, in 1933.

*Verity*, to a certain extent, played the part in 1932–3 that J. C. White filled so well on the 1928–9 tour in Australia, for he kept an end going even when not taking wickets. But he went further than that, and in the fifth Test at Sydney in 1933 accomplished a great performance in the second innings. Australia had 119 runs on the board with Bradman and Woodfull well set—and Larwood off the field with a badly injured foot. At this critical point Verity bowled Bradman and then ran through the rest of the side. He may be said to have won that match for England. Verity had a beautiful action and could bowl all day. He startled the cricket world in 1931 when, almost unknown, he took all ten wickets against Warwickshire. He accomplished this feat again in the next season, against Notts, and, as before, at Leeds. He was a keen thinker, and a close student of the game, who was always planning a method of attack. But his greatest performance was in the Test Match at Lord's in 1934 when he obtained fifteen wickets for 104 runs, thus excelling Rhodes' fifteen wickets for 124 runs at Melbourne in 1904. With the turf false Verity kept a perfect length and made the ball turn and lift. He was backed up by brilliant fielding, Hammond and Hendren being superb. I am told that one very famous

P

Yorkshireman thinks Verity was an even better bowler than Rhodes. It is unnecessary to argue the point here, but there is this to be said—that Verity could bowl to the great Bradman with a silly point on a perfect wicket and keep him quiet, and I wonder whether Rhodes could have done that. Like Rhodes, he bowled first and went in first for England. He was always a safe catch and no one who saw it will forget his magnificent catch at backward point which got rid of McCabe in the Test Match at Lord's in 1938.

Verity was mortally wounded in Sicily as he led his Company to the attack. His last words were 'keep going.'

*Voce* is a far better bowler when he bowls a length with two slips than when he crowds the leg-side with fieldsmen. A magnificently built man his left-handed action is easy and fluent and he is an impressive bowler to watch. His pace varies from fast to fast-medium and he can both make the ball go with his arm and čome back. At his best he is a great bowler, and G. O. Allen tells me that in Australia in 1936–7 he bowled splendidly in the first three Test Matches. Afterwards he was handicapped by a strain. On the previous tour in 1932–33 he was an important factor in England's success, he, Larwood, Allen, Verity, and Hammond making up a fine combination. Voce is a fine fieldsman with a fast low return.

Between 1922 and 1929 *Maurice Tate* was a great bowler. Fast-medium right hand, he made tremendous pace off the ground, and though not a spin bowler he could make the ball do a little both ways. At his best he bowled the ball which comes with a right-handed bowler's arm perfectly. Very powerfully built he possessed great stamina, and his bowling in Australia in 1924–5 won tremendous praise. On that tour he obtained 38 wickets in the Test Matches for an average of 23·15 runs—this being the highest number of wickets taken by any bowler in a series of Test Matches. He has three times taken over 200 wickets in an English season, and in eight seasons in succession between 1922 and 1929 he scored over 1,000 runs and obtained over 100 wickets. He has, indeed, been a fine all-round cricketer, for, if a slow field, he was a safe catch near the wicket. I never knew a cricketer who worked harder or more keenly. He put his whole soul into every ball he bowled. Tate was a fine hitter, and his 100 not out for England v. South Africa, at Lord's in 1929, when runs were badly wanted, was a remarkable innings.

Tate was, and is, a great personality. He is as brown as a berry and must be nearly six feet in height, with large hips and enormous feet which are the delight of the caricaturist. He is always smiling and is exceedingly popular with both English and Australian crowds. His father before him played for England.

A keener cricketer than *R. E. S. Wyatt* never lived. He would willingly play every day all the year round. Always very fit, he is an invaluable member of a side, for besides being a sound and reliable batsman he is full of grit and courage. He is generally regarded as a defensive type of player, but he has plenty of strokes, and hit three sixes in his very fine first innings in the Adelaide Test of 1933, when he and Leyland retrieved a desperate situation after four wickets had fallen for 30 runs. He has made great improvement since that tour in Australia and is now a great batsman. He is also a useful medium-paced right-handed bowler. His fielding has improved immensely—and he saves many runs at deep third man by quickness and strong throwing. He never tires, no day being too long for him, and his enthusiasm is unending. He captained England v. Australia at the Oval in 1930, v. West Indies, also at the Oval, in 1933, and against South Africa in England in 1935. A lover of

Maori and Hawaiian music, he possesses a fine collection of gramophone records which he will play at any hour of the day or night. Wyatt is a great traveller and a good companion.

*M. Leyland* played two great innings at Adelaide and Brisbane in 1933 which helped very materially to win the two matches for England, innings which somehow have not received quite their full meed of praise. He played O'Reilly, Grimmett, and Ironmonger particularly well, his value as a left-handed batsman being emphasized against bowlers of their style. He liked Grimmett's bowling, and was always on the *qui vive* to move out of his ground to drive him. As a general rule, he blends caution well with aggression, though his natural game is that of an attacker. In 1934 *v.* Australia he made 109 at Lord's, 153 at Old Trafford, and 110 at the Oval, and altogether he has made seven centuries *v.* Australia, and two *v.* South Africa. No one plays O'Reilly quite so consistently well as he does. He seems to be O'Reilly's master and I fancy that great bowler would not greatly cavil at the suggestion. He is a great Test Match player. He is a fine deep field and is built on Yorkshire lines—short, strong, and sturdy. Leyland has music in his soul and sings a good song.

*J. C. White*, 'Senor Blanco,' as the dressing-room attendant on the Belgrano ground at Buenos Aires, used to call him, has been the mainstay of Somerset for twenty years and more, and during the course of his career must have sent down many thousands of overs. A slow left-handed bowler of quite exceptional accuracy and clever flight, he has commanded the respect of the best batsmen; and it was his skill and stamina which won the exciting Test Match at Adelaide, by 11 runs, in 1929. Even on the perfect Australian wickets he could 'shut up' an end and get men out, and he was one of the successes of that memor-able tour. He has also played for England *v.* Australia in England, and captained England *v.* South Africa. He has taken ten wickets in an innings, and as many as sixteen in one day. Somerset, for whom he made his first appearance in 1910, owe him more than they can ever repay.

White is a fine field to his own bowling, and a useful slip or mid-off. Jack is of a fair complexion, well-looking and of a pleasing aspect, and Dame Nature has given him a most amiable disposition. A better companion on a cricket tour it would be hard to imagine. Those who are versed in the mystery of cards tell me that he is no mean poker player.

In the summer of 1931, *F. R. Brown* was one of the finest leg-break googly bowlers I have ever seen. His pace was a little quicker than slow and he could spin the ball tremen-dously. His bowling, on a difficult wicket, in the Gentlemen *v.* Players match, at Lord's, won unstinted admiration from Sutcliffe, and on many occasions that summer he attained to greatness. Latterly he has fallen away, but there is no reason whatever why he should not recover his form. Like many bowlers of his type he needs encouragement, super-vision, and careful handling. Brown is a magnificent fields-man and a beautiful natural hitter. An innings of 200 for Surrey *v.* Middlesex, at the Oval, is an abiding memory with me, and it is on record that for Surrey *v.* Kent, at Black-heath, in 1932, he made 168 out of 206 in 125 minutes; at one period he made 50 runs in fifteen minutes.

The news that *K. S. Duleepsinhji* would be seen no more in first-class cricket was heard with the deepest regret by the cricketing world, especially as his early retirement was due to illness. As to his ability there can be no doubt at all that he was a great batsman and a great slip-fielder—a worthy successor, indeed, to his uncle, the famous 'Ranji.'

He was essentially a stroke player, who was always attacking the bowler, and his beautiful method, quickness of foot and eye, and his supple wrists made him almost as attractive to watch as Woolley, who, to me at any rate, remains the most attractive of all batsmen.

As a player of googly bowling in particular 'Duleep' was unsurpassed, as R. W. V. Robins and Freeman will readily admit. His presence would have made a great deal of difference to the M.C.C. team in Australia.

The first time I ever saw Duleep bat was when, as a boy of 15 or 16, he was playing in the Schools' Week at Lord's, and one was immediately taken by his exquisite late cutting and his easy methods.

At a later date he owed much to the late Major G. A. Faulkner, a superb all-round cricketer himself and a master coach, who set to work to cure him of a slight weakness which he at one time possessed outside the off-stump. Faulkner, of course, realized that he had got hold of a genius, and used to delight in bowling to him in the nets at the school which still bears his name. I remember in the spring of 1927 Faulkner saying to me: 'Come and have a look at Duleep. It isn't only a question of how to get him out, but how to stop him scoring 60 runs an hour.' That was in April, and cricketers will remember Duleep's magnificent batting for Cambridge in the early weeks of that season, until he was struck down with pleurisy after playing a glorious innings of 200 and more v. Middlesex—an illness which nearly proved fatal.

Of his deeds for Sussex, the Gentlemen, and England it is not necessary to speak, they are known to all; but it may be added that he made a most admirable captain for Sussex, managing his side with tact, discretion, and ability.

It is very sad to think that all this great skill—a skill which had not yet come to its full maturity, for Duleep was only twenty-eight when he retired—has been cut short by illness. But though we shall not again see him on the cricket field, everyone will hope for such a restoration to health that we may meet him on our grounds and in our pavilions in the years to come. He has written his name in letters of gold in the history of the greatest of all games, and we shall think of him not only as a splendid cricketer, but as a man whose demeanour and character evoked both affection and respect.

One word more. Ranji, of course, took the keenest possible interest in his cricket, perhaps at times too keen, for his standard was very high. I once remarked to him that he must be very proud of his nephew, and he replied: 'Yes, he's good, but he's careless.' A few minutes later Duleep was splendidly stumped on the leg-side by Oldfield, off Hornibrook, whereupon Ranji turned to me and said: 'There you are, Plum, what did I tell you? Duleep is careless, very careless.' 'Anyway, Ranji,' I replied, 'you are very proud of him.' And, with a charming smile, he said, 'Well, yes, I am.'

*C. J. Barnett* made his first appearance for Gloucestershire in 1927, when he was only seventeen, and I remember seeing him make a very good 50 *v.* Surrey, at the Oval, a year or two later. He is a most attractive batsman. Powerful, confident and free with a wealth of strokes—an attacker of the bowler from first to last. He has played some unforgettable innings, notably his 126 *v.* Australia, at Trent Bridge, in 1938; on that occasion, he made Fleetwood-Smith look a very ordinary bowler. He gives one the impression that the bowler is there to be hit, and hit uncommonly hard. He seems to like every kind of bowling, but has he not a weakness to a good length fast rising ball on the leg-stump? He is apt to take his eye off this type of ball, and with it, his bat, but so naturally great a player could easily remedy this defect.

Gloucestershire are lucky in having two such attractive batsmen as Barnett and Hammond, for they are great 'box office' draws.

Barnett is a safe catch and an active fieldsman at mid-off, in the deep, or at short-leg, and no bad medium-paced bowler. Both his father and two uncles played for the county so he is very much a Gloucestershire man.

It is interesting to note that four of the most 'crowd-compelling' cricketers hail from the West Country, Hammond and Barnett from Gloucestershire and Gimblett and Wellard from Somerset, not to mention the Champion and the Human Catapault of an earlier generation. In 1935, *Wellard* hit no fewer than 72 sixes—a record in first-class cricket since hits over the boundary have been so reckoned. A very fine figure of a man, his drives 'climbed the sky' and as he was also an excellent fast-medium right-handed bowler and a keen fieldsman, his value to Somerset was immense. Indeed it is scarcely an exaggeration to say that he was half the side. At Wells he hit Armstrong, of Derbyshire, a slow left-hander, for five sixes in succession. Somehow Kent overlooked him. He made heaps of runs and took lots of wickets for Bexley, but for some reason he failed to catch the eye of the county authorities. He has played for England and the Players, at Lord's, and his 38 in England's second innings *v.* Australia at Lord's in 1938, has not been given its full due. England were in the toils and he, with Compton, saved us. I shall not forget one of his hits, an on-drive into the balcony of the grandstand which a spectator stood up and caught with easy grace.

I recall W. Findlay, the then Secretary of M.C.C., asking me to 'have a look at *W. Bowes,*' who had but recently arrived at Lord's from Yorkshire Council Cricket, the County

Committee for once in a way having failed to 'spot' him. I had retired from first-class cricket several years earlier, but, greatly daring, put on my pads and went to the nets. There I found a very tall strongly built man, who, I thought, bowled very well. A purist might have said that his action was a trifle too full-fronted, but his arm was high, and he made the ball come quickly off the ground. He is easily the best fast-medium bowler in the country, and at Leeds and the Oval, *v.* the Australians in 1938, he touched greatness. Like David Harris of old he is often grinding the batsman's knuckles and, if I were playing to-day, I should be inclined to dislike his bowling. His length is accurate, he varies his pace, and there is 'ginger' in him. Bowes is not what would be called a good fieldsmen, he is a bit too far from the ground for that, but he is a very safe catch, and few men judge and hold a 'skyer' better.

Had he been available for all the Test matches here in 1938 I believe we should have won instead of drawing the rubber that season. Unfortunately he was injured and played only in the Test Matches at Leeds and the Oval.

Bowes looks like some very learned Oxford professor, and if he is not so learned as all that, he is a well-read man. Has not R. C. Robertson-Glasgow written: 'The evening before an Australian Test of 1934, he presented for my solution a geometrical problem, he might as well have invited Professor Einstein to field for him at close short-leg!'

The first time I saw *Denis Compton* play was in a match of Lord's between the Elementary Schools and Mr. C. F. Tufnell's XI. He was then about fourteen and made a splendid century. As he was a Londoner I was 'after him' like a flash of lightning! He made his first appearance for Middlesex against Sussex, at Lord's, at Whitsuntide in 1936, and before the end of July people were talking of him as a candidate for Australia. His style is easy and absolutely

natural. The hall-mark of genius is all over him. He is a
beautiful timer of the ball and gives one the impression of
having the best bat that ever was made, the ball flying off
it with apparently little effort. Before he was twenty-one
he had made 102 for England against Australia, at Trent
Bridge, and in the next Test Match, at Lord's, he scored 76
not out, most of them on a none too easy wicket at a time
when O'Reilly and McCormick had their tails in the air and
defeat stared England in the face. Bradman thought the
world of him. Since then he has gone from strength to
strength and but for the war, he would by now have been
proclaimed a veritable Champion. He and Hutton are the
best young batsmen who have appeared since Walter Hammond was a boy. Compton is also quite a good slow left-
handed bowler who can flight and spin the ball, and a fine
and very fast fieldsman as one would expect from an Arsenal
and England outside-left.

Many hundred years ago *W. J. Edrich's* ancestors used to
raid our shores, but he came to Middlesex via Norfolk, who
suggested that he was a cricketer who would find better
opportunity to display his skill in a higher class of cricket.
I believe, I am not sure, that Kent might have had him,
but it was a lucky day for Middlesex when he threw in his
lot with us. After duly qualifying, he appeared in the
County eleven in 1937—a year later than Compton—and it
was a gift of the gods that these two should have arrived
soon after J. W. Hearne had retired and Hendren was on
the eve of doing so.

The limelight has beaten fiercely round Edrich because of
his failures *v.* the Australians in the season of 1938 and until
the last Test Match, at Durban, *v.* South Africa, in 1939,
but when his fortunes, so far as International cricket go,
were at their lowest, he came out with a superb innings of
219—a tribute to his grit and courage—a courage which has

since been proved in the grimmest of all spheres and which has brought him high honour.

The selectors in 1938 were 'caned' for sticking to him, but it should not be overlooked that he was something of an all-rounder—'good at the bits and pieces' as Hammond put it. He could field magnificently anywhere and as a bowler he 'let her go' for a few overs at a genuinely fast pace. Indeed he bowled like a mighty rushing wind, kicking up the dust and scattering the leaves off the trees as Neville Cardus put it.

Short in height but strongly built—a born athlete—quick, well balanced, and bursting with energy—Edrich is a personality with a love of the game which is reflected in every movement on the field.

As a batsman, he is always on the look-out for runs, with a tendency to overdo the hook stroke. A hard hitter, he is particularly adept in forcing the ball past the bowler and, unless the bowling is very accurate, he scores at a great pace.

A thorough cricketer and a man of character and charm.

A man who can score two centuries in the University match, do the hat trick in Gentlemen v. Players, at Lord's, and for Middlesex v. the Australians is no mean cricketer, and H. J. Enthoven was clearly such an one. He was captain of Harrow, Cambridge and Middlesex, and though his general record is not conspicuously good, every now and again he would set the cricket world talking by an outstanding performance as, for example, his masterly century v. Lancashire, at Lord's, and his double century, 123 and 115, v. Sussex, also at Lord's. On the first occasion the manner in which he drove McDonald recalled Jessop. As a batsman he had little grace of style but his defence was good and he hit the loose ball hard. He knew exactly how much to attempt. He bowled slow-medium right and flighted the ball cleverly. The 1926 Australian team thought highly of him.

The first time I heard of *K. Farnes* was at Lord's during the summer of 1930. I was lunching with the Middlesex and Kent teams, and towards the end of luncheon H. T. W. Hardinge came across to me and said, 'Mr. Warner, I have seen an England bowler.' He then went on to talk enthusiastically of the way in which a boy of nineteen, by the name of Farnes, had bowled; how tall he was, and how finely built. Since that day Kenneth Farnes fully supported Hardinge's judgment, for he played for England both here and in Australia, and also against South Africa, while he was an indispensable member of the Gentlemen's and Essex elevens.

Some of the best fast bowling I have ever seen was by him, G. O. Allen, and Captain J. W. A. Stephenson in the Gentlemen *v.* Players match at Lord's in 1936, Farnes in particular bowling at the pace of a Kortright, another Essex man, and sending the bails flying and the stumps somersaulting. It was tremendous in its speed and 'devil.' With his great height, 6 ft. 4 in., splendid physique and figure, Farnes was not only a fine bowler but an impressive one to watch. His arm seemed to come out of the sky, and his deliveries hit the ground uncommon hard. That must have been a rare piece of bowling of his in the fifth Test Match, at Melbourne in 1937, when he bowled 28 overs (eight balls to the over) and five balls, and obtained 6 wickets for 96 runs in a total of 604. Other outstanding performances of his were 10 wickets for 179 runs in the Test Match at Trent Bridge in 1934, and 11 wickets for 103 runs for Gentlemen *v.* Players at Lord's in 1938.

He was killed flying.

In his first county match, for Somerset *v.* Essex at Frome

in 1935, *H. Gimblett* scored 123 in an hour and twenty minutes, and since those days he has played for England and the Players without quite fulfilling the hopes that were entertained of him. He missed selection in the M.C.C. tour in Australia in 1936–7. He was not then the splendid fieldsman he subsequently became, and his dropping two easy catches in the slips, off Gover, in the Test Match *v.* India, at Old Trafford, no doubt influenced the selectors. I do not think he is by nature a slip fieldsman, but that is where he had been fielding for Somerset and that is where, when asked, he said he preferred to field. Selectors do take trouble about these sort of things! When he played for England in 1939 *v.* the West Indies, at Lord's, he had become a splendid fieldsman anywhere away from the slips, and greatly distinguished himself by making a magnificent catch at cover-point and throwing beautifully from the deep field.

As a batsman he has a touch of genius about him. He is a very powerful driver, and hooker of a short ball, and when he makes runs, he is impressive to watch. He is a natural attacker of the bowler and in one of the war-time matches at Lord's, he made a century which sent the crowd roaring with delight.

That sound critic, R. C. Robertson-Glasgow, in his *Cricket Prints*, writes: 'The selectors'—he is writing of 1939—'did not give a full trial to their idea of playing an original and interesting batsman for England and Gimblett was unlucky to have been the shuttle in this unsatisfactory game of to-and-fro.' And adds: 'There is time yet.' Gimblett was born in 1914.

*J. Hardstaff* is a son of the Hardstaff who was so successful a batsman in the Nottinghamshire team during the first twenty years of this century, and who batted very well for the M.C.C. 1907–8 Australian team under the captaincy of

A. O. Jones. The elder Joe was short in stature, but well knit and sturdy. He was an attractive, wristy, quick-footed batsman, and incidentally a fine out-field who the Australian crowd called 'Hotstuff,' but it is no disparagement to him—and he would rejoice in it—to say that 'Young Joe' is an even finer batsman. Considerably taller than his father, Young Joe was for a time something of a disappointment. Amidst ability and brilliancy were to be found a few chinks in his method, but experience in the hard Australian school, in India and elsewhere, eventually smoothed out the creases and he is now a star in the firmament of cricket. Hardstaff is a lovely bat to watch. Standing well up and using a long handle, he is a powerful and fluent stroke player with a particular aptitude for forcing a ball just short of a length through the covers. Blessed with supple wrists and a sense of balance the ball flies off his bat with apparently little effort. He is a fine deep fieldsman with a strong return.

*L. Hutton* made 0 and 1 in his first Test Match *v.* New Zealand, at Lord's, in 1937, and I recall how bitterly disappointed he was and how unhappy he looked in the dressing-room. But his complete failure on that occasion was due to the fact that he was dead tired having scored 271 not out *v.* Derbyshire and 153 *v.* Leicestershire during the previous six days, had fielded while Leicestershire scored 458, and had travelled all night from Hull to London. This was too much for one of none too robust frame who had but recently recovered from a severe illness. The Selectors took note of this and in the next Test Match, at Old Trafford, he made 100.

It is unnecessary here to recall his many triumphs, including his record score of 364 *v.* Australia at the Oval in 1938. It is sufficient to say that he now stands forth as a batsman splendidly equipped at all points—one worthy of inclusion in the first flight of batsmen of any generation.

Sutcliffe years ago wrote that he was 'a marvel, the discovery of the generation,' and that he was 'certain to be England's opening batsman,' and a prophet won renown in his own country. Hutton's technique cannot be faulted and his off-drive is a thing of joy. The war has robbed him—and others—of six years' first-class cricket, but in recent matches at Lord's he looked as great a batsman as ever. May the day not be far distant when he will be seen in Australia. I am certain he will plague the Australian bowlers. He is a fine out-field and no bad leg-break bowler.

The purist in style or technique would not place *E. Paynter* amongst the foremost batsmen, but in determination, coolness, and knowledge of what to attempt, and what not to, he would probably award him full marks. Paynter revels in a crisis and amongst 'fighting men' I place him in the front rank. His innings of 83 at Brisbane in 1933 will live in the history of international cricket, and for sheer unadulterated pluck, I have not seen its superior, or indeed its equal, on the cricket field.

He has twice made a score of over 200 in Test Matches—216 in 1938 at Trent Bridge *v.* Australia, and 243 at Durban *v.* South Africa in 1939, while at Lord's in the former year he made 99 *v.* Australia. Left-handed, he is very quick on his feet, likes a half-volley on his pads, and is one of those batsmen who seizes every opportunity of making runs. In the field he is very good. I have never seen him in the slips, but anywhere on the off-side, in the deep field, or deep third man, he has few superiors. A great mistake was made in not sending him to Australia in 1936–7. His previous record in Australia, his ability to bat at No. 1 or 3 or 5 or 7, and his excellence against bowlers of the type of O'Reilly and Grimmett should have gained him a place in the side. I pleaded strongly for his inclusion but my views did not prevail.

In 1932 Yorkshire needed a new captain and the choice fell on *A. B. Sellers*, the son of Arthur Sellers, a well-known Yorkshire batsman of the 'nineties.' In his first season he won 18 and lost none of the 25 matches in which he played, and at the end of the 1939 season, he could claim to have led Yorkshire to the Championship five times in seven seasons—a notable record indeed. Sellers is a great fieldsman especially on the off-side, or at silly point, in which positions he has made many magnificent catches. With his tall athletic figure and long well-shaped legs, he looks every inch a cricketer. He is a personality and Yorkshire with one accord speak well of his leadership. He understands his men and gets every ounce out of them. He leads but does not drive and his own fine fielding inspires them. He ought to be a better batsman than he is as one would expect from a man who made a century against the Australians in 1934, but for some reason he has not come on in his batting. In spite of the fact that Grimmett was amongst the Australian bowlers off whom he made a century, he never seems at home to leg-break bowlers. None the less, he has made a good many runs and, at a crisis, he is a 'good man.' A pleasant and agreeable companion, he invariably imparts an amusing atmosphere, for he has a great sense of humour and can make even so solemn a body of men as a Selection Committee laugh!

There never was a keener cricketer than Colonel *J. W. A. Stephenson*. As Leyland said of him: 'He's a rare lad. He hates six-thirty and as for Sundays, he can't abide them!' An acrobatic and cat-like fieldsman, an untiring fast-medium right-handed bowler, and a busy aggressive batsman, he is an outstanding figure. Before he had played against him, Bradman said to me, 'I am looking forward to meeting Stephenson,' and when Stephenson a few days later clean beat him with two successive balls which literally shaved

W. BARDSLEY GETTING WELL OVER THE BALL

*G. W. Beldam*

W. W. Armstrong
Finish of a drive

the stumps in the match between the M.C.C. and the Australians at Lord's, in 1938, I can see Bradman (who eventually made 278) looking down the pitch at him with renewed interest and admiration. And in this game Stephenson's fielding at backward point and to his own bowling was magnificent. He bowled very finely indeed in the Gentlemen and Players' match, at Lord's, in 1936, taking ten wickets in a row—nine in the first innings—and, to my mind, a mistake was made in not sending him to Australia that autumn. He would probably have made at least one Test Match winning catch, and I believe his bowling with its pace off the pitch and his fiery energy might have made just the difference between victory and defeat. It is my regret that I lived in a different cricketing generation to his. I should have loved to have had him on my side. It was he who made the famous remark after one of the one-day wartime matches: 'I thought I was dead and had gone to Heaven. It was so lovely playing cricket at Lord's again.' Colonel Stephenson won the D.S.O. in North Africa. No one was surprised.

*G. T. S. Stevens* played for the Gentlemen at Lord's in 1919, when he was still a boy at school. In his first innings of 24, he hit Parkin into the pavilion for 6, obtained a wicket and made a brilliant catch at short-leg. Later he was to score two centuries in this match, 122, in 1923, and 129, in 1925. He was an automatic choice for the Gentlemen, played for England *v.* Australia in 1926, and captained Oxford. He was a great man for Middlesex. As a batsman he had a pronounced short back lift, but his defence was sound, he hit the loose balls hard, and he was at his best in times of stress. On his day his bowling touched greatness, for with a lively approach to the crease and a high action he made his leg-breaks jump and his googly was difficult to detect. At short-leg and at backward-point he made

Q

many fine catches, and in these two places he almost invariably fielded, for he was neither a fast runner nor a good thrower. He retired from first-class cricket at an early age, but he had done enough for fame.

C. F. Walters' early retirement from first-class cricket was an embarrassing blow to the Selection Committee, for he was a beautiful batsman with a classic style and a good fieldsman. He played many a fine innings v. the Australians here in 1934, but he was not available v. the South Africans in 1935 until the last Test Match, at the Oval, when after accepting the invitation to play he had to cry off owing to an injured thumb. He was very much needed for the Australia tour of 1936–7, but though every influence was brought to bear on him, he could not be lured from his tent.

D. V. P. Wright of Kent is a leg-break (with an occasional googly) bowler of whom I hold a high opinion. I have not seen more difficult bowling than his against Gloucestershire at Maidstone in July 1939, since the days of S. F. Barnes. In that summer he obtained 141 wickets for 16·81 runs each—remarkable figures for a bowler of his type. No leg-break bowler except S. H. Emery, the Australian, ever bowled at his pace, medium. Some have urged that he would be an even better bowler if he reduced his pace. I am not at all sure of this. A medium-paced leg-break is clearly more difficult to play than a slow one. On his day Wright can win a match on his own as he very nearly won the fourth Test Match in that great game at Leeds, in July 1938. Fairly tall with long arms and fingers and a lively action, Wright spins the ball tremendously, and I know that Bradman and his team held him in high estimation. He was approaching greatness when war broke out. He has done the hat-trick five times in his short career, for he only began to play regularly for Kent in 1937 after Freeman's retirement.

# CHAPTER XI

## SOME CRICKETERS OF MY TIME: AUSTRALIAN

WHENEVER I think of *Victor Trumper* my mind goes back to a certain afternoon at Sydney some forty years ago. R. E. Foster had played his wonderful record innings, and the star of Australia seemed setting, when a lithe and graceful figure appeared on the scene. What an innings he played! Such style, such ease, such dash, such power! Against a magnificent and varied attack he put the ball where he liked, and I remember Hirst saying to me: ' It's not much use trying to place the field when that lad's going.' He played as one inspired, and no wonder the thousands who thronged that lovely ground went wild with delight. Undefeated at the finish, he gave his side a chance of victory. Indeed, had Hirst been caught from a difficult catch to short-leg before he had scored, the Australians might well have won. But they deserved almost as much credit as the victors, for I cannot recollect another instance of a side which, going in 292 runs in arrears, eventually sets its opponents nearly 200 runs to win. It was a monument of grit and courage, and a glorious tradition for future generations.

During the summer of 1902 Trumper scarcely ever knew what it was to fail. The state of the wicket made no difference to him—runs flowed from his bat; but of all the wonderful innings he played on that tour, those against the M.C.C. at Lord's and the Players at the Oval will ever remain within my recollection. He just did what he liked with the best bowlers of the day. One straight drive literally 'went through' Braund in the Players' match and hit the far screen first bounce with a lovely thud. All bowling came alike to him. The way he hooked good-length balls was amazing and his driving and late cutting were brilliant in the extreme. Exceptionally quick on his feet he did everything with perfect ease. He died on 28th June, 1915, and his death did not pass unnoticed even in the midst of war. His name is held in veneration by all cricketers. Trumper stood alone. He was like no one, and no one was like him, and he was as modest as he was magnificent as a batsman. No one ever played so naturally. Batting seemed just a part of himself.

*George Giffen* has been called the Grace of Australia, and if never in quite the same class as our champion, his name is writ large in the annals of cricket. He first came to England with W. L. Murdoch's famous 1882 team, which beat England at the Oval by seven runs, and the last time he was here was in 1896. As late as 1904, however, he played for South Australia against the M.C.C. team at Adelaide, and batted and bowled well enough to show what a giant he must have been in his prime. He was a very sound batsman who could, when he liked, drive hard, and his bowling was remarkable for a peculiar flight, the ball always dropping much shorter than one anticipated. His performances with both bat and ball, especially in Australia, are exceptional. He could not play Richardson in England in 1893, the famous fast bowler dismissing him time after time for a small score, but in the Australian season of 1894-5 he had his complete revenge. He was not a good captain, for he bowled himself far too much.

It is questionable whether *M. A. Noble* was not a better all-round cricketer than Giffen ever was. His career did not last so long, but between 1897 and 1909 it would have been difficult to find his superior. He could bat, bowl, and field, at point, almost equally well, and he was the best captain Australia has ever produced. His batting was characterized by judgment and safety, his style was excellent, and if, on the whole, a defensive player, he had plenty of strokes, being especially good at cutting, and in off-driving and playing off his legs. With his nasty swerve, variation of pace, and 'life' in every ball, he was thought by the best judges to be one of the greatest exponents of medium-paced right-hand bowling, and as a point he stood alone, his nearest rivals being his fellow Australian, F. Laver, Ranjitsinhji, and L. G. Wright, of Derbyshire. Noble nearly always gave of his best when things were going against his side, and determination was a distinct feature of his cricket.

Fine captain as he was, I have always thought that he made a mistake in having third man up to save the single when R. E. Foster was playing his record innings. Had third man been back to save the four it is hard to see how Foster could have made as many as he did. As it was, that superb cutter got the ball repeatedly to the boundary past third man. Judged by his method here in 1909, Noble would have had third man back very early in Foster's innings. Noble was a splendid sportsman, as true as steel, a generous winner and a generous loser.

*Clement Hill* is, perhaps, the finest left-hander the world has yet seen, though many think Woolley at least his equal. He was a very attractive batsman, for, being quick on his feet to a degree, he was always 'rushing' the bowler. He was a wonderful player on the leg-side both in his ability to glance straight balls to leg and in forcing the good-length ball wide of mid-on, while he was a most skilful puller, and he could drive very hard on both sides of the wicket; also he possessed a square cut. Indeed, it would be hard to discover a stroke he could not play, and this made it very difficult to place the field for him. He threw with his right hand, and was a fine long-field with a lovely return.

Hill has done many great things in Test Matches—he once scored 97, 98, and 99 in three consecutive innings—but his greatest was undoubtedly his 188 on 29th January, 1898. 'Felix'—T. Horan of the 1882 team—has given a graphic account of it:

In the annals of Australian cricket there is no batting performance to surpass that by Clem Hill to-day. It was magnificent, unique. Like another Coriolanus, he might fairly say, ' Alone I did it.' All the way in Clem was cheered, the climax being reached when he got inside the pavilion gate, borne by the joyous crowd. You may take my word for it that Clem Hill's innings on 29th January, 1898, will be talked of when the smallest boy who saw it will be white with the snows of time.

Some Australians place him on a par with Trumper, pointing to his record which is second only to that of Bradman in Test Matches.

*J. J. Darling*, at his best, was but little inferior even to Hill as a left-hander. He was, indeed, a more punishing player, the strength of his driving being terrific, but he scarcely possessed Hill's defence and soundness. Darling's greatest innings was at Sydney in March 1908, when he scored 160 out of 252 in two and three-quarter hours for Australia against England.

He hit the fast ones of Richardson (says an Australian account), in a way that has never before been approached in Australia save by one man—H. Graham in the second Sydney Test Match of 1894. And that was merely an approaching, not a parallel, bit of cricket. He powerfully drove the fastest ones straight past the bowler to the fence along the turf, then over the heads of the field at mid-off, next past extra-cover, and again past cover. The onlookers were astounded with the extraordinary strength of the man. He seemed to have the devil in him. He square cut the ball so that it travelled like lightning. and back cut with electrifying effect upon the public pulse. Still Richardson kept at him, was pounded to the fence, until one, even though dazzled by the magnificent play of the batsman, felt a thrill of admiration for the bowler, who, pasted as he had perhaps never been before, and perhaps never will be again, showed no traces of giving in. MacLaren's keeping him at the bowling crease in the face of such punishment was surprising. The spirit of the bowler was great, but Darling was Richardson's master that day. It was a battle between giants, and one never felt more admiration for the pluck of any bowler. Darling's innings was beyond praise. It ranks with Clem Hill's 188.

Darling captained the Australian elevens of 1899 and 1902 with great skill, but in 1905 he allowed Armstrong to go on fielding in match after match at slip, a position he was obviously unsuited to at that time—a mistake in tactics which cost his side dearly.

*Warwick Armstrong* was a great cricketer. Very tall and very powerful, he was built for long driving. Essentially a forward player, he forced the good-length ball away in a manner equalled by few, and in general style he was attractive to look at, being a fine square-cutter as well as an extraordinarily powerful driver. His innings of 248 not out against the Gentlemen of England at Lord's in May 1905 was a typical instance of his best methods of play, the power of his driving on that occasion being so great that four outfields stationed fairly near to one another were unable to prevent his hits reaching the boundary. A drive he made off Bosanquet in the Test Match at Nottingham that year I shall not easily forget. It was the last ball of the day, but Armstrong jumped a yard or two down the pitch, and hit a slow, high-tossed delivery on the half-volley over the bowler's head clean over the grand-stand. Ninety-nine batsmen out of a hundred would have played for 'keeps' at that period. It is batting like this that appeals to the imagination of the public; but one trembles to think what Darling would have said to Armstrong had he missed the ball!

Armstrong was an extraordinarily accurate bowler—a more accurate bowler never lived—and it was really wonderful how over after over he could drop the ball within an eight-inch square. When it came to a matter of keeping down runs the greatest of batsmen were reduced to scoring an occasional single, and though he did not break the ball as much as the majority of leg-break bowlers, he could make it do just enough to worry the batsman. He did not bowl exactly a googly, but occasionally an apparent leg-break came straight on and very fast off the pitch. He delivered the ball from nearly the full width of the crease, so that, as he brought his arm over quite high, the ball which pitched on the leg-stump comes across the line of the wicket from the off, somewhat after the manner of Barnes. He batted superbly in the Test Matches in Australia in 1920–1, and he possesses the unique distinction of having captained Australia in ten Test Matches, and of never having lost one.

*Hugh Trumble* was one of the greatest bowlers that that great bowler-producing country, Australia, has sent forth. Very tall, he made use of every inch of his height, kept a wonderful length, with a deliberate and easy action, and on a pitch that helped him got a lot of work on the ball. On a sticky Melbourne wicket he was to all intents and purposes unplayable, but he was very far from being only a sticky wicket bowler. On a good wicket there was nothing, at first sight, very striking about his bowling—indeed it has been said of him that 'from the pavilion he looked to be bowling half-volleys!' But out in the middle one found that half-volleys were few and far between, and that he gave that impression from the pavilion because he delivered the ball from a great height, followed by extremely subtle variation of pace. Trumble, like J. T. Hearne, believed in 'the little difference that often does so much,' and he was a perfect master in tempting a batsman to play his favourite stroke at a ball which originally appeared suitable, but which was not in reality so. A more thoughtful and brainy bowler there has seldom been.

Trumble played for Australia for fourteen years, and the last time he took part in a Test Match he 'did the hat trick,' a fitting wind-up to a great career. He used to make some wonderful catches at slip with his telescopic reach.

*S. E. Gregory* played in more Test Matches than any other cricketer. He played his first in 1890, and his last at the Oval, in 1912, and he scored 2,193 runs in these games with an average of over twenty-five, his highest score being 201 at Sydney in December 1894. This is a wonderful record; but Gregory's usefulness to his side did not end with his batting, for he was a great run-saver as well as a great run-getter, ranking as an extra-cover in almost the same class as Jessop. He was extraordinarily quick on his feet, and had a lovely below-the-shoulder return which he obtained as much by a flick of the wrist as by arm swing. He fielded almost as well on his last visit to England, when he was in his fortieth year, as ever he did. Gregory was rather apt to be caught in the slips or at the wicket on first going in to bat, but once he had got set he was a magnificent cutter. He was also very good at hooking and playing on the leg-side, and on a bad wicket was often seen to the greatest advantage. He took plenty of risks and scored at a good pace, and though very short in height liked fast bowling.

*W. Bardsley* and *V. Ransford* have been very prominent in international cricket. The former holds the record of scoring a double century in a Test Match, and both made hundreds against England at Lord's, the ground above all others on which, because of its great traditions, an Australian desires to excel.

Both were left-handed, but they differed in style, Bardsley

standing up very straight to his work, while Ransford crouched somewhat over his bat. Bardsley was the better of the two. Very quick on his feet, he was a master of many strokes, and his bat was very straight. Ransford was just as good as Bardsley in making the left-hander's stroke past cover and past point, but he had not Bardsley's straight drive, and I question whether he was quite so sound. No safer catch or more untiring worker in the deep-field has ever been seen than Ransford, his running, picking-up, and throwing (left-handed) being a positive delight. Bardsley was a good field, but he cannot, in this respect, compare with Ransford. No other Australian batsmen on a first visit to England have ever done so well, Bardsley scoring 2,180 runs with an average of 46·39, and Ransford 1,783 runs with an average of 43·48, and in a *wet season too.*

Bardsley batted superbly here in 1912, and again in 1921 and 1926, and he has good claims to be considered among the best left-handed batsmen in the world. The then editor of *Wisden*, Mr. S. H. Pardon, had a great opinion of him, saying that England had never won until Bardsley was out.

*J. M. Gregory* came of a famous cricketing family. His uncle, David Gregory, captained the first Australian eleven which visited this country in 1878, and he is a cousin of S. E. Gregory, who played in over fifty Test Matches for Australia. J. M. Gregory was one of the great personalities of Australian cricket. In his day he would have been selected for a world eleven. A fast bowler with a high action, a superb fieldsman in the slips, and a dashing left-handed batsman, he played the game with tremendous energy and enthusiasm.

*E. A. McDonald* might well have served as the model of a fast bowler. He had a beautiful run up to the wicket, an easy action, and he kept a length and could do a good deal with the ball. He also had at his command a particularly good slow-medium yorker. His bowling was one of the best features of the 1921 Australian tour in this country. At one time he was easily the best fast bowler in the world. Qualifying for Lancashire he did great work for that county for several seasons.

*C. G. Macartney* first appeared for Australia against England at Sydney in December 1907, and from that date until 1926 he was one of the first choices in an Australian eleven. He was a most delightful batsman to watch. He attacked the bowling from the start. He was confident, daring, and possessed a perfect magazine of strokes. Very cleanly and actively built, he was the possessor of an extraordinarily powerful forearm and steel-like wrists, wielded his bat as an expert swordsman does his rapier, and was wonderfully quick on his feet. He was never coached. He was one of the best batsmen in the world, a beautiful field at mid-off, and in his earlier days a first-class left-handed bowler.

He made five centuries for Australia *v.* England, and in 1926 he scored 133 not out at Lord's, 151 at Leeds, and 109 at Old Trafford—three hundreds in succession. He also scored 99 *v.* England at Lord's in 1912, and was then caught on the leg-side by the wicket-keeper. I have never seen a greater innings than his at Leeds. He pulverized all the bowling except Tate's. Such stroke play as he showed on that occasion is seldom equalled, never surpassed. It is said that Macartney once asked, when someone had been eulogizing Victor Trumper: ' What did he do that I can't do? ' And there was no adequate reply, for Macartney was as fine a batsman as has ever lived. Macartney was a very pleasant companion on and off the cricket field.

*H. L. Collins* was captain of the Australian Imperial Forces team and afterwards of Australia. He was a very dogged and determined fighter with great powers of defence, patience, and concentration, and if his style was not attractive he was an invaluable No. 1—and a rare man to hold a breach. He was an excellent and painstaking captain who managed his bowling ably. The two teams which he captained in England were very popular.

*W. H. Ponsford* has been a tremendous run-getter. He twice made scores of over 400, twice over 300 runs, and three centuries for Australia *v.* England, one of them on his first appearance. His 110 at the Oval in 1930 was, perhaps, the best of all—a truly great innings. He crouched somewhat in his position at the wicket, but he possessed many strokes and, incidentally, courage, and was an interesting batsman to watch. He was blessed with a wonderful eye, timed the ball well, and had a good square-cut and a forcing stroke wide of mid-on. He was a master in playing slow leg-break or googly bowling, and his bat looked uncannily broad to the bowler. He had a wonderful season in England in 1934.

*V. Richardson* is a real personality, a beautifully built man, and his influence on South Australian cricket has been great, his captaincy and general attitude towards the game having had a very happy influence. He was a superb fieldsman who never by any chance showed off. He was very quick, possessed a sense of anticipation that amounted almost to genius, with the safest of hands and a very quick return. He deservedly ranks amongst the best fieldsmen in the game. He was a most attractive bat—not especially sound—but full of attack and courage. A noted all-round athlete, he was immensely popular.

*A. A. Mailey* was a great exponent of googly bowling. He imparted a tremendous amount of spin to his deliveries and he could make his leg-break 'dance' off even an Australian 'shirt-front' wicket, and jump up like a tennis ball. A clever brain which was always planning and scheming made him a very interesting and dangerous opponent, and he was quite indifferent to punishment. He won many a match for Australia between 1921 and 1926, and the contrast between his slow bowling and that of the swift J. M. Gregory and McDonald, was one of the trump cards in the hands of W. W. Armstrong, the captain of the famous 1921 Australian team. Mailey is a famous caricaturist, and a very sound and knowledgeable writer on the game.

*A. F. Kippax* was one of the great stylists of cricket— almost as good to watch as Palairet or Woolley. He had neat wrists, cut late beautifully, and played well off his legs, but his forte was the off-drive. The best innings I ever saw him play was his 158 out of 227 *v.* Sussex at Hove in 1930. How he came to be omitted from the 1926 Australian side is a mystery, for he was at the head of the averages of the whole of Australia that season. His omission caused tremendous criticism to be directed at the selection committee. Kippax batted very finely here in 1930, scoring 1,514 runs with an average of 56·07; and his style has had considerable influence on his contemporaries. His book on the bowling controversy—*Anti Body-line*—is by far the best of the many that have been written. It avoided personalities and gave the Australian point of view fairly, courteously, and convincingly.

*W. M. Woodfull* first came to England in 1926, and was captain of the 1930 and 1934 Australian elevens which won the rubber. He has made six centuries *v.* England. He was not a pretty batsman to watch, his style being rather stiff, but he had a certain amount of wristiness in his stroke at the last second, a remarkable defence, and was a cool, collected, and determined player. As a captain he managed his bowling excellently and was a skilful placer of the field; and he was very popular here. He has been one of the mainstays of Australian cricket since 1926, liked and respected by everyone. There never was, in fact, a more popular and better-liked Australian captain in this country, his pleasant manner making him hosts of friends both on and off the field. In the field he was not such an outstanding personality as some captains, but he was a good one, cleverly varying his bowling and strategy.

*S. J. McCabe* has a splendid variety of strokes and is a most attractive batsman to watch. He is a particularly fine straight driver and hooker; and the manner in which he hooked short-pitched deliveries of Voce in a Test Match at Sydney was tremendous. To keep him quiet it is necessary to 'bowl tight'—as the Australians put it—that is a good length. He developed into a great batsman.

He batted very finely in England in 1934, scoring 2,078 runs with an average of 69·26, and his innings of 232 *v.* England at Trent Bridge in 1938 was one of the greatest ever played. He scored his last 72 runs in 28 minutes.

He is essentially a stroke player and is always on the attack. He is a masterly player of googly bowling.

*D. Bradman* is the world's greatest batsman, a complete master, his stroke play being magnificent and brilliant in the extreme. In facing Larwood in Australia during the 1932-3 tour he adopted a most original method, for he used his exceptional quickness of foot and eye to move away from the wicket, and hit balls, which pitched on the middle- and leg-stumps, and even off the leg-stump, on the off-side with a horizontal bat. In doing this he forced Larwood to strengthen his off-side field by bringing over two of the seven on-side fieldsmen; and if there were critics who disliked his method and even accused him of running away, the answer to this was in the runs he made. Both at Brisbane and at Sydney, in 1933, he got out when he looked as if he was definitely on top of the bowling; and if his methods appeared unsound he was probably evolving a new idea in dealing with a type of attack to which he was unaccustomed. A good example of his genius was to be found in his playing of Ironmonger in the inter-state matches. Ironmonger, a most accurate left-hander, invariably kept men entirely on the defensive, but Bradman smote him hip and thigh, and scored his century in a couple of hours or less. Many of his strokes live in one's memory, in particular an off-drive off Hammond, at Sydney. Never have I seen a ball go so fast to the ring. Short in height Bradman has long arms, wrists of steel, a very strong forearm, and a wonderful eye. He seldom plays forward. He is either right back or feet out of his ground attacking the bowler—indeed he is always attacking.

Bradman is a glorious fieldsman. A long, strong, and most accurate thrower, he is exceptionally fast, and he picks the ball up with unfailing accuracy. The catch which dismissed G. O. Allen in the Test at Sydney in 1933 was extraordinarily fine, for he turned round at extra-cover, went after a mis-hit at full speed and held the ball with arms outstretched to their full length. His deeds need no recapitulation here. It is sufficient to say that on figures alone he stands far above any batsman of any age.

*C. V. Grimmett* is one of the few instances of a cricketer attaining to eminence after the age of thirty; but in his first Test Match at Sydney in 1925 he bowled out our men in both innings and did the same thing for his State, South

Australia, a few days later. Since then he has been the mainstay of Australian bowling. His action is low and he lowers his shoulder when delivering the ball. Since the old round-arm bowlers I should think there has never been a bowler with a lower action. Very accurate in length his leg-break is his most dangerous ball, but he occasionally sends down a googly—though it is rather more of a top spinner than a googly. He has always struck me as rather an unlucky bowler who is more dangerous on our wickets than in Australia. He has a fine cricket brain and heaps of perseverance and I always enjoy immensely his duels with Hammond. Both are attackers. Hammond is undoubtedly his master on Australian wickets, but I should not like to say the same thing on English wickets. Grimmett is a good field and a useful bat, but he does not like fast bowling.

*T. Wall* was a good fast bowler with a very big heart and a pleasant personality. He never gave in and was very apt to 'come again' at the end of a tiring day, a proof of the grit and determination of a man who was not over-strongly built for fast bowling. He took a very long time to bowl an over, for his run up to the crease was nearly twenty-five yards, and he walked back very slowly to his starting point. Including a follow-through of ten yards he must have run and walked seventy yards every ball he sent down, or roughly, 420 yards in an over of six balls, or well over a mile in five overs. I have seen him make some clever catches near the wicket.

*W. J. O'Reilly* is the best bowler in the world to-day. Standing six feet two, he stoops as he delivers the ball and so does not make the most of his height, but he has complete control of the leg-break googly and top-spinner, and he changes his pace and flight without apparent change of action. His length is always perfect and his stamina and energy are amazing. His leg-break is, perhaps, bowled at a slightly greater pace than his off-break, but his most dangerous ball is the top-spinner which 'lifts,' and unless a batsman drops his wrists quickly in playing back he stands in danger of being caught by one or other of the short legs.

O'Reilly seems to rejoice in every ball he sends down, and only once have I seen him completely mastered, and that was by Hammond at Lord's in that unforgettable innings of 240. Not once did he succeed in beating this great batsman.

*W. A. Brown* first appeared for New South Wales during the Australian season of 1932–3, and against the M.C.C. team he batted admirably for 69. He was very successful here in 1934, scoring 105 in the Test at Lord's, and four years later he was second only to Bradman. At Trent Bridge in the first Test he made 133, and at Lord's in the second, 206 not out, carrying his bat through the first innings. Brown bats in a polished style. He relies on his strong back play in defence and it is a waste of time, and of runs, to bowl on his pads.

He also has a good square cut and there are few better opening batsmen. He is a very fine fieldsman and something of a sprinter. In the years to come, I should not be in the least surprised to find him captain of the Australian eleven.

# CHAPTER XII

## South Africans

*J. H. Sinclair* gained his South African cap against Lord
Hawke's team in 1895–6 when he was only nineteen years
old. He made the first century ever hit for South Africa
in international cricket, 106 against Lord Hawke's eleven at
Newlands, Cape Town, in March 1899, and in the same
match he took six wickets for 26 runs in the first innings.
Against the Australians in 1902 he scored three hundreds in
eight innings, two of them in the Test Matches. Standing
nearly six feet four inches, Sinclair possessed tremendous
punishing powers. The bat looked like a cane in those
brawny hands, but his hits flew like golf drives from the tee.
In one of his hundreds against the Australians *he drove the
ball no fewer than eight times out of the Newlands ground*,
while against Lord Hawke's eleven he found the pond yards
over the ropes. In both innings in that game he fell to
wonderful long-field catches by Tyldesley and F. W.
Milligan. Sinclair was a more than useful medium-paced
right-handed bowler who varied the pace and flight of the
ball with no little skill, and between 1897 and 1904 was far
and away the finest all-round cricketer in South Africa.
He was a member of the 1901, 1904, and 1907 South African
teams in this country, and in 1910–11 was one of P. W.
Sherwell's side in Australia.

*G. A. Faulkner* was one of the world's best cricketers. He

242

first appeared in the South African eleven in January 1906, and did very well, his bowling in particular making a great impression. In this country in 1907 he was a great success, taking seven wickets for 16 runs in the Test Match at Leeds, and scoring on that tour 1,288 runs with an average of 30·66. His batting in South Africa against Leveson-Gower's M.C.C. team in the winter of 1909–10 was remarkable for its consistent excellence, and in Australia in 1910–11 he set the world talking, his play in the Test Matches rivalling that of Trumper himself. Clem Hill told me that no one has ever batted better in Australia than Faulkner did. Apart from his batting and bowling, Faulkner was a remarkably fine field in the slips. In his prime he would have been a very strong candidate for a place in a world eleven.

The prowess of *G. C. White* and *R. O. Schwarz* as bowlers has been mentioned in a previous chapter, but both were batsmen and fielders as well, White in point of pure style being, in his day, the best batsman in South Africa. In the South African season of 1905–6 he batted magnificently, scoring 82, 46, 147, and 73 in the Test Matches, his 73 scored out of 97 for six wickets, being the kind of innings that one does not easily forget. White did not like the wet wickets which were so prevalent during the summer of 1907, but on a fast pitch he was a delightful player to watch, his chief strength lying in the power and variety of his off-side strokes.

R. O. Schwarz was an attractive batsman, very quick on his feet, and a good off-driver. He made 102 for South Africa against an England eleven at Lord's in 1904, and was always likely to make runs. He was a good field. He used to play for Middlesex before he went to South Africa, and in those days was a very ordinary fast-medium bowler. He was a great half-back at Rugby football and played for England.

*A. D. Nourse* is the veteran of South African cricket. He played consistently for South Africa for a quarter of a century. A left-handed batsman with a splendid defence, he was always a most difficult man to get out, while he was a very fair fast-medium left-handed bowler and a superb field, in which respect he was enormously helped by the possession of the biggest pair of hands I have ever seen. It is said that he once missed three catches in one day on the Johannesburg ground, but I never saw him miss a catch. He did splendidly on tour in Australia with P. W. Sherwell's team in 1910–11, and in England both in 1907 and 1912, and he played very finely indeed against the Australians in South Africa in 1921.

*H. W. Taylor*, the former South African captain, was one of the best batsmen in the world. During the visit of the M.C.C. team to South Africa in the winter of 1913–14 he displayed wonderful form. The way in which he played the superb bowling of Barnes evoked immense admiration. To most of the other batsmen Barnes was unplayable, but Taylor in match after match scored runs, and his record in the Test Matches was extraordinarily fine. Taylor was a great back player, and there has seldom been a more powerful or certain hooker of any ball the least short of a good length. Taylor's method was so perfect that he might well have served as a model for a young cricketer. He was always delightful to watch: neat, aggressive, and correct. He made seven centuries for South Africa *v.* England, six of them in South Africa.

*S. J. Pegler* was the best bowler in the South African eleven which came here for the Triangular tour in 1912. He had a high action, could turn the ball both ways, and had a deceptive flight. He was not a googly bowler, as it was possible to detect whether the off-break or the leg-break was on its way, but he was a really fine bowler of the more or less orthodox type, and he was held in high repute by batsmen here.

*H. B. Cameron* was a very fine wicket-keeper—one worthy to rank in any company. His work here was always up to a very high standard, and he was also a fine batsman who hit the ball hard and was at his best when runs were wanted. He drove beautifully with a very long carry, and cut well. He played a great innings *v.* England, at Lord's, in 1935, scoring 90 out of 126 in an hour and a quarter, hitting three sixes and six fours. At Scarborough that season, against H. D. G. Leveson-Gower's XI, he made 160 in 140 minutes, with two sixes and twenty-six fours amongst his strokes, and against Yorkshire at Sheffield in an innings of 103 not out, he hit Verity for 30—4, 4, 4, 6, 6, 6 in one over (8 balls). On that tour he averaged 41·65 with an aggregate of 1,458.

There have been few, if any, greater wicket-keepers. Both as a catcher and a stumper it is not overpraising him to say that he was magnificent, and he takes a place amongst the great wicket-keepers in the history of the game. His death soon after his return to South Africa was a tremendous loss to the game. He was worth two men to a side.

*H. G. Owen Smith* was something of a genius as a cricketer. He was first and foremost a great fieldsman on the off-side, or in the deep, and indeed anywhere. Very quick in starting, no hit was too hard for him to stop, he had the safest of hands, and his return was as quick and as accurate as can be imagined. In a long day's fielding he saved literally scores of runs, and his activity and keenness were an inspiration to his comrades and a tonic to the spectators. As a batsman no one would dream of calling him sound, but he had an eye like a hawk, hit a half-volley a long way, using his wrists, left shoulder, and every ounce of body swing, and he could cut and hook. With his nimbleness of foot he was always 'after' the bowling. Quite the best cricket I saw in 1931 was in the University match when he and the Nawab of Pataudi were batting to the bowling of F. R. Brown, K. Farnes, and A. G. Hazlerigg. His slow googly bowling was not always of a good length, but on his day he could be very difficult to play. He was essentially a cricketer for a big occasion. A noted boxer, he was a superb full-back at Rugby football. Altogether an exceptional athlete. He, like S. M. J. Woods, has represented one country at cricket and another at football.

*B. Mitchell*, G. A. Faulkner, and H. W. Taylor are the best batsmen South Africa has so far produced. Mitchell during a short career has scored four centuries *v.* England, and in the season of 1935 he batted splendidly, making 164 not out, at Lord's, and 123, at the Oval, *v.* England.

His style is graceful and he seems to have plenty of time in which to play the ball, and he is nimble on his feet. His back play is very sound and his off-drive is beautifully made. He is essentially a steady defensive batsman, but his method of play is so correct and easy that he is seldom dull to watch. He is a slip fieldsman of high class and a more than useful googly bowler—a thorough cricketer.

## West Indians

*G. Challenor* in his day was the idol of Barbados—where he was known as Lord ' Runs-come.' He was, indeed, a great batsman, with style, hitting power, and strong defence. Runs flowed from his bat in a delightful manner. Strongly built, with powerful shoulders, he attacked the bowlers from the start—did he not hit a six over cover-point's head off the first ball in a Test Match at Georgetown, British Guiana? He was a happy combination of attack and defence, his off-.

driving and cutting being particularly good, and his brilliant play used to send the enthusiastic West Indies crowds mad with delight. He came to England with the West Indies teams of 1906, when he was not quite eighteen, in 1923 and 1928; and in 1923 scored 1,556 runs with an average of 51·86. He was the first great batsman the West Indies produced, and he set a tradition and a style which had a great influence on his own and the present generation, and which will not wane as the years pass.

*L. H. Constantine* was born at Diego Martin, a village about four miles from Port of Spain, Trinidad. His father was a good cricketer as was his uncle on his mother's side, V. Pascall, and on one occasion, the three of them played for Trinidad in an inter-Island match. Constantine is the most famous cricketer the West Indies has produced and, next to Bradman, the greatest 'draw' of any living player. He is the finest fieldsman the world has ever seen. This may sound extravagant praise, but men like Hammond and Hendren, who know all there is to know about fielding, are emphatic that Constantine stands alone. His activity has to be seen to be believed—he can literally catch anything anywhere and he throws with the speed of a bullet. He is twice as active as the proverbial cat, and as lithe as a panther. To see him in the field is sheer joy. He is supreme in any position, and to attempt a run until the ball is past him is suicide, for the amount of ground he can cover is amazing.

As a batsman he is *sui generis*. His exceptional quickness of foot, the keenest of eyes, long lissome arms, and steel-like wrists have enabled him to develop his batting on his own lines. He is not a stylist like Hobbs, Hammond, or Woolley, and yet he makes the most glorious, and indeed, thrilling strokes. Two, in particular, I shall always remember, both of them off G. O. Allen in the Middlesex *v.* West Indies match, at Lord's, in 1928. The first was when he played back and forced the ball along the ground between the bowler and mid-on with such power that, after hitting the pavilion rails, it bounced over the seats against the pavilion brickwork; and the second was when he half drove, half cut —call it what you will—a widish good-length ball, over extra-cover's head, full-pitch into the seats of the grand-stand. That was the match in which he scored 86 and 103, and took six wickets for 11 runs in six overs and three balls. Another stroke which only he could bring off was when he hit a full-pitch to leg, off Bowes, who was on at the Nursery end, over the flagstaff by the professionals' dressing-room at Lord's. Never before had a full-pitch been hit so far in so fine a direction.

Great natural cricketer as he is Constantine has a poor record in Test Matches. In Australia in 1931–2 he scored but 72 runs in ten innings and his eight wickets cost 50·87 runs each, and in England only twice has he played an innings of over 50, 64, at Old Trafford, in 1933, and 79, at the Oval, in 1939. It cannot be denied that he makes the most appallingly rash strokes often before he has got a sight of the ball, and it is no exaggeration to say that he throws his wicket away time and time again. He would enjoy himself so much more if he could curb his enterprise on first going in, and so would the spectators! His bowling, at times, as for instance in the Middlesex match and in the Test Match at Lord's in 1928, was of a very high excellence. On this last occasion Sutcliffe told me that he had never played better bowling on a good wicket than that of Con-stantine, Francis, Griffith, and Browne. Constantine plays in a delightfully happy and carefree, and yet enthusiastic, manner. He is typical of West Indies cricket, and West Indies cricket to-day is a potent influence for good in a game which, in recent years, has become too serious and too antagonistic.

*G. Headley* is short in height and slightly built, and one wonders how a man of his stature can impart such power to his strokes. The answer is to be found in his perfect physical co-ordination. Then, like all his countrymen, he is blessed with a quick eye, a sense of timing the ball, and he is as quick on his feet as Hobbs or Macartney in his prime. He learnt his cricket in Jamaica and his feats there, and in England and Australia have earned him the title of 'the Bradman of the West Indies.' In spite of a badly strained ankle he showed magnificent form here in 1933, scoring 2,300 runs with an average of 66·28. Some of his innings were masterpieces of the art of batting, but he has probably never played more finely than when he scored 131 *v.* Victoria at Melbourne. Australian critics were enthusiastic, describing his innings as 'one of the grandest exhibitions of batting that had been seen for many a year.' Like the cover-point hitter in the famous Rugby and M.C.C. match in *Tom Brown's School Days*, Headley is always out of his ground to a slow bowler, and possesses a command of stroke given to few cricketers.

He is a fine late and square cutter, hooks well, and although, as has been said, he is quick on his feet, he plays the greater majority of his strokes off his back foot and does not often employ the orthodox off-drive as played by Bradman, Hammond and Hutton amongst the moderns, or by L. Palairet, Jackson, Spooner and Hobbs of the past.

He was at his very best in England in 1939, scoring 1,745 runs with an average of 72·70, and making a 106 and 107 *v.* England at Lord's, being the first batsman to score a double century in a Test Match at Lord's. He carried his side on his shoulders. C. B. Fry has suggested that his second christian name which is Adolph should be changed to Atlas. Headley has scored seven centuries for West Indies *v.* England, two of them scores of 223 and 270 not out, both at Kingston, Jamaica.

He bats very naturally and very easily, and ranks in that very small class of stylists which include Hobbs, Woolley, Kippax, and Hammond. He is an extremely fine fieldsman.

The brothers *Grant*, *G. C.* and *R. S.*, of Trinidad, have taken a prominent part in West Indies cricket. Both Cambridge Blues, G. C. captained the West Indies team in Australia in 1930–1 and in England in 1933, and R. S. in England in 1939. Their fielding was the best feature of their play, both being really magnificent in positions near the wicket such as short-leg and backward point, and both were more than useful batsmen, G. C. stylish and full of pluck, and R. S. a powerful hitter. In the Test Match, at old Trafford, in 1939, R. S. going in first on a difficult wicket, went for the bowling, actually scoring 46 out of 56 and hitting Goddard for three sixes and four fours before being caught in the deep field. 'The whole crowd, including everyone in the pavilion, rose to him,' says *Wisden*. In the Test Match at the Oval he made a brilliant catch at short-leg to dismiss Hammond, and he must be ranked amongst the great fieldsmen with a very safe pair of hands and a long reach. The chroniclers of those years give unstinted praise to both brothers, who were also admirable captains, enthusiastic and energetic, and playing the game in a manner and spirit which earned their elevens great popularity.

## Indians

The Indians were late in entering the international field of cricket, but before that Ranjitsinhji, Duleepsinhji, and Pataudi had shown us that they were stars of the first magnitude; and there is no doubt that the athletic Indian has a natural aptitude for cricket. Indeed, C. B. Fry is of the opinion that 'they have on the average a greater natural aptitude for batting than any people.' Certainly they are graceful in their methods and lithe and active in their movements. Their best cricketers, so far, excluding the three mentioned above who learnt their cricket in England, have been C. K. Nayudu, Amar Singh, and V. M. Merchant.

Tall and well built, *Nayudu* was blessed with supple wrists and, like nearly all his countrymen, a keen eye, and he was a strong player in front of the wicket, his driving being clean and powerful. He was also a clever slow-to-medium bowler who could spin the ball and flight it, and a very fine fieldsman. In his best days, he was worthy of a place in almost any side.

*Amar Singh* was a great cricketer. Active as a deer, he had a lovely loose action and could make the ball do a little in the air both ways, and he was always full of vim and devil. His bowling *v*. England, at Lord's, in 1936 was of a very high excellence; and he was consistent and determined. I rank him high amongst fast-medium right-handed bowlers, and I believe most modern batsmen would back me up in that view. He was a beautiful fieldsman and a natural hitter who used his wrists as well as his arms and shoulders, but he was apt to throw his wicket away. An innings of his was worth going a long way to see. Potentially, he was one of the best all-rounders in the world. His early death was almost as great a loss to Indian cricket as Cameron's was to South African.

*V. M. Merchant* was by far the best batsman in the Indian side which visited England in 1936, scoring 1,745 runs with an average of 51·32, including a very fine innings of 114 *v*. England at Old Trafford, when he and Mushtaq Ali (112) put on 203 runs for the first wicket in the second innings. Only five feet seven inches in height, he is quick on his feet, strong on the on-side and cuts well. His defence is sound and he gets into position quickly to play the ball. In recent years he has shown fine form in India.

### New Zealand

*C. S. Dempster* stands out as the best batsman New Zealand has given to the game. He is short in height but strongly built and his beautiful grey eyes see the ball very quickly. There are few more exact timers of the ball and he possesses all the strokes. He is neat and compact, uses his feet well and is one of the best and most consistent batsman in cricket to-day.

For years he was the mainstay of New Zealand batting; 1,778 runs with an average of 59 in the wet season of 1931 was a great performance, and since he qualified for Leicestershire, he has made heaps of runs.

*T. C. Lowry* we knew in England as captain of Cambridge and a member of the Somerset eleven, but he is a New Zealander by birth and residence and made a most excellent captain of the first New Zealand team to visit England in 1927. He has done much for New Zealand cricket, and when he came to the premature conclusion that his playing days were over, he came here as Manager of the 1937 side, and just to show that his hand had not lost its cunning, scored 121 *v.* Nottinghamshire. Very powerfully built, he was a fine batsman who excelled particularly on soft wickets. He drove very hard and was adaptable and versatile.

His fielding, too, was very good and he was a dead sure catch. Full of courage and originality in his tactics as a captain, no side could dream of being slack or indifferent when he was about. He played for the Gentlemen *v.* the Players' at Lord's, and in one season scored over 1,000 runs for Cambridge. A personality and very much of a cricketer.

*K. C. James* is a wicket-keeper of high class, and his method could not be improved on. To him must belong what I believe to be a record for in a recent match at Lord's he caught the first four batsmen off the same bowler, Mathews. He, like Dempster, threw in his lot with an English county, Northamptonshire, and has done fine work for them.

## *American*

Had *J. B. King* been born an Englishman or an Australian instead of an American his fame as a cricketer would have been more widely known. As it is he is recognized by all those who played against him as one of the greatest of all bowlers. He was at his best between 1894 and 1904 at a time when cricket in Philadelphia was of a high standard. It is not easy to make the modern cricketer believe this for, alas, little or no cricket is played in America to-day, but between the years I have mentioned the Gentlemen of Philadelphia defeated the Australians on two occasions and invariably held their own with various English teams. King was a tall wiry man, small-waisted and with good shoulders, who bowled fast right-hand with a marked inswerve of the ball to a right-handed batsman. He made full use of his height, bringing his hands together over his head before delivering the ball, kept an accurate length and direction, and did not rely only on his inswing, or body break, for his wickets, for he made the ball occasionally go straight or move a little away from the bat. He invariably bowled on a true wicket with a couple of slips and did not overdo the leg-side fieldsmen—a couple of short-legs and a mid-on were enough.

King had tremendous 'ginger' and was a rare striver, and his intended yorker was a yorker and no half-volley or full-pitch. Everyone who played against him was tremendously impressed. There can be little question but that he was a great bowler.

The cricketers of whom I have written in these pages cover a period of roughly fifty years. During that long time, both as player and spectator, I have honestly enjoyed almost every minute of my participation in the game both on and off the field. I love the atmosphere, and the memory of all these good men and true will linger happily with me until the end.

# CHAPTER XIII

## THE GREATEST GAME I EVER PLAYED IN

IT is not a little curious that two of the most exciting games of cricket I have ever taken part in should have been against the South Africans. On the first occasion I was playing for Middlesex, and on the second for the team sent out to South Africa by the Marylebone Club. The result of the Middlesex and South African game was a tie, and that of the M.C.C. v. South Africa a victory for our opponents by one wicket. On paper the first match would appear to be the more exciting, but the second was of greater importance to the general public of the two countries and to the individual cricketers in the two elevens, and was at least as full of thrilling moments. I have therefore selected M.C.C. v. South Africa as the most exciting game in my cricket career.[1] In both matches I happened to be acting as captain, and, therefore, am not likely to forget either, and especially the second, in which every stroke, I had almost said every ball, in that long three days' battle is still fresh and vividly painted on my memory.

And now for my 'greatest game.' To begin with, I will give the names of the two elevens who were drawn up face to face on the red-dust Wanderers' ground at Johannesburg on January 2, 1906. I give the order of going in.   M.C.C.—

---

[1] In many ways, of course, that wonderful game at Lord's in 1920 with which I wound up my playing career, was my greatest cricketing experience. But, although it was a great game in every sense, the end was not so exciting as that recounted here, and, in any case, it was too *personal* an experience to justify my claiming it as the 'greatest game I ever played in.'

P. F. Warner, F. L. Fane, Denton, Capt. E. G. Wynyard, Hayes, J. N. Crawford, Relf (A. E.), Haigh, Board, Lees, and Blythe. *South Africa*—L. J. Tancred, W. A. Shalders, M. Hathorn, G. C. White, S. J. Snooke, J. H. Sinclair, G. A. Faulkner, A. D. Nourse, Vogler, R. O. Schwarz, and P. W. Sherwell (captain).

Marylebone won the toss and made 184: three wickets fell for 15 runs, and only Crawford batted really well.

One hundred and eighty-four was generally considered to be far too small a total, but South Africa replied with 91. Lees, Blythe, and Crawford bowled splendidly, and everything came off for us. Indeed it was a triumph for our bowling and fielding. Lees and Blythe went on over after over sending down the most perfect-length deliveries, from which scoring was extremely difficult. The batsmen played carefully and patiently to tire the arms of our bowlers. But they refused to be tired. When the six-foot-four-inch Jimmy Sinclair—all arms and legs to look at him from a distance, though a closer view reveals a magnificent breadth of beam and shoulder—was seen walking slowly to the wicket a great shout went from the ten thousand spectators who by this time were sitting five and six deep round the cycle track beneath the giant gum trees. Here at last is one who will knock these amazingly accurate professionals off their length.

There is a hush, so intense that one feels that one would hear a pin drop, as he prepares to face Lees. The long-striding bowler sent in a fast and rather short-pitched ball. Up goes the bat, looking like a walking-stick in those brown and sinewy hands, there is a dead silence for the fraction of a second, 'Catch it, Walter,' shouts someone, and Jimmy is on his way to the pavilion. And so things go our way. Seven are out for 44 runs. Then Vogler, so like the George Hirst of twenty-five years ago in build, and with the same pronounced energy as the famous Yorkshireman, whether

batting, bowling, or fielding, makes a drive or two off
Blythe, and Crawford takes Blythe's place. He catches the
ball eagerly, and the next moment Vogler's leg-stump is
down on the red sand, laid low by a beautiful-length break-
back. At six o'clock South Africa had eight men out for
71 runs, and the crowd passed out of the ground talking
eagerly and enthusiastically about the day's cricket—as
well it might, for there had not been a single dull moment.

On the second morning the South African innings was
soon over for 91, Nourse carrying out his bat for 18. He
was in for an hour and twenty minutes—a sure proof of the
quality of the bowling—and showed fine defence, and a grit
and stubbornness which, as the sequel showed, was to con-
tribute very materially to our ultimate undoing.

With a lead of 92 runs, at one time in our second innings
we had 160 runs on the board with only five men out; but
the tail went down before Faulkner.

South Africa was left with 284 runs to win and at the
drawing of stumps had made 68 runs for two wickets—
Tancred and Hathorn. Next morning everything went
right for us at first. Shalders was run out, Snooke leg before
wicket, Sinclair splendidly caught at long-on by Fane, who
ran some distance and took a hard drive high up on the left
side, and Faulkner run out. This run out deserves a detailed
description, as it was so characteristic of Board, our wicket-
keeper. Point was standing a good deal deeper than the
legitimate position requires, when White played a ball a
little to the right of where point would have been standing
in the ordinary way. He called Faulkner for a run, and
Board dashing after the ball threw the wicket down in
brilliant style, and Faulkner was out by feet. Six wickets
were now down for 105 runs, and the game looked to be
ours.

Then Nourse and White added 121 runs in two hours and
a quarter before Relf bowled White with a fine ball. During

s

this long stand the cricket all round was of the highest class, the fielding being superb and a stern duel going on between batsmen and bowlers. When he had made 11 Nourse gave an extremely difficult chance to extra-slip, but it would have been a marvellous catch had it come off, and indeed the fieldsman deserved great credit for getting his hand to the ball, which was travelling very high and wide on his left side.

White was in four hours for his 81 and never looked like getting out. The position of his side and the admirable bowling compelled him to play a purely defensive game; and it was his superb defence and judgment that helped to wear down our bowling.

The score was 226 when White left. Vogler was clean bowled by Hayes four runs later, and at 239 Schwarz was caught and bowled; and with 45 runs to get and one wicket to fall the odds would have been almost anything on M.C.C. if the last man in the South African side had been of the calibre of the usual eleventh man. But Sherwell is a capital bat, and from the first ball he received, which he hit for four, appeared perfectly at his ease.

Runs came faster than at any other period of the innings, the bowlers, whether it was owing to the excitement or to the long physical strain they had undergone under a hot sun on a hard grassless ground, losing something in their length and direction; and as each run was scored the crowd roared with delight as the idea began to dawn on it that after all, perhaps, South Africa might win. When eight runs were wanted, Crawford sent down a very fast ball which Sherwell snicked between first and second slip, and the spectators literally yelled with joy at this lucky escape.

Nourse then made a three on the leg-side off Relf, and the game was a tie. The fielders were now brought in round the batsmen, and three balls were bowled by Relf to Sherwell, who played two and left the third alone. Then Relf

sent down a full pitch on the leg-side, and Sherwell seized the opportunity and hit it to the boundary.

Nourse played a magnificent game. His back play was exceptionally strong, and he had a beautiful half-drive, half-cut behind point, while he was also very strong on the leg-side. He scarcely ever drove straight, but made most of his runs just in front or just behind point, and on the leg-side. His level-headedness and sterling cricket won the match for South Africa.

Sherwell deserves just as much praise as Nourse, and no one could have played more calmly and coolly. Everything depended on him.

If he failed the match was lost to his side, and the way he rose to the occasion and snatched a victory from the game of defeat stamped him as a big-hearted cricketer. One envied him his feelings at the end of the match. He had led his men with discretion and judgment in the way of placing the field and changing the bowling, and then, when an extraordinary effort was demanded of him, he emerged with flying colours. No captain ever inaugurated his reign of office with a more striking or happier result; for up to this date, January 4, 1906, a South African team had never got the better of an English eleven in what is now commonly called a Test Match. 'Twas, indeed, 'a famous victory,' achieved by magnificent and splendid pluck in the face of grave difficulties, and in all my experience of cricket I have never seen a side fight a better rearguard action. With six wickets down for 105 runs in face of a necessary 284 to win the match, the last few men on the South African side might well have been excused had they failed; but, so far from doing so, they stuck to their ground with that grit and courage which we are so fond of saying are inherent in the British race, and though naturally the first person to regret the result, one could not but appreciate the splendid qualities which brought victory to our opponents.

And we too, I think, deserved as much praise as our conquerors; for, handicapped on the last day by the absence of Haigh, owing to sudden indisposition, we fought with splendid determination, the fielding being so close and keen that scarcely half a dozen runs were given away, and the bowlers working with such courage and goodwill that it took South Africa just on five hours to get the 284 runs.

Never have I witnessed anything like the scene at the finish. Men were shrieking hysterically. Some were actually crying, and hats and sticks were flying everywhere. When the winning hit had been made the crowd 'tackled' Nourse and Sherwell and carried them into the pavilion, while, for half an hour after it was all over, thousands lingered on, and the whole of the South African eleven had to come forward on to the balcony of the committee room.

And so we were beaten, but defeat in such a struggle was glorious, for the First Test Match will be talked of in South Africa as long as cricket is played there.

## M.C.C.

| | | | | |
|---|---|---|---|---|
| P. F. Warner, c Snooke, b Schwarz | 6 | b Vogler . | . | 51 |
| F. L. Lane, c Schwarz, b Faulkner | 1 | b Snooke . | . | 3 |
| Denton, c Faulkner, b Schwarz | 0 | b Faulkner | . | 34 |
| Capt. E. G. Wynyard, st Sherwell, b Schwarz . | 29 | b Vogler . | . | 0 |
| Hayes, c and b Vogler | 20 | c Schwarz, b Snooke | | 3 |
| J. N. Crawford, c Nourse, b Sinclair | 44 | b Nourse | . | 43 |
| Relf, b White | 8 | c Sherwell, b Faulkner | | 17 |
| Haigh, b Faulkner | 23 | l.b.w., b Nourse | . | 0 |
| Board, not out | 9 | l.b.w., b Faulkner | . | 7 |
| Lees, st Sherwell, b White | 11 | not out | . | 1 |
| Blythe, b Sinclair | 17 | b Faulkner | . | 0 |
| B 6, l-b 9, n-b 1 | 16 | B 23, l-b 8 | . | 31 |
| | 184 | | | 190 |

## SOUTH AFRICA

| | | | | |
|---|---|---|---|---|
| L. J. Tancred, c Board, b Lees | . | 3 | c Warner, b Blythe . | 10 |
| W. A. Shalders, c Haigh, b Blythe | | 4 | run out . . . | 38 |
| M. Hathorn, b Lees | . . | 5 | c Crawford, b Lees . | 4 |
| G. C. White, c Blythe, b Lees | . | 8 | b Relf . . . | 81 |
| S. J. Snooke, c Board, b Blythe | . | 19 | l.b.w., b Lees . . | 9 |
| J. H. Sinclair, c and b Lees . | . | 0 | c Fane, b Lees . . | 5 |
| G. A. Faulkner, b Blythe | . . | 4 | run out . . . | 6 |
| A. D. Nourse, not out . . | . | 18 | not out . . . | 93 |
| Vogler, b Crawford . . | . | 14 | b Hayes . . . | 2 |
| R. O. Schwarz, c Relf, b Crawford | | 5 | c and b Relf . . | 2 |
| P. W. Sherwell, l.b.w., b Lees | . | 1 | not out . . . | 22 |
| B 9, l-b 1 . . . | . | 10 | B 6, l-b 2, n-b 7 | 15 |
| | | — | | — |
| | | 91 | | 287 |

## BOWLING ANALYSIS

### SOUTH AFRICA

| | O. | M. | R. | W. | | O. | M. | R. | W. |
|---|---|---|---|---|---|---|---|---|---|
| Schwarz | . | 21 | 5 | 72 | 3 | . | 8 | 1 | 24 | 0 |
| Faulkner | . | 22 | 7 | 35 | 2 | . | 12·5 | 5 | 26 | 4 |
| Sinclair | . | 11 | 1 | 36 | 2 | . | 5 | 1 | 25 | 0 |
| Vogler | . | 3 | 0 | 10 | 1 | . | 11 | 3 | 24 | 2 |
| White | . | 5 | 1 | 13 | 2 | . | 4 | 0 | 15 | 0 |
| Nourse | . | 1 | 0 | 2 | 0 | . | 6 | 4 | 7 | 2 |
| Snooke | | | | | | 12 | 4 | 38 | 2 |

### M.C.C.

| | O. | M. | R. | W. | | O. | M. | R. | W. |
|---|---|---|---|---|---|---|---|---|---|
| Lees | . | 23·1 | 10 | 34 | 5 | . | 33 | 10 | 74 | 3 |
| Blythe | . | 16 | 5 | 33 | 3 | . | 28 | 12 | 50 | 1 |
| Crawford | . | 7 | 1 | 14 | 2 | . | 17 | 4 | 49 | 0 |
| Haigh | | | | | | 1 | 0 | 9 | 0 |
| Relf | | | | | | 21·5 | 7 | 47 | 2 |
| Wynyard | | | | | | 3 | 0 | 15 | 0 |
| Hayes | . | | | | | 9 | 1 | 28 | 1 |

# CHAPTER XIV

## AN HONOURS SCHOOL OF CRICKET

In talking of cricketers of different generations, the question is often asked: 'Was Grace a better batsman than Bradman, Jackson than Hammond, Ranji than Hobbs? Was Spofforth a greater bowler than Barnes, or Peel than Rhodes or Verity, or Noble than J. T. Hearne?' And again, who was the best fieldsman, or the best all-rounder, or the best wicket-keeper? It is, in my opinion, impossible to answer such questions, and I thought the best manner of solving a difficult problem was to consult a group of experts of different generations and to select twenty-five batsmen, twenty-five bowlers, twenty-five fieldsmen, twenty-five all-rounders, and ten wicket-keepers, and place them in one class only, Class I. I have taken the last fifty years—1894-1944—as the period of time.

The names of the 'Examiners,' if they may so be styled, may not be disclosed, but they numbered seven, not including myself—five England cricketers, one a University and County cricketer, and the other not a first-class cricketer, but a rare judge of the game with a historical sense and a rare perspective. They were imbued with that sense of responsibility which the examiners in, for example, the Honour School of *Lit. Hum.* must feel, but it was great fun, if it did entail much concentrated thought and quite an amount of study of *Wisden* and other works. It was suggested that we should increase the Honours List from 25 to 30, except in the case of wicket-keepers, but we came to the conclusion that this would tend to make our task less fascinatingly difficult.

How the examiners approached their task is described by one of them.

'Examiners and those who sit in judgment on their fellows are usually unpopular people—so ruthless, pontifical and wrong. So they often prefer to remain anonymous, thus avoiding lynching and even gaining among simpler folk some prestige for their verdicts. *Omne ignotum pro magnifico.* The board of examiners, which has drawn up these lists of the best cricketers of the last fifty years, claims no infallibility. It is composed of diverse elements; all that we have in common is a long acquaintance with and love for the game, and our respective achievements in it range from the famous to the infamous. But we can say, one and all, that we have expended much time, argument and ink on weighing every one of these names. It would insult the reader's knowledge of human nature to say that the board was always absolutely unanimous, but in the end agreement was fairly complete, and there will be no minority report.

'The first twenty names or so in each department were easy enough; they practically chose themselves. But it was the choosing of five out of the next ten that has thinned our hair and multiplied our wrinkles; and so when complete deadlock threatened, some external opinion, massive with experience and prowess, has been sought. But even so, some of the rejections have been made almost with blood and tears. How could it be otherwise? Dr. Johnson said there was no settling the precedence between a louse and a flea. It is the same at the other end of the scale. Which was the stronger, Hercules or Samson?

'The war has in one respect been something of a blessing in disguise, and made our task easier. For the last five years have added no new names, while at the other end the years 1889-94 would have brought us more headaches in the shape of great players who in 1894 were past their majestic best—such, for instance, as J. M. Blackham, W. Gunn and W. G. as an all-rounder.

'So here are our names. The first reaction of the temporarily ungentle reader will undoubtedly be amazement and wrath at the omission of his pet hero, and belittlement of some of ours. He must take the board's word for it that all claims have been fully weighed, and we may hope that he will find on further reflection that his idol—judged of course by the highest standards—had, if not feet, at least a toe or two, of clay—some weakness on a tricky wicket perhaps, or against a certain type of bowling, some tiny inadequacy to the great occasion; or merely it may be, a lack of " that stellar and undiminishable something," which is called genius, the hall-mark of which is transcendent mastery of one kind or another. And even if this further reflection does not convince him of our rightness or our reason, it will not greatly matter, for however harsh his words, we shall remain smug and unruffled in our anonymity, knowing that in all his obloquy, as Bill Walker said to Major Barbara, there is " nothink passonal." '

## BATSMEN

Taking the *batsmen* first, many famous names are naturally missing and we may expect criticism from Australia partisans at the omission of McCabe, and from Yorkshire patriots at the non-inclusion of Leyland. We thought, however, that Hendren, a versatile batsman on all wickets, with a plethora of strokes and with a record of 57,610 runs and 170 centuries, deserved preference over S. J. McCabe, without a doubt a superb stroke player with some glorious innings to his credit such as his 232 for Australia, at Trent Bridge, in 1938, and his 178, at Sydney, six years earlier, and over Leyland. The Yorkshireman's record in Test Cricket is very good indeed, and one does not like to see an England eleven without his name. That broad bat with an equally broad back behind it has held the pass on many occasions. Both he and McCabe are to be sympathized with on just missing a first. The Australians have six representatives: Bradman, no argument here: the great left-handers Bardsley (England had never won until he was out), and Clem Hill, 'Sir Clement of the flashing blade, the pride and joy of Adelaide': Macartney, at his best the equal of anyone: Ponsford, of the broad bat: and Trumper, incomparable in his prime, and whose grace and prowess are still an abiding memory in the minds of all who saw him play.

Among the Englishmen, some may say that W. G. was past his best by 1894. This is true, but he was good enough to score 1,000 runs in May 1895, to go in first for the Gentlemen, at Lord's, until 1898 (in 1899, going in No. 7, he played an innings of 78, run out, in this match), and to open the innings for England up to 1899. After all he was the Champion and the maker of modern cricket. From Grace to Compton and Hutton cuts across the years, but we make no sort of apology for giving a First to these two young cricketers. They have crammed into a few seasons mighty deeds and both have a touch of genius in their play.

Taylor is the South African representative, and Headley, the Bradman of the Caribbean, speaks for the West Indies. He, like Compton and Hutton, has done much in a few years.

*Hayward* was a great batsman. He was tremendously sound with an array of powerful strokes, and most reliable against every type of bowling except the googly which he encountered at a period when he was putting on weight and was rather past his best. But no batsman, except C. B. Fry, showed to real advantage against the South African bowlers during the sticky wicket season of 1907; and it is generally conceded that the most difficult type of bowling to play is the googly—when bowled to a length, as it was by Vogler, Faulkner, Schwarz and Co.—on the many difficult wickets which prevailed during that summer.

There have been better batsmen than Hayward on false turf, but none the less he stood forth as a player of the highest class, and against the very powerful Australian attack of 1899, and on various tours in Australia his cricket was of the finest quality.

If *Duleepsinhji* was not so secure against fast bowling at the beginning of an innings as his uncle Ranji, he was a great player who, before illness cut short his cricketing career, had done many big things, including a double century in Gentlemen *v*. Players, at Lord's, and a century in Test matches versus Australia and New Zealand.

He had style and genius as had R. E. Foster, who, until Bradman came along, held the record for the highest individual score in England *v*. Australia matches, and who, like Duleep, scored a double century for the Gentlemen, at Lord's. His cricketing life was comparatively short, but he made the most of it.

Few will question the inclusion of Ranji, Fry, MacLaren and Jackson, the four greatest batsmen of what has been called the Golden Age, and Arthur Shrewsbury, if below his greatest best in the period under review, was still a great batsman up to 1902, his last season, when he headed the averages with an average of 50. He might well have played for England that year as it was a wet season and he was a master on false turf.

There can be no quarrelling over Hobbs and Sutcliffe, the best first-wicket pair England has ever had, or over Hammond, and Tyldesley was great on good, and quite magnificent on sticky, wickets. Woolley sometimes appeared to have a hole in his bat and though his record in Test matches is not quite what one would have expected from so outstanding a cricketer, it is, if carefully examined, good, and who that saw them will forget his double 90's at Lord's, v. Australia in 1921, when all around him were falling like leaves in an autumn gale, and his 133 not out, and his 123, at Sydney, on two tours in Australia.

## BOWLERS

As for the *bowlers*, we feel confidence in the selections. J. B. King's name may surprise a few, but all who played against him, or saw him bowl, recognized his ability. He did many great things on his two tours in this country, clean bowling some of our greatest batsmen—Ranji, L. C. H. Palairet, Sir T. C. O'Brien, A. C. MacLaren, and Sir Stanley Jackson amongst them—and in Philadelphia, he was almost invariably successful against English and Australian teams. He was a personality on the cricket field if ever there was one. He had the electric quality.

## FIELDSMEN

The fieldsmen include the three Australian ' greyhounds,' Ransford, Pellew and V. Richardson, S. E. Gregory, great at cover-point with a return like a flash of lightning, and Bradman. Some Australians aver that Bradman is not a dead-sure catch, but whether this be an accurate estimate or not, his speed, anticipation, clean pick-up and powerful and accurate return cannot be questioned.

Chapman—no one would question his inclusion—or that of Owen-Smith. A. Mitchell is a quite exceptional fieldsman in the slips, or at short leg or at silly point and Yorkshiremen swear by him. John Tunnicliffe, ' Long John of Pudsey,' with his telescopic reach made over 700 catches at slip, and no modern cricketer, or spectator, would gainsay the choice of Robins.

*H. Ashton* gave up cricket at an early age, but he was an exceptionally good batsman and a fieldsman of the highest class in any position. At short-leg he made a great name for himself, but he was equally good on the off-side or in the slips, and he was very fleet of foot in the deep. He was activity incarnate, and could galvanize a side by his own example. Had he continued playing he might well have captained England. He was the best young captain I ever saw.

*Braund* was a great short-slip, and the combination of MacLaren, A. O. Jones and himself in the slips during MacLaren's tour in Australia in 1901–2 has never been surpassed, if possibly equalled by that of Jones, Braund and Hutchings six years later when Jones captained the M.C.C. team. Hutchings was also a great deep fieldsman with a magnificent return and a very safe pair of hands.

*Hendren* was ubiquitous in the field. It mattered not where he was placed—he was brilliant anywhere and his feet twinkled over the grass.

*Hobbs* was great at cover-point. He always had his feet in the right position for his rapid return—he ran out 15 men during the Australian tour of 1911–12—and he was a dead-sure catch. We recall one catch of his in the Second Test at Melbourne in 1912. Cotter 'let fly' at F. R. Foster and the ball climbed the skies, swerving about in the wind. Hobbs followed the varying phases of its flight and held it safely.

*Jessop* was a glorious extra-cover. He stood rather deep to slow left-handers like Dennett, but woe betide the bats-man who took a liberty with him, for he would pounce on the ball like a cat and an arrow-like return sped to the wicket-keeper. After a particularly good catch by him, at extra-cover in the Gentlemen v. Players match at the Oval in 1908, A. C. MacLaren, the Gentlemen's captain, chaffingly remarked, ' There you are, Jessopus—standing on your heels again!'

*MacLaren* was in his early days a fine long-fieldsman—his catches at deep square-leg off Jephson's lobs in the Gentlemen v. Players match at Lord's in 1899 not only brought the spectators to their feet, cheering wildly, but caused the champion to walk towards the Mound Stand in order to shake hands with him. In the slips he was equally safe and was brilliant with either hand.

We should like to have been able to award a First for fielding to the brothers Grant of the West Indies, S. H. Saville, J. W. A. Stephenson, and J. W. A. Davies, as well as to the Australians, Trumper, Hill, Duff and Fingleton, the South Africans, A. D. Nourse, B. Mitchell and G. A. Faulkner, and the Indian Lal Singh, a picturesque figure in his light-blue turban, but as already explained the number of Firsts was limited.

## ALL-ROUNDERS

*G. O. Allen* was a bit of a puzzle to the critics. When they were saying he was not worth a place in the England XI, he would take five wickets for 13 runs as at the Oval, v. New Zealand, in 1931, or 57 runs v. Australia, at Lord's, in 1930. He almost invariably bowled well in Gentlemen v. Players, at Lord's, and he is one of the comparatively few bowlers who has taken 10 wickets in an innings. Then he was a very fine fieldsman at short-leg, both in front of the wicket and behind it—a difficult place. In 1936, he bowled very well both at Lord's and the Oval, *v.* India, and on his two tours in Australia he played a prominent part.

*Amar Singh's* First amongst all-rounders may cause some raising of eyebrows. He had not the opportunities of taking part in as much first-class cricket as are afforded to Englishmen, Australians and South Africans, but he made much of his limited opportunities. He was a fine bowler of the Maurice Tate type and only a little inferior to him. He was all whipcord and his lovely loose free action was a delight to watch. His bowling in the Test matches at Lord's in 1932 and 1936 made a great impression, especially on the latter occasion, when he looked almost unplayable in England's first innings. He was tall and beautifully built, with big shoulders and a slim body, and he looked every inch a cricketer. As a batsman, he was over-rash, but he was a lovely natural hitter with a rare combination of wrist, shoulder and swing. Add his beautiful fielding and you have an outstanding all-rounder.

*George Giffen* was in his day the W. G. of Australia. Many feats as an all-rounder stand to his credit, the greatest of which was in the South Australia *v.* Victoria match, at Adelaide, in November 1891, when he scored 271 and took sixteen wickets for 166 runs. He came to England in 1882, 1884, 1886, 1893 and 1896. He was a very good if not a great batsman, and a slow medium bowler who flighted the ball and spun it. His action was easy and when he delivered the ball, almost as much of his back as his front was visible to the batsman. He was therefore very difficult to see and many mistimed strokes were made off him. As a captain, it was said of him that he bowled himself too much, and one extraordinary analysis is worth recording. At Adelaide in 1895, between South Australia and England (Stoddart's team), he bowled 87 overs (6-ball) for 309 runs and five wickets. Stoddart's team made 609. There has seldom been a keener cricketer and in his old age, in 1911, he used to bowl for hours at the nets to the English team, and bowl very well too.

*Bosanquet* was the inventor of the googly with which he won two Test matches for England, at Sydney, on March 3, 1904, and, at Trent Bridge, on May 31, 1905. On the first occasion his analysis in the second innings was O.—15, M.—1, R.—51, W.—6, and at Trent Bridge, also in the second innings, O.—32, M.—2, R.—107, W.—8. He was also a good and resourceful batsman with no particular grace of style, but with powerful forearms and shoulders, and was especially reliable on sticky wickets. He was the master of medium-paced right-handed bowlers and left-handers. We recall the manner in which he dealt with Rhodes in the match at the Oval in 1908 between Yorkshire, the champion county, and the Rest of England. He made 214, and seemed able to drive the same ball from Rhodes either through the covers or pull-drive it wide on the on-side. He was also a very safe catch in almost any position in the field. It was said of him that 'he could argue on any point and at any distance from that point.' Be that as it may, his was an original and inventive mind and he was a pioneer of the game.

*Hammond* in 1928 made 78 catches and for Gloucestershire *v.* Surrey, at Cheltenham, in the same season, he made ten catches—a record. In the next match *v.* Worcestershire he obtained fifteen wickets, nine in the first innings for 23, for 128 runs. In Test matches he made 101 catches. It would be difficult to imagine a finer slip.

*Jessop* was the most consistent by far of all the great hitters, his fielding needs no comment and for a few years

he bowled fast and well from round the wicket, and in a
Test match, at Sydney, in 1902, he obtained the first four
wickets, Trumper, Hill, S. E. Gregory and Trumble, for a
score of runs.   In the same year he began the bowling for
England at Lord's.   During his first-class career he obtained
873 wickets for 22·77 runs each.   Later in life he was a
useful bowler with his medium-paced off-spinners from
round the wicket.

Of *Tarrant* it may be said that round about 1910–14 there
was scarcely a better batsman in England with the exception
of Hobbs.   As a left-handed bowler he was reliable on all
wickets, but better in proportion on a true wicket than on
a sticky one, for on the latter he used to try to spin the ball
too much and his length sometimes suffered in consequence.

During Stoddart's tour in Australia in 1894–95, *Albert
Trott* set Australia, and England too, talking.   Not selected
for the first two Tests, in the third going in No. 10, he
scored 38 not out and 72 not out, and took eight wickets
for 43 runs in England's second innings.   In the fourth he
made 86 not out, but did not bowl a ball.   In the final
Test he failed as a batsman, but in a big-scoring game he
obtained six wickets for 134 runs, England winning the odd
game of the rubber by six wickets.   It is fifty years ago but
I recall vividly how we fought round the notice board in
Vincent's Club to get a glimpse of the latest cablegrams,
and Albert Trott's name was on everyone's lips.   But for
some reason he was not chosen for the 1896 Australian tour
for England, and in high dudgeon he came here on his own
and was given a place on the M.C.C. ground staff.   In due
course he qualified for Middlesex and during the summers of
1898, 1899, 1900, he was a great all-rounder—a bowler of
infinite resource and variety, a splendid fieldsman at extra-
slip, where the most difficult catches found a safe resting-

place in his enormous hands, and a hitter of tremendous power. Unfortunately, if something of a genius, he had little headpiece and gradually lost his form. But during the years mentioned he was a big personality and an outstanding cricketer.

*Noble* was an even better all-round cricketer than Giffen, and *Armstrong* was probably better than Giffen, while the excellence of *Macartney's* bowling is sometimes forgotten in the glory of his batting. His eleven wickets for 85 runs won the Test match, at Leeds, in 1909 for Australia, and his fielding at mid-off was marked by a very safe pair of hands and a quick return.

Some description of *George Lohmann's* cricket has been given in the chapter on bowling, so there is little more to be said of him here. That he was, after W. G., first choice for England many years is a fact, for he was a magnificent extra-cover, a great bowler, and a dashing hitter who was at his best when runs were wanted. Some of his catches are historical, as for instance the one which dismissed A. C. Bannerman, the Australian, in a Test match at the Oval. I remember S. H. Pardon telling me that ' Bannerman talked of nothing else for the rest of the day '— and Bannerman was a silent man. 1896 was his last season, for consumption had begun to lay its fell hand on him, but in that year he and Tom Richardson bowled out the Australians on a ' plumb ' wicket in the Test match at Lord's. He loved cricket and during the tour of Lord Hawke's team in South Africa in 1898–99 we used to talk cricket by the hour as we sped across the Karoo and over the Orange and the Vaal on the way to the Golden City. An already enthusiastic cricketer was made even more so, and I learnt much from him. He was a tall nice-looking man with a fair moustache—very much of the Saxon type—and ' Our

T

George,' as the Surrey crowd called him, was a tremendous personality.

If *Woolley* was ' the Pride of Kent ' to the modern generation, *J. R. Mason* occupied much the same position between 1894 and 1910. He never played for England in England, but he was reserve to the famous XI, captained by Mac-Laren, which played at Birmingham in 1902. He was a fine upstanding batsman with a free style and many strokes, a medium-paced right-handed bowler with a high action who made the ball ' lift,' and a superb short-slip with a long reach who made difficult catches look easy. It sounds like an exaggeration but I personally never saw him miss a catch. An admirable captain and a sound judge of the game, he was immensely liked and admired by friend and foe. In first-class cricket he scored 17,40. runs with an average of 33·92, took 845 wickets for 2. 85 each, and made 340 catches.

*J. M. Gregory* in his day, between 1919–26, was a great all-rounder. He and McDonald were the spearhead of the bowling of the famous 1921 Australian team in this country, their great pace disconcerting many a batsman. He was also a slip-fieldsman who with his great reach made many a catch which at first sight looked impossible, and a dashing, daring, hard-hitting left-handed batsman. He had a wonderful season in Australia in 1920–21, scoring 100, 78 not out, 77 not out, 76 not out, and 93 in the Test matches, and taking 23 wickets for 24·17 each.

*Crawford, Douglas, Fender* and *J. W. Hearne* form a group of cricketers of whom Hearne, had he been blessed with better health, would have been comparable with almost any other all-rounder of his time. *Jackson* admits of no argument, nor do *Hirst* and *Rhodes*.

Apart from his batting, *Woolley* on a sticky wicket was very nearly as difficult a bowler to play as Blythe, and he was a fine short-slip. On the M.C.C. Australian tour of 1911-12, he made many splendid catches, and the total for the whole of his career was 890.

In considering the all-rounders, *Constantine* was something of a problem. Potentially and naturally he is great, but as has already been mentioned in the chapter ' Some Cricketers of My Time,' he has a poor batting (and bowling) record in the biggest matches through attempting the rashest strokes before he has ' got his eye in.' This weighed against him in considering whether he should be given a First or not, but whatever his failures, on his day, as in the Middlesex *v.* West Indies match of 1928, he was a vivid personality, with that indescribable something which we will call 'genius.' That he is the greatest of fieldsmen is not to be disputed and a big innings by him—which, alas, is all too rare—is not readily forgotten—while as a bowler he is full of enterprise, originality and fire. But he misses a First.

## Wicket-Keepers

Because of the comparatively small number of wicket-keepers only ten Firsts are given in this department of the game. South Africa gets three, Halliwell, Sherwell and Cameron, and Australia two, Carter and Oldfield. Opinions may differ as to the other five, and some no doubt may favour H. Martyn, of Oxford and Somerset, and Duckworth, but it would be difficult to say who should stand down for them.

Huish has a fine record of consistent excellence. He was equally good standing back to fast bowlers like W. M. Bradley and Fielder as to slow bowlers like Blythe and

Carr. In all Kent matches he caught 906 and stumped 356. Twice he obtained over 100 wickets in a season.

Duckworth was often brilliant, especially on the leg-side, but not always sound—though I have seen him keep magnificently, and Martyn's feat of standing up to Knox and Brearley in the Gentlemen v. Players match, at Lord's, in 1906, is still remembered. But our decisions have been taken and now we must be prepared to face the critics who, we hope, will deal with us with a difference which will amount almost to a deference!

## HONOURS SCHOOL OF CRICKET

| BATSMEN | BOWLERS | FIELDSMEN | ALL-ROUNDERS | WICKET-KEEPERS |
|---|---|---|---|---|
| W. Bardsley | S. F. Barnes | H. Ashton | G. O. Allen | L. Ames |
| D. G. Bradman | C. Blythe | D. G. Bradman | Amar Singh | H. B. Cameron |
| D. Compton | G. A. Faulkner | L. C. Braund | W. W. Armstrong | H. Carter |
| K. S. Duleepsinhji | F. R. Foster | A. P. F. Chapman | B. J. T. Bosanquet | E. A. Halliwell |
| R. E. Foster | A. P. Freeman | L. Constantine | L. C. Braund | F. H. Huish |
| C. B. Fry | C. V. Grimmett | D. Denton | J. N. Crawford | A. A. Lilley |
| W. G. Grace | J. T. Hearne | R. E. Foster | J. W. H. T. Douglas | G. MacGregor |
| W. R. Hammond | G. H. Hirst | A. E. R. Gilligan | G. A. Faulkner | W. A. Oldfield |
| T. Hayward | E. Jones | S. E. Gregory | P. G. H. Fender | P. W. Sherwell |
| G. A. Headley | J. B. King | W. R. Hammond | F. R. Foster | H. Strudwick |
| E. Hendren | H. Larwood | E. Hendren | G. Giffen | |
| C. Hill | W. H. Lockwood | J. B. Hobbs | J. M. Gregory | |
| J. B. Hobbs | G. A. Lohmann | K. L. Hutchings | W. R. Hammond | |
| L. Hutton | E. A. McDonald | G. L. Jessop | J. W. Hearne | |
| F. S. Jackson | A. A. Mailey | A. O. Jones | G. H. Hirst | |
| C. G. Macartney | M. A. Noble | A. C. Lohmann | F. S. Jackson | |
| A. C. MacLaren | W. J. O'Reilly | A. C. MacLaren | G. L. Jessop | |
| W. H. Ponsford | R. Peel | A. Mitchell | G. A. Lohmann | |
| K. S. Ranjitsinhji | W. Rhodes | H. G. Owen Smith | C. G. Macartney | |
| A. Shrewsbury | T. Richardson | C. E. Pellew | J. R. Mason | |
| H. Sutcliffe | M. W. Tate | R. W. V. Robins | M. A. Noble | |
| H. W. Taylor | C. T. B. Turner | V. Ransford | W. Rhodes | |
| V. Trumper | H. Trumble | V. Richardson | F. A. Tarrant | |
| J. T. Tyldesley | H. Verity | J. Tunnicliffe | A. E. Trott | |
| F. E. Woolley | A. E. Vogler | J. T. Tyldesley | F. E. Woolley | |

## CHAPTER XV

### CRICKET DURING THE WAR

It is curious, but how like the 'mad English,' as we have been called, that during the war, cricket should have enjoyed a boom. For instance, crowds of over 30,000 watched the cricket each day, at Lord's, on Whit Saturday and Whit Monday, 1944. During the war years a large number of splendid matches, nearly all of them restricted to one day, have been played at Lord's, and in other parts of the country; in the North, the South, the West and the Midlands. These matches were arranged with the approval of the Service authorities and the leaders of the Government, who realized that they provided a healthy and restful antidote to war strain, and incidentally produced large sums of money for war charities.

During the past five years, Cabinet Ministers and distinguished sailors, soldiers and airmen have snatched odd hours to watch these games, and even Mr. Curtin, the Australian Prime Minister, managed to spend a few hours at the Headquarters of cricket in May 1944. Did he not say in one of his speeches that Australians would always fight for those twenty-two yards at Lord's, and that Lord's belonged to Australia as much as to England? And not only in England has cricket flourished during the war years, for our Servicemen have indulged in the game in such unlikely places as the moat of a Polish Castle, on the lava-strewn rock-like ground of Reykjavik, at Carpriquet aerodrome within range of the German mortars, on the beach at Salerno, and, naturally, in Egypt, Palestine, India and South

Africa. It would be difficult indeed to name a district visited by British Servicemen which has not witnessed some attempt, however primitive, at a game of cricket.

There have been many appeals for cricket gear for our forces overseas, but this is no new feature. It is, perhaps, not generally known that troops were appealing for cricket gear over 130 years ago. In 1810, for example, when our troops were in the Iberian Peninsula, an officer of the Light Dragoons under General Crauford wrote: 'We found things pretty slow, kicking our heels in idleness in Lisbon. So one of us got a kindly carpenter to make us some cricket implements. He did very well, but the difficulty was the ball. He turned a piece of wood about the size and shape of a cricket ball, but this missile proved more deadly than the enemy's fire, and, after several of us had been more or less seriously wounded, we abandoned this form of amusement. Later, however, the game was resumed when proper implements had been received from England.'

Few of these one-day, and, occasionally, two-day, wartime matches compare with the standard of a first-class game in peacetime, but, on the other hand, they have been of value to many young players with little or no first-class cricket experience prior to 1939. The Northern Leagues, in which many famous players have appeared during the last few years, have also proved an admirable training ground, and there are good accounts of many players.

Of those who have appeared in the more important games, the best batsman is undoubtedly R. T. Simpson, of Nottinghamshire. He is very correct and neat, and gives the impression of having plenty of time in which to place his strokes. Another point in his favour is that he is a first-class fielder. H. Halliday, who played a few times for Yorkshire, in 1939, is tremendously strong with all the concentration of his county. He is also a splendid fieldsman, and so, too, are T. E. Bailey and A. W. H. Mallett, two all-rounders about whom the experts are apt to differ. Other players the war has brought to the front are T. G. Evans, the Bedser twins, and J. R. Bridger. Evans is already hailed as an England player, and in one of his early games, at Lord's, he played a capital innings of 50.

A. V. Bedser played in several of the Lord's matches after returning from France in 1940 and before being drafted overseas again. He is one of the most promising fast-medium bowlers of the war period, and his determination and enthusiasm may one day bring him fame. His twin brother, E. A., has the makings of a sound batsman and is by no means a bad off-spin bowler. J. R. Bridger is not an attractive player to watch, but he has made runs as an opening batsman for Cambridge and other teams during the past five years.

At the conclusion of the 1914–18 war, an Australian Service side—playing as the Australian Imperial Team—toured England during the summer of 1919, and they provided a number of players for the most successful Australian XI's of 1920 to 1924. Names such as C. E. Kelleway, H. L. Collins, J. M. Gregory, J. M. Taylor, W. A. Oldfield and C. E. Pellew occur. The course of this war has necessitated that the Australian Army should be employed far from European fields and relatively few Australian cricketers have been in England during the last four or five years, but none the less, Australia's cricket reputation has been worthily upheld by the R.A.A.F. who have introduced some most attractive cricketers, several of whom should be candidates for the next Australian XI.

In K. R. Miller the R.A.A.F. have a batsman of high class. Perhaps one can give him no higher praise than to say that in the second ' England ' v. ' Australia ' match, at Lord's, last summer, his innings of 85 was not overshadowed by W. R. Hammond's 105. Miller is beautifully built and

CRICKET IN WAR-TIME

Army *v.* R.A.F., Lord's, July 29, 1944. A flying bomb is heading for the ground. The batsman is Captain J. D. Robertson, wicket-keeper P/O E. A. Wilson, slip Sqdn. Ldr. W. J. Edrich, D.F.C., and Flt. Lt. A. D. G. Matthews in the gulley. Robertson's next stroke was a six

DENNIS COMPTON AND M. S. NICHOLS
(Army *v.* A Lord's XI, September 6, 1941)

CRICKET IN WAR-TIME

Section of a war-time August Bank Holiday crowd at Lord's watching W. J. Edrich and D. Compton
batting for Middlesex and Essex v. Kent and Surrey

L. Hutton and W. J. Edrich
(England *v.* Australia, Oval, 1938)

has strokes all round the wicket.  D. K. Carmody, now a prisoner of war, has played some very good innings, notably a magnificent century, at Hove, in 1943, and R. M. Stanford has made runs whenever he has played.  Last May, D. R. Cristofani had a great triumph against the R.A.F., at Lord's, when he took seven wickets for 39 runs.  He has spin—his top-spinner puzzled many batsmen—and flight, but if punished is apt to bowl too fast.  Probably the best Australian bowler in wartime England is the slow left-hander, R. S. Ellis.  Bowling over the wicket, he kept a length and spun the ball, and impressed no one more than W. R. Hammond, who lost his wicket to him on four occasions in 1944—the last occasion admittedly when he was endeavouring to force the pace directly he came in.  Ellis is said to bowl with more confidence than he did in Australia before the war.  S. G. Sismey's wicket-keeping has been one of the features of the R.A.A.F.'s cricket and if, as suggested, he had developed a tendency to 'snatch' before he left Australia, he has eradicated that fault since he came to this country.

The Army, the R.A.F. and the Civil Defence Services put capital elevens into the field from time to time, and last summer the Royal Navy were clearly on the way to victory over the Army when rain fell.  The Buccaneers, who were in existence before the war, were able to command the services of several good cricketers, a result largely due to their enthusiastic and hard-working secretary, G. Moore. The war has been responsible for the foundation of such sides as the British Empire XI, London Counties XI, West of England XI, and the Surrey Colts. The first three elevens have contained a large proportion of first-class cricketers, and have not only been instrumental in raising large sums of money for war charities, thanks to the co-operation of the clubs against whom the majority of their fixtures have been played, but they have also given many people the opportunity of seeing first-class cricketers taking part in an actual match. As a county Surrey have not participated in any wartime cricket, but, under the leadership of A. Kempton, the formation of the Surrey Colts has been an outstanding success, and it will be surprising if some of these Colts do not ultimately find their way into the Surrey XI.

The standard of school cricket has understandably been lowered by war conditions, but M.C.C.'s policy of sending sides against schools whenever feasible has done much to encourage school cricket which has also benefited by the efforts of the Forty Club, the Public Schools Wanderers, Buccaneers, Grasshoppers, Hornsey C.C., and others.

Club cricket has held its own amazingly well, and not a few clubs have even been able to continue their cricket weeks. Perhaps the most serious problem facing the clubs at the present time is the reconditioning of their grounds. Some are of almost pre-war excellence, but in many instances it will be advisable to consult a turf expert; the preparation of a cricket ground is no task for the inexperienced. During the war, the Club Cricket Conference, the largest organization of its kind in the world, has lost its secretary, E. A. C. Thomson, and G. W. Hammond, a past president, who was Chairman of the Conference when he died in 1943. Despite these losses, the C.C.C. has continued to watch over the welfare of club cricket in the South and, further, has managed to play a number of representative matches.

Oxford and Cambridge, in the face of great difficulties, have played an annual one-day game, at Lord's, except in 1940, and Cambridge, who have many more men in residence than their rivals, arranged quite a good list of fixtures. It should be remembered that at both Universities the average age is considerably lower than in peacetime.

# INDEX

U